Where Is Home Papa ?

Where Is Home Papa?

by Bernice Green Isaacson

NODIN PRESS
Minneapolis

ISBN 0-931714-45-1

Nodin Press, a division of Micawber's, Inc.
525 North Third Street
Minneapolis, MN 55401

Printed in U.S.A. at
Gopher State Litho, Minneapolis, MN

Preface

I vividly recall the day when the first 500 copies of "Where Is Home Papa?" were delivered to my home on May 10, 1983. It was the day of my 33 year old son's funeral. He died from the disease of addiction to alcohol and other drugs. Family and friends filled the house to support my wife, Helen, and me in our time of grief. Helen was in treatment for her addiction to prescription drugs at the time (she's doing fine today).

These events provided a tragically appropriate backdrop for the introduction of "Where Is Home Papa?", the story of a father who wants desperately to provide a proper home for his daughters, but his addiction to alcohol stands in his way.

"Where Is Home Papa?" tells the adventures of two young girls during the three years following the untimely death of their mother. My mother, Beeny Cooney (the author) was age 7 and her sister, Dubby, was age 9 when their mother died.

Their adventures take place in Iowa and Minnesota in the early 1900's. They want very much to have a home with their Papa, but close family relatives feel he cannot provide a proper home for them, because of his addiction to alcohol; nevertheless, he persists in trying. His jobs as a railroad man and logger take him from place to place. His daughters go with him and have many exciting experiences that are vividly marked in my mother's memory to this day. She especially remembers the time her papa looked at her seriously and told her "some day you are going to write about this." To her, that was a sacred assignment.

Today, Bernice Green Isaacson is a very active, alert lady of 96 years. She happily lives alone, cooks all her own meals (she likes to have me stop by for lunch whenever I can), keeps abreast of current events, particularly political events throughout the world. She enjoys the challenge of lively discussions about timely events of all kinds.

My mother could look back and reminisce about a very full and satisfying life, but she doesn't do that—she doesn't have the time. In addition to pursuing her intense interest in world affairs, she enjoys painting and reading. All of the illustrations in this book are her art work.

When my Mother started writing her story some 50 years ago, she thought of it as something only her children, grandchildren and close friends might enjoy reading. With urging from friends who read the manuscript, I had 500 copies of "Where Is Home Papa?" printed in 1983, so that others could enjoy reading its heartwarming stories, Those books have long since been sold or otherwise distributed.

I continue to receive requests asking for copies of "Where Is Home Papa?". So I have entered into a joint-venture With The Nodin Press in Minneapolis to publish the book. Hopefully, many more readers will be able to enjoy "Where Is Home Papa?" I'm sure you will find the stories very interesting—so turn this page and start reading!

Fenton R. Isaacson
The Author's Son

I dedicate this book to all who would have an interest in knowing how life was lived in the north woods at the turn of the century and to grandchildren - Terry, Kristy, Janet, Jim and their children.

Bernice Green Isaacson

Contents

1

Life Becomes Different

A surrounding quietness comforted our silent group as we stood before an open grave watching a black casket being lowered. Everywhere, white Mayflowers bloomed in this wooded cemetery in Iowa.

I was just seven and sister Dubby not quite nine. I stood next to Papa Frank close in front, and Dubby was on his other side as we wept at our Mama's grave. When I was led away it seemed all wrong to leave Mama there — I had been told she was now with God, but that was so hard to understand.

Afterward, when the family was back again in the now halfempty parlor of Mama's parents, Papa Frank prepared to say good-by quickly to his inlaws.

This was a most unhappy hour for me and for Dubby. Mama was gone, and now Papa was leaving. But first, he took us to the back bedroom to say goodby in privacy. As we sat beside him on the bed, he put his arms around us and spoke softly.

"Darlings, Papa can't take you back to Minneapolis right now but I want you to know that I'll always be planning to somehow get a home where I can be with you again. Right now your Aunt Carrie wants to take you home with her for a little visit. Don't you think it will be nice to do that — go for a little visit?"

I couldn't answer. I felt so strange, sitting in the room where we had sat during the service and listened to Gathering Home and Nearer My God To Thee, with everyone crying. It wasn't easy to think about days ahead, but Dubby agreed it would be nice to go.

"There is something else I want to tell you," he continued. "Mama is watching over you. She is right there with God and I'm sure she will ask Him to take care of you. She would want you to be good girls and mind Aunt Carrie. And I know you will be good girls for Mama's sake, and for my sake too, for I love you very much. Always remember that."

After hugging and kissing us tearfully, he joined the family to explain that he must catch a train. Then he left.

When the door had closed I heard someone say, "I'll bet he just wants to get away so he can hit the bottle."

Mama's mother said to Aunt Carrie, her daughter, "I'm so glad you are going to take the girls home with you. I don't know how that man can ever hope to look after them — unless he changes his ways."

Aunt Carrie was one of Mama's five sisters and five brothers at the funeral. And they soon began talking about Papa Frank, saying unkind things. One of the brothers reminded them, "He'd be a mighty fine man, if he could just leave that booze alone."

Hearing all the talk helped me understand why Papa didn't want to stay this day. Aunt Carrie sounded hopeful when she said, "Let's give him a chance — Maybe he will change now that the responsibility is all his. And I think he does love the girls an awful lot."

Aunt Carrie was a younger sister of Mama's. She lived on a small farm at Eldora, Iowa with her new husband and his parents who owned the farm. The next day she took Dubby and me home with her for that visit. We had a nice 75 mile train ride. Her husband - tall, young, slender and dark eyed - welcomed us, as did his parents whom we would call Grandma and Grandpa Wright. They too, were slender, even wiry — and very English.

Our visit became lengthy, but we were content. Fanny, their shepherd dog, raced with us every day and trotted along when we started for the cows at night. Grandpa Wright taught me to fish for bullheads in the nearby Iowa River. I was his daily companion all summer and fall, and loved it.

In that way a whole year sailed by. It was spring again, and we were still at the farm! Papa Frank hadn't come. He was in Minneapolis, Minnesota where he had gone after the funeral. We had been living there when Mama died. In his letters he told us he was lonesome, and the endings always said "I love you very much."

Most of the time I played outside. Anyone passing, especially on Sunday morning, would see a long rope swing, yellow in its newness, traveling back and forth swiftly in the quiet front yard of this little farm house. I could stand on the narrow board seat, gaily confident, and clutch the ropes with tightened fists, while I worked my knees vigorously to pump the swing high. Looking down, I liked to watch the pleated flounce on my Sunday skirt as it sucked against me on the forward down sweeps. It was almost like being a circus girl I thought, except that no crowd was watching.

In the meantime, strange things were happening at the farm. Dubby and I might not stay here long. The Wrights were considering selling the farm and moving to northern Minnesota where land was being given away. They wouldn't go, however, unless they could find land they liked.

Aunt Carrie and Uncle Ed would move with them. The family had talked about the adventure ever since hearing from their former neighbor who had gone there the year before. He liked the wonderful country where tall pines could be sawed into boards for houses and where immense lakes were full of choice fish. All could be theirs if they

Almost Like Being A Circus Girl

would go and live on the land. That would be homesteading.
They would be homesteaders. Dubby and I begged to be
taken along and promised to help with all work.

Swinging high this Sunday morning, I wondered how
much taller the trees could possibly be in that wild country.
My toes were almost touching the branches when Dubby
came running from the porch.

She was wearing her French dress with pleated flounce
like mine for we all were going to church in town as soon as
everyone was ready and the horses hitched to the surrey.
Dubby was very chubby, especially around her middle, and I
was almost runty for eight years. We didn't look alike.
Dubby's beautiful eyes and hair were brown, but I had hazel
green eyes, and my hair was taffy color — though dark
streaks were showing.

I stopped pumping to slow down, for I knew Dubby
wanted to swing. Besides, she looked distressed and was
trying to tell me something. In broken whimpering tones she
blurted, "They aren't going to take us homesteading."

I braked the swing to a full stop, and Dubby climbed on to
pump double. As she grabbed the ropes above my hands, she
poured out what she had overheard:

"Uncle Ed told Aunt Carrie she would have to take us to
Minneapolis."

I couldn't feel bad about going back there. I wanted to go
homesteading too, and do all the things I'd heard about, but
Papa was still in Minneapolis and so was Donald, my good
playmate, my real "fellow." Aunt Nellie was there too, and
lived right across the street from Donald.

"We'll keep teasing to go along," Dubby decided. Dubby
always did the deciding. She thought being almost ten gave
her that privilege.

We bent our knees in turn and pushed the board with both feet until the swing was moving again. I almost slid off each time Dubby straightened up and pressed against me. Swinging double wasn't as much fun. The swing wouldn't go as high.

Within a few minutes Uncle Ed had the team hitched and waiting near the gate. King and Lady, standing in their polished harness, were beautiful animals of the same size and color. The family was proud of the matched dapple-gray team, especially when the horses were hitched to the black fringed-top surrey with shining patent leather guards over the wheels.

Grandpa Wright didn't go along with the family, for the surrey's two seats were filled, with Grandma in the back seat between Dubby and me, and Aunt Carrie and Uncle Ed in front. Sunday school was important to this family because Uncle Ed was the superintendent. But that is what would make the ride home afterward so saddening to me, for I didn't know that anyone could act like a saint for an hour and then be a devil right afterward. Uncle Ed couldn't control his nasty temper, and he always got his own way in everything. I found that out later.

At the church, we entered with others primly dressed in Sunday clothes. I liked the music part because Aunt Carrie played the piano, and Uncle Ed led the singing up front. Everyone seemed pleased.

But on the way home, all was so different. Uncle Ed didn't act like a Sunday school superintendent. He cursed the horses for no reason I could see, and, leaning forward, whipped the ends of the reins over their backs. Poor King and Lady. I couldn't understand it; he had led the praying only a short time before.

As I watched him I wondered why everyone hated Papa Frank when Uncle Ed was so much worse, and he was even looked up to at church. Papa Frank was a good man and believed in God. I knew that. It was most difficult to understand.

On Tuesday Grandpa Wright and Uncle Ed took the train north to look at land. A week later when we met them on their return, Uncle Ed's first words, as he stepped from the rain, were, "Well, we're going."

Riding home, all six in the surrey, the men told how they had ridden a full day on the train going up, and then had driven a day with a hired team to reach the free land. They had stopped two nights at the home of their friend and former neighbor, John Anderson.

"That's fine country up there," Uncle Ed said, and his father sounded just as ready to go saying, "We found some land right next to John's that he thought hadn't been taken, and I'll tell you we hurried back to Brainerd to file for it. And it's really ours. No one had beat us to the Land Office."

King and Lady trotted along as if they too, were happy. It was now mid-April, and so much to be done! The farm must be sold. They would move and begin "proving up."

As soon as we were home, two maps which the men had brought were spread on the square oak table in the dining room. One was of the state of Minnesota, and the other said CROW WING COUNTY at the top, with the date 1903. This one was more interesting to me because it showed every lake and every road. There were many pencil marks in the upper part of that one, marks put there by Uncle Ed.

I stretched on tiptoes from the edge of the wide table to see where he was pointing. The longest wiggle mark showed the wagon trail that wound through forty miles of wilderness. He ran a finger up from the town marked Brainerd to where an X meant John Anderson's homestead. It touched the shore of a large lake. Right next to it, heavy marks outlined the area of Uncle Ed's and Grandpa Wright's claims.

"This is where the land is," Uncle Ed announced, almost as if telling where Paradise lay. "It's just about forty miles north of Brainerd."

Grandma Wright leaned over to study the map. "Why, I can't see a railroad anywhere," she said after a moment.

"No," Grandpa said slowly. "There isn't any. Everything has to be hauled in by team."

No towns on that forty miles. Only two names, Cross Lake and Emily, were even near the homestead. But there were many lakes.

Grandpa Wright smiled as he peered closer, and took his pencil to show Grandma. "See this smaller lake? That's Blue Lake. That's partly on our land. That's like our own. Our land touches John's right here. So we're not far from big Crooked Lake either. There's fine fishing there."

Grandma smiled too, as she looked at him knowing how much he liked to fish. She was a person who moved quickly and never seemed to tire. She was ready for the new venture.

The women knew they would be going north to please the men. Uncle Ed liked to hunt, and wanted to shoot bigger things than squirrels and rabbits and wild ducks, which were all he could get on the Iowa farm.

I hoped to be Grandpa Wright's fishing partner. I liked to jerk my pole when the bobber went down and find a bull-head on the end of the line. But Grandpa Wright wanted bigger fish.

Aunt Carrie sat thoughtfully now, with arms around

Dubby and me standing beside her. She seemed to be wondering how she could ever take children to a place like that. It was frightening even for grown-ups.

Uncle Ed was saying, "Here is our nearest town." He grinned when he said "town." "We'll get our mail here, at Emily. There is one store and a blacksmith shop and a school, besides two or three houses. It's only six miles from us."

I looked quickly at Aunt Carrie. The nearest town and school six miles! How far is six miles I wondered — could people walk that far?

Then Aunt Carrie said, "That's too far for the girls to go to school."

Uncle Ed straightened to say, "Oh, I forgot. There is a school quite near our land. I think it would be only about two miles — depends on where we locate our house."

"But is there a road to the school?" Grandma Wright wondered. "It looks wild to me."

The men laughed and showed her that the road from Brainerd passed right through the new claims. It had taken them past the school. And they could build their homes squarely beside the road.

"What do people do if they need a doctor?" Grandma Wright sounded worried. Grandpa squinted, and gave her a doubtful half-smile as he said, "I suppose you would have to drive to Brainerd for one. It would take at least two days to bring a doctor up there." He didn't seem to like that thought, either.

Dubby had been whispering to Aunt Carrie, anxious to have her say we could go because a school was near. But now all she said was, "People would think we were crazy — taking you girls along to a place like that."

Dubby drew back, wide-eyed. Had all teasing failed? By now I was sure I wanted to go because in Minnesota we would be closer to Papa.

"Oh Aunt Carrie, dear Aunt Carrie," Dubby begged. "Please — we don't want to live with anyone else. Please."

Aunt Carrie Wright looked to the others for help, but they gave her none. After a few minutes, she patted Dubby's shoulder and said, "We'll see. I'll write to your papa tomorrow and see what he says."

* * *

By the end of the third week the farm had been sold. Inside the house we could scarcely weave our way through the clutter. Open boxes and barrels, half-filled, centered the space where rugs had been before. Walking across the bare boards caused strange unnatural hollow sounds. Even that sacred area — the front room — was noisy confusion, with only the lace curtains remaining in place.

Dishes were bedded in straw to withstand the long ride over rough roads later on. Dubby and I carried them to Grandma Wright as she sat beside the barrel, packing each dish her own way — the plates standing on edge and all heavy dishes on the bottom.

Good news had come from Papa Frank. He said he would be happy to have us taken to northern Minnesota. We would be close to him and he might go to the northwoods too, later on, and work near us.

So all was settled. We were now really part of the family, going homesteading where pine trees towered to the sky and wild animals roamed.

Finally, our last Sunday came, and everything not needed on the homestead had been sold, even the surrey. It couldn't be used in the timber — the top and the fringe would soon be ruined. Besides, not many homesteaders used fine surreys.

But the surrey was still Wrights to use until they left. Grandma wanted one more ride in it. So at the table at noon she said, "I'd like to go to the concert tonight. It might be a long time before we hear another concert."

The boys of the reform school in this Iowa town played every Sunday evening during summer on the lawn of the school. Because whatever Grandma Wright wanted done was done, we knew we would get to go and we were happy.

Right after an early supper Uncle Ed rolled the surrey from the barn. We were all going except Grandpa Wright, who said, "I've been to enough band concerts before."

It was a warm, quiet summer evening. The horses stepped lively, and the surrey fringe rippled overhead. Soon Uncle Ed was passing teams and stirring up dust along the last mile to the school beyond the town.

After tying King and Lady at the hitching rail far out front, our family joined others on the long, petunia-lined walk leading in. A commanding building of yellow brick stretched wide, towering in front of us, hiding all else. Its long rows of lofty, narrow windows watched across the front, evil-eyed.

We didn't go in, but followed a side-path around to the rear lawn where the concert was to be played. The only boys in sight were those arranging chairs for the musicians. It was difficult to believe that more than a hundred boys lived in the lonesome looking houses farther back.

Presently doors began opening on the porches. Boys appeared, not running and laughing and talking, but with supervisors beside them, and moving slowly, forming double lines before marching down the front steps. They came along the board walks to the concert area and settled to the ground

Sunday Concert At Reform School

in groups.

The band members emerged from that big front building carrying instruments and walking in orderly fashion to the chairs waiting for them. With quick, precise movements — and no talking— they arranged themselves behind racks and music, then leaned back, and from their somewhat raised platform, gazed over the others proudly.

People were still crowding onto the lawn. Dubby and I sat on the grass, quite close to the band. The groups of boys, with housemothers, were seated nearby. We watched them thoughtfully and wondered why they were in a place like this instead of their own homes. They appeared no different from other boys; a few looked not older than eight or nine. What could they have done?

We had been told these were bad boys who wouldn't mind their parents. They were here to be "reformed." Some of those on the grass did seem to be pouting, but would grin happily when we smiled shyly at them.

Many of the visitors moved around between numbers, and children ran playfully. It seemed too terrible that the reform school boys had to remain seated and separated so they couldn't even talk to visitors.

When the concert was over, they all rose to march back as they had come. I thought the grounds looked lonely again.

As Dubby and I followed Aunt Carrie, leaving with the crowd, we were ever so grateful we didn't have to be in a reform school, or even an orphan's home. We couldn't know then all that would happen in the next two years.

Of all the teams at the hitching rail, the one Uncle Ed untied was the most beautiful. He patted King's smooth gray neck to quiet him, for he had begun to paw the ground when he saw his master coming. Lady, too, was prancing, anxious to start even before everyone was seated.

It was still not dark when the lively animals whirled the
surrey around and started off at a swift pace. Uncle Ed held
the reins tightly so they wouldn't run too fast. In a few
minutes, however, even when they were trotting so swiftly,
the heads of two other horses came up alongside trying to
pass. When King and Lady saw them they leaped ahead,
jerking the surrey and all of us. They knew their master
never allowed other teams to pass when they were trotting.
He was too proud for that.

Quickly, Ed Wright looked back to the man driving the
other horses and saw that he was urging his team. Uncle Ed
seemed to think, "All right. If the man wants to race —" He
sat up stiffly and leaned forward, giving the reins to the
horses by allowing them to sag from his hands. As soon as
King and Lady felt the bits in their mouths loosen, they
knew it was the signal to run, and they did.

But the other team was running, too. A race was on! The
road at this spot was wide enough for both teams, but not far
ahead a plank bridge without sides spanned a wide ditch.
Two teams could not cross it abreast, so each driver was
urging his horses to get there first. Both the surrey and
buggy were bouncing dangerously over the rough edges of
the road as it narrowed toward the bridge.

It was frightening for us in the back seat, for no deep sides
held us in. Only thin iron rods, a few inches high, were there
for climbing up. Grandma Wright sat rigidly between Dubby
and me, her arms tightly around us and her feet braced, while
Aunt Carrie, in front, began screaming at Uncle Ed to stop,
"Ed — they're running away!"

By now Uncle Ed knew it, too. King and Lady (no longer
a lady) had started to gallop in their excitement. That caused

the surrey to jump crazily, and Dubby and I, with Grandma Wright, were nearly thrown out.

Uncle Ed pulled frantically on the reins, but the panicking animals kept plunging. Suddenly, their hooves hit the planks like thunder. I twisted in Grandma's arm to look back, afraid the other team had tipped over. But the driver had slowed just in time.

We were nearing town now, where a run-away was bad. Lady stopped galloping, and that made King stop. They were still running fast, however, and careening the surrey around other rigs.

Aunt Carrie turned again to see if we, in the back seat, were still all right. Her face was gray with fright, and anger, too. Behind Uncle Ed's back you could see her lips say, "Just showing off."

The horses changed to a proper trot when they came to town streets and houses, as though they knew what they were doing.

That was our last ride in the surrey. Grandma said, "Jim surely would have been furious if we had wrecked it after he had it sold."

2

Happy Days Back Home

All plans were complete. Aunt Carrie would go with
Dubby and me to Minneapolis to visit our Aunt Nellie,
Papa's sister, and we would be with him there while the new
house in the timber was being built. Grandma Wright would
remain in Iowa with her married daughter during that time.

A boxcar had been rented at the freight depot to haul the
farm things north. Animals, furniture, everything could go in
it. There were several cows, a flock of chickens, and a few
hogs, also four sheep, besides King and Lady. And, of
course, there was Fanny to bark and scare away wild animals.

There was the wagon box and wheels, the hayrack and
bobsled runners, the grindstone, plow, and many tools,
besides all the furniture. Even the piano was being shipped.

Finally, the day came when the boxcar was loaded, ready
for the freight train to hook on to it. Grandpa Wright and
Uncle Ed would ride along, right in the freight car, to take
care of the animals. They had arranged a separate open space
in the center for themselves, near the sliding doors, and had
put two of the rocking chairs out to use.

On that same day, after seeing the men settled comfortably, Aunt Carrie, with Dubby and me, took the passenger
train to Minneapolis. Aunt Nellie met us at Union Depot.
Such a special meeting — so much to be said! We sat down
to visit in the crowded waiting room until our checked
baggage came.

It was afternoon, and the streets were full of hurrying
people when we walked to where the right trolley car would
come by. As we stood watching the lines of passing street-

cars, a comfortable feeling spread over me — for I was home again.

When the home trolley came in sight it seemed to be smiling. I smiled back at the familiar letters "COMO HARRIET" on the scroll high in front. I climbed the steep steps eagerly.

Aunt Nellie cuddled me beside her in the cane woven seat and looked down tenderly as the car gained speed. "Donald has been asking about you every day," she said, and smiled as I looked down embarrassed.

The back yard of Donald's house was across the street from Aunt Nellie's. Donald and I had built a playhouse in his yard — and had great fun.

Once he had given me a valentine with a verse I had read so many times I hadn't forgotten it:

> More than when first I singled thee,
> This only prayer is mine,
> That in the years thou yet shall be
> My happy Valentine.

I had given him one, too, but had run into so much trouble delivering it I didn't want anyone to talk about it afterward. I had rung Donald's doorbell and laid it on the porch, then jumped to hide in the bushes below, waiting for the door to open.

While I was hiding, Donald and his mother came along the sidewalk. And they saw me! I had thought they were in the house.

Donald's mother pretended not to see me, and she marched Donald inside, which was a good thing, for it had given me a chance to run for home. Afterward, he told me the Valentine I gave him was beautiful, and he didn't tease me about hiding, though I was sure he had seen me.

As I thought about the backyard playhouse, while the streetcar sped along and Aunt Nellie's arm tightened around me, I wished I were not going homesteading ever and could stay in Minneapolis and be with Papa. Dubby seemed happy too, sitting with Aunt Carrie and looking out the open window.

It seemed such a short ride, in spite of the many stops. Already we were coming to our old neighborhood. Dubby watched for the corner where the tan-colored brick school could be seen a block away. She said she wanted to show Aunt Carrie the big Calhoun School we had attended.

I saw the school first, and the street we had walked on to get there. We always passed a group of stores that seemed like a separate small town.

Suddenly, as the trolley rolled across an intersection, I caught sight of the monstrous green pickle hanging from an iron rod over the sidewalk a half block away. I remembered walking under it often and wondering why the beautiful thing had the number 57 on it. The sign was made of tin that quivered and crackled when the wind blew hard. That was the meat market!

The streetcar turned the corner and hummed west three more blocks; there we got off. As the trolley left us and whined on down the track, we gathered our luggage to tug it the one block to Aunt Nellie's house.

Soon Dubby and I were running excitedly up Humboldt Avenue to see if old playmates were home. I couldn't see Donald anywhere as we passed his house. And I didn't want to stop and go to the door. Not right away.

In such a little while Aunt Nellie called and told us to

watch for Papa who would be coming from work. What excited waiting! Suddenly we saw him, far down the street. We raced to him, were caught in his reaching arms and hugged warmly. It had been a long time since I had felt his arms, and I wished I could stay right there and have a home with Papa even if I wouldn't get to see the tall pines and wild animals.

I asked, "Why didn't you come and see us, Papa?"

His answer made everything seem better: "It wasn't easy for me to get there, but now that you're going to be nearer I'll be doing just that, you can be sure."

"Did you get our letter?" Dubby asked.

"You bet I did," he said, and patted her tenderly, "and I like to get your letters, and I want you to keep writing after you get up north."

"But Papa, I wish I could stay here with you. Can't you get a home for us like you said you would?" I asked.

He squeezed my hand as we walked and said, "Now don't you worry. The time will come. Maybe it's not so far away. But remember, Mama is always with you, and I know she would want you to be happy wherever you are. You must try to do that."

After supper the big curving front porch was filled with chairs. Everyone was talking homesteading.

It was the next day before I saw Donald. I went to his back yard and he came outside. I had been away many months and we both wanted to play.

None of the boards and bricks or the water pipe from our old playhouse were in sight, but Donald knew where they all were. The boards were stacked in the workshed near the alley and the bricks were piled behind the shed.

Our greatest delight was finding a piece of water pipe

with a faucet attached to one end. It was just what we needed. We had not had a faucet before. At once we started carrying. Bricks and boards soon covered the middle of the back yard. We laid them in rows to outline the walls of a playhouse. We needed but one room. That would be a kitchen, so we could use the faucet.

To make a table, boards were laid on bricks. Three bricks made a chair. Donald propped the water pipe slanting, so that water being poured into the open end would run out when the faucet was turned. Then he found a wooden box on which to rest the faucet. The open box looked a wee bit like a sink.

As before, I was Missus and Donald was Mister. When mealtime came, which was almost right away, we washed carrots from the garden and ate them sitting at our table.

Aunt Nellie called dinner and allowed me to take my filled plate from the table and Donald brought his. Smiling, we faced each other across the low board, eating with mighty manners and pretending that I had cooked the food as any Missus should. Donald told me it was very good.

And never had water tasted better. We drank glassfuls just to have the fun of getting it. It didn't matter that it took a bit of doing. Donald rose from the table each time and carried the pitcher to the open end of the pipe. There he slowly poured in water so that I, going to the "sink," could turn the faucet at the other end and let it trickle into a glass.

* * *

The fun-filled days slipped by too fast.

One Sunday Papa rented a rowboat and took us riding on Lake Calhoun, three blocks away. For a treat he bought a sack of fresh apricots. As the boat moved across the lake, I wished I could fish. I told him about the bullheads I had caught with Grandpa Wright and said, "Papa, I wish you could come with us homesteading. There are lots of big fish up there."

"I wish I could do that," he said, and then looking at us soberly, continued, "Girls, I want you to know something and always remember it. Nobody loves you like your papa does. Someday we will have a home together — somehow. I'm sure of that. And if I can arrange to get work near you next winter, I'm going to do it."

We listened closely as he went on. "In the meantime, you will make Papa happy if you will try to be the kind of girls your Mama taught you to be. She was a fine woman and I want both of you to be just like her."

He sounded so serious and looked so sad as he mentioned Mama, that Dubby and I couldn't think of an answer, but only nodded that we would be good girls.

He smiled at us then and the agreement seemed made.

As he slowly dipped the oars he looked at me tenderly and said, "Little Beeny Coony." I wondered if I would always be called by that nickname. It was he who had caused me to get the name. When I was not quite four and couldn't sound my "r's," he liked to hear me say my name — Bernice — for I could only say Bawn-us. One day when he came from work, he stopped beside me in the yard and asked again, "What's your name?"

I knew what he was expecting, but instead of drawling "Bawn-us," I made up a name never heard before. Stomping my foot impatiently with each word, I spurted, "Beeny Coony - Snakey Biddle - Bum Bum Bum."

He had gone into the house laughing and told Mama. Then to tease me afterward, he called me that. But the silly name was too long and he soon shortened it just to Beeny

Coony. Mama never did call me that except for fun once in awhile, but so many others did that now it sounded as natural as my real name.

Dubby got her nickname in a simpler way. It was what I called her before I could say Concetta, which was Dubby's real name.

As he now watched us lovingly, he must have thought the names fit well enough — chubby Dubby — and racing, rope-jumping Beeny Coony. "I wish your Mama could have lived to see you grow," he said.

It was late afternoon when we left the water, planning to have another ride soon.

* * *

The days with Aunt Nellie were soon to end.

Uncle Ed had written only twice, for he was so busy. His first letter had said that all the animals and chickens had stayed alive on the trip; it had taken four days to get them over the rough crooked trail. He and Grandpa had built a pen for the pigs, but a barn couldn't be built until after the house was finished. He said they were almost killing themselves working, although John Anderson was there — hauling lumber and helping build.

In the last letter, he said the boards of the roof would be on by another week and we could come — if we wanted to live in the house while the shingles were being put on and the outside walls covered. He told Aunt Carrie he and Grandpa would meet the train and reminded her we would all have to ride on a load of furniture if we did come so soon.

Aunt Carrie said she knew all the furniture had been left at the freight depot while the house was being built, but she wanted to go, even if she did have to ride on top a big load and move into an unfinished house. It was now the first of

August and we had waited six weeks. Fall days, and school days, were near. She and Grandma could help, cooking good meals for the men. So Aunt Carrie wrote she was coming and told them which day to meet the train.

A week was allowed before leaving, as the letter might lie in the post office at Emily. The men were too busy to go for mail, and, after getting it, would need a day and a half to drive to the depot. Aunt Carrie had been told that neighbors always brought each others' mail and the road passed the new house. She wrote Grandma Wright too, and in a few days Grandma came to go with us.

The long exciting days ended. I had to tell Donald good-by, but promised I would come back some day.

Papa Frank went along to the depot. It was a bright forenoon. On the platform, as we watched for the train to come in, he put his arms around Dubby and me and told us, "Remember, you are your Papa's little girls and I love you very much. You know that, don't you? When I can, I'll come to see you, and we'll have a home together some day. So you'll be good girls for Mama's sake, won't you?"

Later, he helped us into the coach and onto the red plush seats.

All during the ride, Aunt Carrie wondered aloud if Uncle Ed had received her letter in time and would be at the depot. It was midafternoon when, finally, the engine puffed into Brainerd, ringing its way to a slow creep. There, with the crowd on the platform, stood two familiar tall, lean men in blue overalls, watching the slowing coaches.

Aunt Carrie exclaimed with relief, "Oh, he got my letter!"

Dubby and I hopped from the conductor's stool, with Grandma Wright and Aunt Carrie close behind, so glad to see their husbands. Greetings overflowed.

Uncle Ed seemed waiting to groan, "You'll never know how hard we've worked." Grandpa Wright nodded the truth of that, and said, "Yes, and we aren't half through either."

I saw King and Lady, hitched to the empty hayrack, farther over, and ran ahead to reach up and pat their smooth gray necks. Good King and Lady — they were part of the family, too.

The men had driven since morning and part of the day before. We would stay in Brainerd overnight. So now we carried the luggage around the depot to where green grass, trees and benches beckoned, to consider plans. Across the street a sign said "ROOMS."

"That's a nice clean rooming house over there," Grandpa Wright said. "We stayed there before. Maybe we better take you women over now, and then go and get our loading done. We must get all of it done today and get an early start in the morning."

After the men left to load, the rest of us hunted a grocery store and bought food supplies to pick up later. Then we hurried to the depot. Down the tracks by the freighthouse we spotted the hayrack backed against a high platform in front of a wide door. The men were carrying out boxes and furniture.

When Grandpa Wright saw us coming he called, "You're just the guys we need. Come over here." He was reading the penciled writing on the boxes. "We'll never be able to get all of it on. You'll have to tell us what you need most and we'll leave the rest for another trip." Some things had already been hauled by John Anderson.

"What's in all these boxes?" Uncle Ed asked, as he placed still another one out on the loading platform.

It was hard to decide what to leave. The piano would stay.

That had been planned all along. They sorted the boxes, to find those with bedding, clothes and needed things. Grandpa even asked if the dressers should be taken. But Grandma insisted she needed hers — besides, she had packed so many things in the drawers of it.

It was surprising how well everything fit on the load. Boxes filled spaces between legs of furniture. Chairs were sandwiched together, seat to seat. When the rack was packed, everything but the piano and one barrel of dishes was on it. Even the clumsy rocking chairs were tied at the back end, upside down. The bedsprings and headboards extended above, along the sides. They had loaded it evenly and well so it wouldn't upset.

Last of all, the two spring seats were boosted up and settled solidly on the flat boxes at the front. There was room for three persons in each seat. Everything was ready for the wheels to roll north at daybreak.

Grandpa grasped Lady's bridle and led the team, pulling the load to one corner of the freight yard. There the men unhitched the horses to take them to the livery barn where they would be watered, fed and bedded. The loaded rack would be safe until morning, for trainmen were always around the busy depot. A good meal and a night of rest was what we needed now. It was almost dark.

3

Learning The Way Of the Wilds

The morning was clear and very still when we awoke. The two men slipped out before the rest of us to get breakfast and be on their way to the livery barn. First, they stopped at the grocery for the box of food. By the time the rest of us walked into the freight yard, King and Lady were hitched and waiting.

As Aunt Carrie stood looking up to where she was to sit, she said, "Ed, I don't see how in the world we are ever going to get up there." "I could drive over by the loading platform, but you're going to have to do it from the ground the rest of the way," Uncle Ed replied. Climbing to the top of that load would be a struggle for the women, with long skirts wrapping their ankles.

Uncle Ed swung himself up and then reached a hand down to assist. Squeezing behind the horses, Aunt Carrie stepped on the heavy wagon tongue and reached for the ladder-like strips above, jerking her skirts up before her. Grandma followed. Mounting a loaded hayrack was a thing they had never done. It took a lot of pulling and doing. Dubby and I scrambled up like a pair of squirrels. We had ridden with Grandpa Wright at the farm.

Soon all of us were seated high, Dubby on the front seat between the men and I behind her, tucked in by the women. Uncle Ed lifted the reins andKing and Lady pulled forward into their harness. The piled hayrack creaked alarmingly, then slowly began to move.

Two large tin pails hung on the rack. Water might have to be brought to the horses. A bag of oats was on the load. Grandma Wright's black umbrella, the box of food and jug

Ready To Roll From The Freight Yard

of water were all handy right behind the seats. If it rained, or if the sun blazed too hard, we would need the umbrella. Everything had been remembered.

As the rig swayed through ditches behind the pulling team, Aunt Carrie said, "Well, this surely makes you think of the pioneers. All we need is a covered top." She couldn't know when she said that, how much harder she was going to work than many settlers ever had, for she was a pioneer to that little part of the world.

Dubby and I didn't say much. Everything was so new, we were content only to listen and watch. The men were telling about their trip with a load of livestock. "Honestly, Carrie," Uncle Ed said, "there are some spots where I thought we'd never make it."

Grandpa Wright turned and grinned as he added, "Yes, you may get swiped right off this load if you aren't careful. The branches come straight out over the road farther up. We may have to stop and cut away some for this high load."

It grew very warm riding in the sun. Grandma Wright's umbrella came in handy. Its black canopy completely covered those of us on the back seat.

Half the forenoon was gone and we had met no one, and no one had passed. Now a team was coming. We had known something was near even before it could be seen. King and Lady had pointed their ears, listening as they walked. A black dog had trotted into sight from the bend ahead and stiffened as it looked up and saw the strange load.

In the approaching rig a man was alone on the buggy seat. As soon as he saw the loaded rack he drove off the road and stopped. Teams couldn't pass everywhere on this trail. When Uncle Ed had driven alongside, he too stopped, then said, "How do you do Sir?" and smiled.

The man answered pleasantly, "How do you do?"

Here in this lonely country, families expected to become acquainted, so they talked. By the time we were ready to drive on, the man knew we were moving to claims near Emily, and that we had come from Eldora, Iowa. We had learned that the man had homesteaded for three years near Lake Pelican which was about fourteen miles farther on.

As he said good-by, he reminded us, "Now it's the road turning off just before you come to Pelican and if you need anything at all, stop at the house and the wife will fix you up."

The teams pulled slowly apart and soon the road was lonely again — and empty.

Later on, when everyone was hungry, we cautiously watched for a lake, pond, or stream to have water for the horses. A small lake was first to greet us and the roadside was grassy for picnicking. Uncle Ed drove out of the tracks before stopping, just in case some rig should come by. The lake shore was several rods away, with brushy steep ground between.

"I'm not going to carry water all that distance," Uncle Ed complained as he swung himself over the front and down.

"You don't have to," Grandpa said. "We'll just take the horses down there, feed and all." Uncle Ed had already decided to do that and had started to unhook the tugs and fasten them up to be out of the way when the horses walked.

The women somehow reached the ground. Grandpa handed down the water jug and food and tossed the oats bag over before lowering himself.

The horses had stepped away, leaving the heavy wagon tongue slanted to the ground, looking very still, in front of the helpless wheels. Uncle Ed, carrying loops of reins, strode half stumbling behind King and Lady down the weedy slope. Grandpa began pouring oats into two feed bags to follow.

Seeing the tall snake-grass, Aunt Carrie called, "Oh, Ed, watch out for snakes."

When he reached the shore line, the horses, without stopping, walked into the water and drank eagerly. Afterward, he brought them to where Grandpa Wright stood, in the shade, waiting with the feed bags. King and Lady knew how to push their noses into the sacks hung in front of them and they were hungry.

Leaving them to nuzzle oats, the men came back to enjoy their own meal, and to sprawl on the ground and stretch. It had been a slow and bumpy ride.

"By this time tomorrow," Grandpa encouraged, "we should be getting near our own neighborhood."

"Well, I'll be mighty glad when I can sleep in my own bed again," Grandma told everyone. I knew what she meant.

Soon the wheels rolled again. A couple of hours later we reached a place where "you might get swiped right off the load." A sweeping branch was in front of us. Grandpa Wright stopped the team and Dubby and I crawled from the seats to the center of the load and covered our heads. The others ducked and lifted the branch away as the horses waited. Then we crunched forward again.

Two rigs had overtaken us by late afternoon. There had been the usual how-do-you-do's and visiting, but no good-bys were said: We would see one another that night. We were all planning to stay at the inn that had been a logging camp at one time and was halfway between Brainerd and Emily.

As the faster travelers pulled away they promised, "We'll tell them you're on the way," and one of them added, laughing, "We'll try not to eat all the food before you get there."

It was after seven when our rack turned into the wide yard. Arms waved a welcome from the bench by the lodge house where the women were sitting, and from the row of men squatting sociably beside the huge log barn. A man in overalls came forward to greet us and take charge of the team.

Everyone else had eaten when we latecomers entered the lodge house. The inn-keeper's wife left the mixing of next day's bread and crossed the room to welcome us.

"We've been watching for you," she said pleasantly. "Have a seat at the table. I've kept food for you."

The large room was very warm, for the big iron stove still held its fire. A long table covered with flowered brown oilcloth extended through the center of the room. The lady hurriedly slid six plates in a row and poked up the fire under the food. The other guests came inside to visit. I fell asleep at the table after eating.

At last, the lady said, "Now come and I'll show you where you are going to sleep." There were no separate rooms and no upstairs. She was proud of all the bedrooms she had created by hanging curtains around the bunks along the walls — forming green tunnels of gunny sack cloth. She was eager to show her special room at the far end, for here was a pink iron bed for herself and her husband. This bed had springs.

Going back to the bunks, she showed us the high fluffy straw ticks she had made, explaining, "We couldn't buy mattresses to fit." The lady was sure everyone would sleep well. Grandma Wright said nothing, but scowled a bit. The lodge lady guessed her feelings and said to Grandma, "Now you and your husband can just as well sleep in our bed. It has springs, and we really like to sleep in the bunks." Grandma Wright didn't argue one bit. We all did sleep well, being so tired.

At dawn the dark air was chilly when Aunt Carrie, with Dubby and me beside her, pumped fresh water to fill jugs for the day. As our bulky rack turned from the yard, other rigs were only being hitched.

The horses had nodded forward an hour when Grandma Wright noticed a road turning off to the left toward a home-stead. "There," she pointed, "I'll bet that's where that fellow lives that we met yesterday." But there was no need to stop — and no time to waste.

As the plump gray horses slowly chewed the miles, far to the right and back again to the left, following the timber road, Grandma Wright said, "We would get there in half the time if we could go straight instead of twisting out of our way so much."

The steady grinding of wheels filled the hours. And the trail grew rougher. It had never been marked to be a road. The wheel tracks we were following were there because someone had found their way around trees, and others had followed until the trail had become a road.

King and Lady strained and struggled through sand-filled ditches and, as the sun poured down heat, their gray skins darkened from much sweating. The wide leather straps of harness across their broad rumps pushed ridges of white foamy lather away, with the constant movement of their bodies.

Soon evergreens again shook hands overhead, and the ground was carpeted with dead pine needles. A single weed here and there poked thinly upward in the shade. Grandpa

The Empty Lonely Trail

Wright pointed to the ground and said, "Now you can see how easy a forest fire could start if anyone dropped a match into that." "You hadn't better knock out your pipe," Grandma Wright cautioned him.

"Don't worry," he mumbled.

"Look over there!" Uncle Ed pointed quickly to a large dark speckled bird on the ground. "That's what you'll be eating a lot of this winter." The large bird resembling a gray barnyard hen, stood calmly looking at us from its shady surroundings.

"Whatever is it?" Aunt Carrie asked.

"That's a partridge. See that little tuft on the top of its head. They are mighty good eating. And this country is full of them. We can have partridge, or squirrel, or fish, anytime we go after it. Venison too, all winter." That thought eased our discomfort for a moment.

Not until we were passing did the bird take a few quick steps away and whirr up into the timber. "Looked like an ordinary prairie chicken to me," Grandma Wright said.

It seemed to Dubby and me we were indeed coming to a wonderland.

At last we were almost there, passing the school Dubby and I would attend. The white building stood on the left, just beyond crossing roads and snuggled against high brush and timber. In front, a large cleared space squared off by the roads provided a playground. School would start in another week. I wondered so much what it would be like.

Within minutes we saw a most charming house sur-rounded by flowers and painted yellow. Other homesteads, the few we had passed, had looked lonesome, with dark houses, and always a crooked hog pen made of poles some-where in the yard. This farm was neat, with a nice barn.

Dubby and I would pass it every day. Surely nice persons must live there. Later we found this to be true.

Every foot of the way seemed long from here on, for Andersons lived off the Emily road where the trail was even rougher. On that last half mile, the clumsy hayrack jerked and swayed with frightening sounds. Grandma Wright groaned as she grasped the end of the spring seat to hang to.

"If I had to ride this rig another hour you'd never take me off alive," she sighed. "I think I'm going to break in two when I hit the ground."

King and Lady perked up. They knew they were nearing home for now dogs were barking, announcing our arrival. It was Anderson's dog, and Fanny, who had been left there and kept tied. Fanny would have followed Uncle Ed and Grandpa Wright.

Mr. and Mrs. Anderson were outside waiting as the horses turned slowly and carefully into the slanting yard. The rack leaned crazily as it came down the slope. It looked for a time as though Grandma wouldn't have a chance to climb off.

Fanny had been untied and was bounding about, whipping her bushy tail. Grandma Wright didn't fall apart when she touched ground, but moaned as if she were going to. So did Aunt Carrie.

Here we were at last, with the water of Crooked Lake lapping at the lower edge of the yard. Dubby and I ran down to the shore and out onto the narrow dock. The lake was large, but the shore wasn't sandy or level. There was a sharp bank instead. When the men came to look across the lake from the bank, Dubby noticed the oddest thing — it appeared they were standing on a road that extended out from the bank.

"What are those tracks?" Dubby asked as she pointed.

"That's a road," John Anderson said. "That's a winter road. People living across the lake drive over the ice in winter. It's shorter for them to come to Emily. We use the road too, when we do our winter fishing. That's something you'll like to see." Then he told the men, "I hope to sell a lot of fish this winter. I think I'll put up a larger fish house and keep two or three holes open. A fellow can spear a pile of fish in one day."

Supper was called and Dubby and I struggled to pull long stockings over wet legs. We had dangled feet from the dock. The highest pile of fried fish we had ever seen greeted us. "I don't see how anyone can get tired of fish like this," Aunt Carrie said after a few bites. "I know I'll never get tired of it."

John Anderson laughed, "You just wait, Carrie, I'll give you two months and I'll bet you'll be turning up your nose at the sight of it." She didn't believe it and she told him so.

4

Making Do Without A Well

The new Wright place wasn't far from Andersons' by the shortcut path through the woods. But on the road, with a team, you needed to go far around — almost two miles.

Grandpa Wright and Mr. Anderson left right after breakfast to walk the shortcut, feed and care for the stock, and work on the unfinished house. Uncle Ed would bring the load over with the rest of us.

When later he barked, "Ge - up," to King and Lady and slapped the reins, they leaned into the harness with heads down, pulling that piled rack up the slope as if ready for another long haul.

Farther along we passed the homestead of a close neighbor. Uncle Ed said they were nice people, and had stopped at the new place several times to offer help. "This is the man I told you about who is going to bring our stovepipe from Emily. He thought he was going to town yesterday or today, so maybe it will be there now."

"I don't see why we couldn't have brought that along ourselves," Aunt Carrie said.

"Why, Carrie, do you realize how much pipe is needed?" Uncle Ed asked. "It has to reach all the way from the stove up through the ceiling and through the upstairs to the roof. There isn't any chimney built in, you know."

Aunt Carrie said, "Oh," trying to imagine a stovepipe running straight up through the rooms.

"And stovepipe," he went on, "is something you can't pack down or roll up, or slide together in any way. It takes room, that's all."

This neighbor's name was Graham and Dubby and I were to know them well.

Going around a bend, Uncle Ed said, "Here's the line."
We had reached our own land! It was dense with trees,
mostly tall Norway pines with smooth reddish bark and
straight trunks, to be sold. The cleared land would grow
grain and vegetables.

In minutes Aunt Carrie would see her new home!
Grandma Wright said she had wished for a small log house.
Now, here she was, to plan just how and where to build it.
She and Grandpa would live with us only for a while.

Uncle Ed had said his house was larger than any nearby,
and that was true: He'd always wanted the biggest and best
of everything. It had an upstairs and was built of new sawed
lumber.

I watched steadily to be first to spy it. So did Dubby. It
was puzzling to know where to look, for the road didn't go
straight ahead, but zigzagged sharply. Soon the spreading
echo of hammering reached our ears, but we couldn't tell
from where. Uncle Ed said, "Keep your eyes peeled now."
In a moment he pointed, not straight ahead, but far over to
the right. We all turned quickly.

There it was! Its raw new boards gleaming almost white
through the trees that seemed to march across it as the horses
walked. It did look big with the high pointed roof. As we
drew closer, it became to us a thing alive and naked with all
its new boards waving a welcome. Then the road angled so
sharply that the house was on our left when we were ready to
turn into the yard. It was well placed with rising ground
behind it. A door and two windows faced the road.

The pounding inside had stopped when Fanny, who had
gone with the men earlier, "woofed" and raced to meet us,
almost as excited as she had been the day before. Grandpa
Wright and John Anderson came outside and waved, then

started picking up boards and building truck that lay before the front door so Uncle Ed could drive there to unload. Before leaving the road, he "whoad" the team and asked his passengers, "Do you want to get off right here?" pointing out the ruts and humps he would have to drive through to reach the door several rods away.

Grandma Wright said, "After all the bumps I've taken, nothing like that scares me now. I'll stay with the ship 'til she docks." We all did.

Inside, curled shavings, sawdust and scraps of boards covered the floor. The partition dividing the downstairs into a large room and a kitchen was only half enclosed. That was where the pounding had come from. The floor of the upstairs wasn't all down, either. Because that floor made the ceiling of the downstairs, it left an opening where we could look to the roof. This uncovered part was above the kitchen.

Enough upper floor was laid to provide for beds and dressers. But there was no stairway! A homemade ladder leaned hopefully against the open edge of the ceiling floor to serve until steps could be built. Aunt Carrie stared at that gapping upstairs and shook her head. It would be a danger-ous place to walk at night. Grandpa Wright, close beside her, teased, "You know, Carrie, we left that open so we could hoist things up easier." And she seemed to believe him. Actually, it was unfinished because they had run out of floor boards.

Unloading couldn't begin until the floor was cleared of building litter. So Dubby and I ran outside and around to the back. The yard here was slanting unevenly and covered with brush. Down, away from the house was the place for ani-mals. Uncle Ed was already there, lifting the harness off the horses.

We circled our way there.

The hogs eyed us from a pen built of sapling poles, with rows of barbed wire near the ground. Next to it, a rough shelter over feed boxes had been constructed for the horses. The cows and the four sheep, however, were nowhere around. Only chickens were in sight, along with the pigs and horses.

"Where are the cows and sheep?" I asked Uncle Ed, hoping they weren't lost or stolen.

"Oh, they're out there somewhere," he said, nodding toward the brushy hillside.

"But won't they get lost?" Dubby asked.

"No, they've all got bells on," he explained. "Don't worry, they always come back to where they get fed."

Up, away from the pen, a queer chicken roost of three poles, looking like a wide and short ladder, was propped off the ground. A chicken house still had to be built and a barn too, before the weather turned cold.

Aunt Carrie opened the new back door and called, "Come girls, change your dresses and then help us."

We cleared the floor of the odd shaped wood scraps and placed them in a box beside the cookstove, which was already set in place, but looked useless without a chimney. I climbed the ladder to clean the upstairs floor and instead began skipping through the long empty space to peer from the end windows into the close branches of the evergreens. Turning, I could look down at the other workers like viewing from a balcony.

Grandpa Wright had a good laugh when it was discovered the women had no broom. Grandma always knew what to do and she flew outside and cut a spray of pine clusters from a young tree. Then she swished the shavings and sawdust across the floor with her witch's broom and told Grandpa, "It's your fault. You must have thrown it away. It was in the freight car you came in."

The men were already bringing in boxes and beds and all else from the rack and piling it just inside the door. Grandma Wright and Aunt Carrie shoved and sorted barrels and boxes to find the most needed articles.

In the afternoon Mr. Graham brought the stovepipe. He was a kind looking man, not tall, but with well muscled arms and neck. He helped Uncle Ed fit the pieces of pipe together into long sections and connect them. Then they poked a blue steel column to the roof and through the hole made for it. Carefully they settled the column down again onto the chimney opening in the stove and moved the stove slightly until the pipe stood straight. It was quite easily done as nothing was in the way between stove top and roof. The upstairs floor would be built around it later.

So many things were needed besides the broom that a trip to Emily was necessary. The next day Uncle Ed put the wagon box on the wheels that had carried the hayrack and took Aunt Carrie, Dubby and me to buy supplies. A six mile ride didn't seem far now.

Emily was marked as a town on the map, but only one large building was there. It was the store. Across the road from it stood a shed with a wide open end where men were shaping iron shoes for horses. They were busy at that blacksmith shop. The owner's home and a few other houses showed beyond it.

Down the road from the store a schoolhouse drew attention. Space for playing ball lay between the store and school house where a few board seats waited for spectators. And that was all of the town of Emily.

But the store! In it was the whole world.

At one end of the long building, built of logs, sacks of flour lay piled high. Boxes of dried fruit, cases of soap and even cookies in barrels left little room for walking. On the walls hung axe handles, tin pails and wash boilers. Also at that end, a section of little square pigeon holes for mail sat on the counter. That area was the post office.

At the other end all space was filled from the ceiling down. You went up a step to this part. Bunches of gloves, caps and heavy speckled socks hung from the low ceiling. Tall Uncle Ed had to duck much of the time.

Tables throughout the room were loaded with bolts of cloth for all needs: calico for dresses, ticking for pillows, outing flannel, everything. In the center, a table held school supplies: tablets, books, gray slates with red felt laced tightly around their wooden frames. I liked the double ones, hinged, to close like a book. Dubby and I lingered here, admiring especially the red cardboard lunch boxes.

Aunt Carrie came and bought two slates and two long thin slate pencils wrapped in striped paper. She seemed sure they could be used at school. "I don't know which books you'll need," she said as we fingered those on the table.

"Won't we need these?" Dubby asked as she held up a red lunch box. It was square, with a leather handle lying flat on top. A canvas strap, buckled around, held the cover on. Knowing we would carry our lunch, Aunt Carrie lifted the little boxes and decided they were nice and lightweight to carry, and bought two.

On the way home we tried out the slates while sitting on the floor of the wagon and were satisfied, even though the slates weren't the double ones. Those had cost more.

* * *

The pressing need was a well. There was plenty of water
for the animals. It could be seen from the back door.
Grandma Wright called it "the slew." But Grandpa said it
was a pond formed by seepage from Blue Lake, our own
lake, just around the slope.

Water for the house had been hauled from Grahams'.
When we were in need of more, Uncle Ed said, "We can't
spend time hauling water. We'll have to use water from the
pond until we get a well." The drillers were to come in
about two weeks.

Aunt Carrie looked horrified, and Grandma said, "You
mean that slew?"

"That's good clear water," he defended, and grabbing a
pail he started out the door. All of us but Grandpa trailed him
all the way to the pond, making quite a parade as we waded
through high grass to its edge. Tall snake-weed and reeds
were reaching up from the water, as well as surrounding it.

Aunt Carrie tried to stop him, and looking at the weedy,
stagnant water, pleaded, "Ed, I'll bet there are snakes and
everything else in there."

But he only laughed and said, "If there are, then we don't
need to worry. If they can drink it and live, so can we. I
know there are frogs in there and they help to keep the water
clean." Dubby and I were squatting low, peering into the
water. It was full of tiny wiggling things!

"Oh!" Dubby yelped as she drew back shuddering, too
horrified to say more.

"It's full of worms!" I decided and tried to look deeper.

Uncle Ed dipped a sample and looked. Black wigglers and
even polliwogs cavorted in the pail. "Polliwogs," he chuckled, "cute little baby frogs. They won't hurt us. You can

strain them out and boil the water. I don't think it will be so bad." He carried a pailful home. Grandma strained it through a dish towel into a kettle to boil it. The wigglers squirmed like everything on the wet cloth on the table.

Having the cows was a blessing. Blackie was giving milk every day, and the men had almost lived on her milk when they were there alone working on the house. Short-tit, the red cow, would "come fresh" soon.

We did get along with boiled pond water for cooking and a little drinking. We just had to get along.

5

Grandma Wright Begins To Build

On Monday school opened. Mr. Graham had said to send Dubby and me over, and his daughter, Ollie, would like very much to take us the first day. She was fifteen and had finished school the year before. When she came running to meet us we thought she was very pretty — a crisp black bow perched atop her head and another flared at the back of her neck. A long dark braid hung down her back. Dubby's ribbons were tied the same way and ever after she wished hers were wide and of taffeta like Ollie's.

This school was so different from our school in Minneapolis. The desks looked like church seats that had long narrow tables in front of them. No piano. No marching in or out. At recess everyone rose and ran noisily outside. There was no one to be quiet for. The trees and the birds didn't care about noise.

We played Ante-Ante-Over, throwing a ball over the roof and racing wildly around the corners to catch one another. I liked that, because I could run faster than the others. At noon, lunch boxes were opened outside. The air was warm, so it was like a picnic. We played Pump-Pump-PullAway and Last-Couple-Out — fast running games, until the teacher rang the little hand bell.

The day went fast and as we plodded home we could barely lift the legs that had never walked so far or played so hard. Grandma Wright had baked bread that day and as we sat by the table she cut fresh crusts from a round loaf and buttered them.

At suppertime there was so much to tell; we jabbered constantly, and we wanted to tell it all to Papa Frank. Aunt

Carrie brought a tablet, though not much was written that night. We couldn't stay awake. After several days there was even more to tell. We knew he wanted to hear about school. His letter had reminded us of that.

* * *

Even though Uncle Ed was often cross, we loved Aunt Carrie and wanted to stay with her. So we carried wood and fed the chickens to please Uncle Ed. The women milked Blackie and did other chores so the men could keep working on the house and get Grandma's log house and the barn built before winter set in.

We had a playhouse on the hill. Dubby was the mama and I was her little girl and had to obey her. Dubby loved this. I would much rather have been in Donald's playhouse where I was the wife and Donald helped me.

I liked better to teeter-totter. We had one near the chicken roost, made of a board across a sawhorse. But Dubby didn't like it. She got only quick boosts, for I needed the longer end to make it balance. So, to keep Dubby from quitting every time, Grandpa Wright centered the board and tied a big stone in front of me to give us an equal ride. That was better.

Every day, coming from school, we heard the ring of hammers. Uncle Ed was on the roof nailing shingles, while Grandpa worked below covering the outside walls with tar paper, carrying long strips of it up the ladder. Nearby, an open keg held shiny tin disks that were being nailed like silver polka dots over the heavy paper.

Grandpa Wright foolishly took two disks and held them together between his lips and breathed to show us what a fine whistle it made. Then Aunt Carrie worried as we ran around the yard with whistling wheels in our mouths. She stopped us, fearing we would choke, and said to Grandma Wright, "Sometimes I almost wish I hadn't brought the girls along. If anything should happen I'd get all the blame." But her mother-in-law said she wasn't too concerned. She expected children to mind and that was that.

Grandma Wright was more interested in planning her log house and was so anxious to have it built that she threatened to cut down trees herself. She did clear brush from a wooded area across the road where she decided her yard and house should be. She raked, and laid stones for flower beds, seeing the house in her mind's eye. "I want my house to face the road and have a beautiful yard all around it," she told us more than once.

To keep her quiet, Grandpa took time to cut a few Norways and drag them to the yard by a chain hitched to Lady. That was as much as he could do right then. He said to her, "Why get the cart before the horse. The cellar has to be dug first."

Grandma had declared she wanted a root-cellar underneath the house. "For," she said, "I don't want to go traipsin' to an outside cave in the winter." The present house had no cellar, so we would all use hers. Grandpa intended to dig it as soon as they finished building the slab barn.

Seeing those trees lying untouched in the yard was more than Grandma could endure. One day she took the axe and started smoothing each one, then measured and marked the lengths needed for the ends or sides of her house. Later on, she began to saw, using the little bucksaw. But it cut too painfully slow.

Aunt Carrie watched her from the kitchen window, out there pushing and tugging by herself, and she said, "Oh, I wish she wouldn't be so impatient, she'll make herself sick."

The Crosscut Saw Wiggled And Jumped

Aunt Carrie decided to help. We followed her outside. "Mother Wright, let me take a turn at that and you rest for awhile." But progress was even slower for Aunt Carrie, having never before touched a bucksaw.

While resting on the pile of logs, Grandma Wright spied the long cross-cut saw hanging by one handle from a tree crotch nearby. That saw was just waiting for two people. "Carrie," she cried, "look!" Pointing to the tree as she rose, she advanced with a purpose and took the shiny metal band from the crotch.

Aunt Carrie stopped struggling, and together they looked it over. A short handle sprouted straight up from either end of the long, wide blade, and they wasted no time grabbing those handles. After placing it across the log, Grandma Wright grasped her end with both hands and pulled the wobbly metal band with determination. Using equal effort, Aunt Carrie jerked it back to her side.

At first it wiggled and stuck and jumped. They were laboring awkwardly for the log lay on the ground, and their long skirts sagged in front of them.

Aunt Carrie straightened and said, "We could do a lot better if we could just raise this log some way."

After tying back the bothersome skirts, they strained to lift the huge log and rest its ends on other logs. That was much better. Soon they were really sawing, pulling in turn regularly, stopping often for breath and to unbend and rest their backs. Aunt Carrie's dark hair soon sagged in loops over her sweating forehead instead of remaining in a neat roll on top.

Blistered palms needed constant attention. They tried wrapping rags around the saw handles, but the rags were forever slipping. Determined, they kept on and, after many days, became experts. No longer were there blisters, but yellow callouses instead. These were rubbed with glycerine every night.

Grandpa Wright cut more trees and dragged the finished ones to the new yard across the road. The men finally dug the cellar and started building, hewing and notching the logs. The women were pleased with themselves. They had sawed all the lengths needed!

Before long, life would be a little easier. Already an iron pump, painted green, stood over the newly drilled well in Uncle Ed's yard. His house was completed except for that upstairs floor. New stairsteps, edged by a handrail, led up the wall of the kitchen replacing the ladder.

At last, with their house finished, Grandpa and Grandma Wright moved from the front room, leaving space for Aunt Carrie's piano which was brought safely from the freight house. Again, Aunt Carrie played for all to sing. The fall days were welcomed.

*   *   *

We liked our schoolmates. There was one girl we thought especially nice. She was part Indian and some of the children called her "the halfbreed." She lived close enough to go home at noon and sometimes, after eating, Dubby and I would hurry down the road to meet her. This gave us a chance to walk with her pet fawn as well. It often followed her and then stayed on the road watching everyone, refusing to go home until she had gone inside.

Her name was Effie and the children would call out, "Effie had a little fawn, its tail was white as snow, and everywhere that Effie went, the fawn was sure to go." And Effie would smile.

She lived in a double-sized house and there was a reason.

We had seen the sprawling building, but had never gone close. Effie knew her home was different and had tried to explain. Two white men had married Indian women and each couple started a family. The men had traded wives and more children were born. So it was most difficult for anyone to remember which children were Effie's full brothers and sisters, or half-brothers and halfsisters, or just step-brothers and step-sisters.

There were two mothers and two fathers and ten children. Each man and his present squaw had their own rooms. The children belonged where their own mother was, but they played together and ran through all the rooms as one big family.

One day when Effie hadn't come to school, Dubby and I ran down to see her. We stopped in the yard when we heard loud quarreling coming from inside. I wanted to run but Dubby was too curious. Effie saw us and came outside wiping tears.

Between sobs she told us, "A terrible thing has happened. My little brother's step-mother hit him so hard she almost killed him." She urged, "Come on," and led us around to a side door to look in. I was afraid because I could hear the two mothers fighting and the children crying.

The side door was open and we could see a little boy sitting on the edge of a bed with his face buried in his arms. A ring of children huddled around him, comforting and consoling. When Effie stepped in and asked him to take his arm down, we gasped. The whole left side of his face was puffed and one eye swollen shut. The awful part was that the red welts were in the shape of a hand showing four fingers.

"That's his step-mother's hand," said Effie. The force of the step-mother's swinging arm had thrown him the full length of the largest room, Effie explained. "He didn't do anything naughty, either," she said as she soothed and hugged him, adding, "and he's my full brother, and only four years old." She was so distressed.

We didn't stay, but promised to come another time. We did, and we saw the larger rooms and all the children with little round faces that looked so much alike.

6

A Logging Camp Is Built

Sometimes, after school, Dubby and I stopped at the pretty yellow house we had first noticed when coming from Brainerd. Sure enough, nice people lived there. Mrs. Steece, whom we came to like very much, often called and handed us cookies from her doorstep, knowing we had a long way to go. If Ollie stood outside waving we'd run down Grahams' lane. But days were shorter so we couldn't linger. Aunt Carrie would be watching and worrying.

One day when we reached home she said, "Don't go out and bother Uncle Ed now. He's been mad about something all afternoon." Just about suppertime, we heard a commotion down by the barn and peeked from the kitchen door to see him whipping King and Lady and cursing loudly with horrible swear words. His nasty temper was showing.

The horses were unhooked from the wagon but still in their harness, and he was holding King's head by the bridle, twisting it sideways and trying to strike both horses at the same time with the long ends of the flat leather lines. The horses, fastened together, were backing and circling away from the cutting straps. But he followed them around and around, lashing their backs.

"Now just look at that man abuse those poor horses," Aunt Carrie said as she watched him whip King and Lady. "I think he had an argument with Grandpa, and this time he didn't get his way."

Fanny was so frightened she came whining to be let inside. Poor Fanny, she was going to have puppies before long.

Uncle Ed was still in an ugly mood as we sat at the supper

table in front of the kitchen window. Dubby always talked a lot and, although that helped sometimes to get acquainted with strangers, it got her into trouble at other times. Right then she was chattering and trying to chew at the same time, when suddenly Uncle Ed turned to her and said, as he pointed out of the window, "Do you see that tree out there?" I too, looked at the smooth trunk of the Norway pine a few feet beyond. It showed clearly, even through the dusk. "Well," he continued, "if you don't shut up, I'll skin you alive and nail your hide out on that tree to tan."

"Oh — Ed —!" Aunt Carrie said, and nothing more. No one said anything more. Dubby stopped talking and stopped chewing too, and cried.

I had heard people say, "I'll tan your hide," but I had never thought it could be as terrible as that and I didn't think anything would have to be skinned while still alive. We tried to stay close to Aunt Carrie the rest of the evening. It wasn't fun being in the room with Uncle Ed. Aunt Carrie didn't play the piano. Nobody seemed to want to sing.

We crept upstairs. Sitting close together on the bed, and pulling off long stockings, Dubby whispered, "I just hate him. Papa would never say anything like that or whip the horses that way. I don't see why they don't like Papa. He's much nicer than Uncle Ed. I wish he would come and get us."

I thought a moment and said, "But Aunt Carrie loves us. She would feel bad if we left her. Maybe Papa will get us a home. He promised us he would."

Downstairs there was arguing in low tones. Once we heard Uncle Ed say Dubby's name. But even with all his meanness, he seldom spoke crossly to me. Aunt Carrie felt badly when he blamed Dubby for everything. He often slapped Dubby if she talked back. And still, she did talk back.

* * *

At last Aunt Carrie visited school. Others came too, for it was a special day. The teacher had planned a spelldown with lines formed along the wall and later chose a group to go up front and add sums on the blackboard.

The one thing I didn't like was arithmetic, if I had to stand and say the answer in a hurry, but the teacher called on me and three other girls to "total a column." It was to be a race!

The teacher read numbers such as 2, 7, 4, 6 , which we all chalked, one below another, into a column. Hearing "Go" we drew a line and started adding.

One girl, who always outdid all the others, was standing beside me right now and my knees were shaking. It was no use, for the girl counted with her chalk, sharply tapping dots alongside each number as if marking a domino. Four dots squared with one in the middle counted five.

The clattering speed was terrifying. From the top down she rapped and mumbled aloud in counting. I lost track each time I was halfway down, and so did the others. The tat-tat-tattat-tat drowned all else. The girl drew attention for she did win every time.

Aunt Carrie was disgusted. After leaving she said, "I think it's just ridiculous for the teacher to allow that girl to count that way. She's no smarter than the others. The next time you get a chance with her, make all the noise you can and rap the same way. I'll bet she won't be able to think either." Just the same, I felt bad for being beaten in anything.

We stopped at Steeces' and were warmly welcomed. Aunt Carrie wanted to thank Mrs. Steece for being so nice to

Dubby and me. Mrs. Steece was a tiny woman and to appear taller she piled her lovely white hair into a highly twisted beehive. Aunt Carrie liked Mrs. Steece and planned to see her again.

Farther along and close beside the road, we had found a patch of red wintergreen berries low on the ground. I ran ahead now and picked handfuls from the waxy leaves for Aunt Carrie to taste. The day seemed very special with her walking beside us. Even the pines stood greener, for fall had sneaked in breathing gold over the brush and coaxing the flaming sumac to glow like ribbons against the lower evergreens.

As we neared home, the clack of Uncle Ed's axe sounded. Every day he was cutting pine trees to sell. At the same time he was getting a cornfield. The cleared space would become field and garden in the spring after the stumps were pulled. Grandpa Wright worked steadily, dragging cut trees to the end of "the field." Clearing the land was everyone's duty. Dubby and I helped — dragging branches and carrying stones to the sides.

There had been the problem of how to get logs to Minneapolis where a sawmill would buy them. Finally, a plan was worked out with John Anderson. They would send their logs along with his to the same company and mark them with his marker. They would keep track and divide the money when it was received - all logs would not reach the mill. In the spring there would be enough water in connecting streams between lakes so the logs could float from Crooked Lake all the way to the Mississippi, and that big river would carry them on to the sawmill.

One day Mr. Anderson came over all excited. The most surprising thing had happened. Even before sitting down he started talking. "We've got something coming now that I never expected to see. Some big company is starting to build a logging camp, almost in our yard."

Uncle Ed, always ready to fight, spoke up. "Well, I'd put a stop to that. How do they have the right to do that? Are you sure?"

"Yes. There's a gang of lumberjacks camping there right now and cutting logs for the building — I talked to them and the foreman says his company has a contract for logging all that territory and there is nothing we can do about it. They're putting the camp right next to my line because that keeps them close to the lake."

"How many are there?" Aunt Carrie wanted to know.

"Oh, at least twenty. And we're wondering if we'll have to stay locked in — we'll never know when some drunken lumberjack might come wandering around." He sounded so discouraged. "And just think how it's going to look. The countryside will be stripped when all those big pines are taken."

And there was more: Now there would be so many other logs in that end of the lake along with Anderson's and Wright's. It was something to be considered slowly. And worked out soberly. Aunt Carrie and Grandma Wright had said they were very curious to see it all, but they held themselves a full day before walking over. Dubby and I went along. We found the camp forming all right. Andersons' thought it was on their doorstep, though really it was over a city block away. None of us stayed outside, even though it was a bright warm day, but we watched the activity from a front window. We sympathized with Mrs. Anderson and promised to come back soon.

* * *

Although Uncle Ed's house looked finished the space above the kitchen was still open to the roof where the floor was not completed.

One night the thing Aunt Carrie had worried about happened. Everyone was sleeping when suddenly a thud, a clatter of sliding wood followed by a scream came from below. I woke up with the first thud, leaped from the bed and reached the steps against the wall even before the scream. I knew it was Dubby, for she wasn't in bed. Then Aunt Carrie cried, "Oh my God — Ed — Light the lamp!" She jumped to make her way toward the stairs. As she passed our empty bed she groaned in horror, "They've fallen!"

Dubby had walked in her sleep and stepped off the open edge, falling on the high pile of stove wood beside the range. When I reached her she was sitting up wondering what had happened.

As Aunt Carrie felt her way in the dark she pleaded, "Girls! Girls! Oh, I knew this would happen!" She thought we were unconscious when all was so quiet.

I called, "I'm down here. I didn't fall." Then the moving lamplight Uncle Ed was bringing showed that Dubby didn't seem to be badly hurt. The pile of sticks had rolled enough to break the fall, but she had barely missed hitting the iron stove!

Aunt Carrie arrived and helped her up, feeling for broken bones, but could find nothing wrong. Dubby was dazed and still half asleep. Uncle Ed said a mean thing — "Well, that's one thing your fat is good for." We all climbed back upstairs and pulled the trunk and some boxes into place to surround that open drop-off, before crawling into bed, thankful we wouldn't have to drive forty miles to a doctor.

7

Uncle Ed Is Heartless

A few days later, Fanny's babies were born. Proud Fanny! She brought a fluffy, light-brown puppy to the back door and excitedly put it down, then raced to the barn for another. As she came carrying them in her mouth, one after another, Aunt Carrie said, "Mercy! How many more?"

I started down the back yard to help, but Aunt Carrie called, "Beeny Coony, don't you touch them. You let her do it. She knows how to carry them. You come back."

Aunt Carrie put some old cloth into the corner near the stove and Fanny placed her puppies on it. When she had put down five she stayed, nudging them happily, and looked up as though to say, "There they are. Aren't they nice?"

Aunt Carrie sighed, "Oh dear, why did she have to get so many. We can't keep all of them." Dubby and I pleadingly promised to care for them. Aunt Carrie said, "We'll try to find homes for them. Uncle Ed would never keep that many."

That evening something happened that helped things a lot. When Uncle Ed came in from doing chores, he said, "The old ewe didn't show up tonight." Aunt Carrie asked if the other sheep were there, and they were.

"That's funny," she said. "Did she have her bell on?"

"Yes."

No one worried about the ewe that night. But the next day she was expected to come home, at least by evening. She didn't. Or the next day, either. Then Aunt Carrie said she thought that here was a chance to drive around to neighbors and give puppies away while looking for the ewe. Although they were too young to leave their mother, it would be better than killing them which Uncle Ed had wanted to do the first day.

Uncle Ed, with Aunt Carrie and us girls, started out on Saturday morning with three of the soft little animals squirming in my and Dubby's laps on the floor of the wagon. Three must be given away. We stopped at several places. No one had seen the ewe. Worse than that, almost everyone had dogs of their own to give away.

As we turned homeward, only one family had taken a puppy. Aunt Carrie had said Dubby and I could each keep one, and those two had been chosen and left at home with Fanny. Now, the two browneyed puppies, crawling over our legs, weren't wanted by anyone. I hugged the one I was holding and begged, "Please — can't we keep these puppies too?"

Uncle Ed snorted. "We'll have three as it is and three grown dogs are too many. People will think Indians live on the place."

"One of them might die before it's grown," Aunt Carrie reminded him. He told her he intended to get rid of two more.

After arriving home, I carried the pups to the box in the kitchen to snuggle with the others, hoping they could stay there. Only minutes later when I looked, two were gone. I couldn't tell which two. Dubby practicing at the piano, said she hadn't taken them. Aunt Carrie told me she thought Uncle Ed had.

I whirled to dash outside and from the back door I saw poor Fanny down by the hog pen begging and whining pitifully. I reached Fanny just in time to see Uncle Ed, standing inside the pen, ready to kill the second puppy. I pleaded for him to stop, but he didn't. He was again showing his meanness. Holding it by the legs, he swung the puppy's head against a post of the pen and tossed it to the muddy ground with the other one that lay killed. He left them with the hogs.

It was too horrible! I ran back to the kitchen sobbing. Aunt Carrie hugged and tried to comfort me, "Oh, why did he have to do it that way. Drowning would have been so much better. How can he be so cruel?" she said.

Dubby hastened out to sympathize with Fanny. She squatted down and hugged her. It had been so awful that Fanny had seen it. Poor, poor Fanny.

We were certain at that moment that Aunt Carrie's husband was the meanest man on earth. We hoped Papa Frank would come soon so we could tell him.

We listened again that evening for the tinkling bell on the lost ewe. Animals shouldn't get lost the way people do. Cows don't get lost. Mrs. Steece had told us that. She said, "If you ever get lost in the woods, listen for a cowbell. When you find a cow, get behind it and chase it. It will take you out of the woods." Mrs. Steece knew that was true. She had been lost, and a cow she chased brought her out to a road.

No sheep bell was heard that evening, but early the next morning, while we were still in bed, there was a tinkle-tinkle-tinkle that Aunt Carrie heard first. "Listen!" she said. "There's that ewe!" It was easy to tell the special sound of her bell.

I jumped out of bed and ran to the window to look down. Sure enough, there she was, picking her way down the rough hillside road on into the yard and up to the tub by the pump to drink, just as though she hadn't been away. No one knew where she had been all those days. She never stayed away again.

There's Your Rug

8

Supper With The Lumberjacks

There was a small rug on Graham's floor, made from the pelt of a black bear that Mr. Graham had shot. Aunt Carrie yearned for one like it, so Uncle Ed kept saying, "I want to go hunting to get Carrie a rug." He had been impatient to go for big game, the real reason he had wanted to come north.

So it was with great excitement that he rode away on horseback with Mr. Graham one morning. I knew he was hoping especially to shoot a bear.

Around the house all day, things seemed strangely different. Aunt Carrie baked a cranberry pie and cookies. We helped lay cooky dough in the pans as we talked of what Uncle Ed might bring. Afterward, in late afternoon when waiting was hardest, Aunt Carrie sat in a low rocker near the front door mending, while Dubby and I played duets at the piano.

We were pounding out "Chop-Sticks" so loudly, the hunters reached the door without being heard. So Aunt Carrie had no warning before Uncle Ed opened the door, leaned over, and rolled a black bear from his shoulder right against her feet. It was soft and limp and dead, but she let out a scream as if it were biting her. It was not a large bear.

"There's your rug!" he announced, and threw his head back laughing, as Aunt Carrie pulled away in terror. But there was more. Outside, a doe was tied atop Mr. Graham's horse. That was the big prize. The trip had been successful.

Later they divided the venison. It tasted like fine beef. No one wanted the bear meat. It look dark and tasted almost bitter, but we tried several times to eat it.

* * *

When it snowed and they could use the bobsled, Uncle Ed and Grandpa Wright started hauling their logs to the shore of Crooked Lake to await spring. At home they talked of skidways, and markings, and key logs, until the women and we girls could hardly wait to see it all. And too, the lumber camp on the shore was now in operation.

On Saturday, right after dinner, we all climbed atop the logs, piled on the low sled-runners. Uncle Ed guided King and Lady through the woods, curving round trees and sliding over quiet untracked snow where no road was ever intended.

We came to Andersons' house first. Uncle Ed let us womenfolk off there to visit and drove on with Grandpa to unload. We could walk over later. Mrs. Anderson seemed much less worried about the camp. She said, "The foreman and the cook came over to get acquainted and they seem to be real nice men."

The road to where Uncle Ed and Grandpa were working led through the logging camp. When later we walked by, the foreman, who was crossing the yard, invited us to look inside the buildings. Grandma and Aunt Carrie wanted very much to do that, so after a polite hesitation, we followed him.

Three long and low buildings, sided with upended slabs, formed the camp. He showed us inside the barn first, being nearest that building at the time. Long rows of empty stalls waited for horses. They would be filled at night.

Then he led us across the road to the rest of the camp nearer the lake. Here was a bunkhouse where the men slept. We didn't go in there. The other building was the kitchen, the grub-house. These two long squatty habitats stood end to end like Siamese twins, separated only by a narrow hall-like space, and connected by a continuous roof. In this open-air hallway, a low bench held a row of granite hand basins. Clean towels dangled ready from nearby pegs on the slab wall.

The courteous foreman invited us to step into the kitchen. Here long tables and benches filled all the area except the far end where open cupboard shelves were nailed to the wall, and where a monstrous table-like iron stove boosted black pipe to the roof.

The cook, working near the stove, smiled pleasantly and started forward to meet his visitors, wiping his hands on the great white towel stretched across his bulging waistline. He invited us to stay for the doughnuts he was ready to make, and told us to "Just call me Bill." He was much pleased to have visitors.

But we decided not to wait. Grandma Wright said, "We might stop on our way back."

When we were far out in the road leaving, the foreman called, "Why don't you eat supper with us? We eat early. And Bill would sure enjoy company. So would all the rest of the men." Aunt Carrie thanked him, promising, "We'll see."

Dubby and I ran ahead, following the tracks of the bob-sled. It was some distance around to where King and Lady were standing, looking big in front of the now empty runners. Here the lake front had fewer trees and was sloping the way it needed to be so logs could be rolled into the water in spring.

I had heard the talk about skidways and sliding the logs into the lake to float. Now, when I saw them unloaded so far up on the bank, I asked, "Why don't you put them nearer the water?"

Uncle Ed stopped working to talk. "They will be near the

water, right on the edge of it, when the time comes. This lake will be so full of water by spring it will come way up the bank to where we're standing." I couldn't believe that until after he explained what Mr. Anderson had told him.

"They have dammed up the outlet over there," he pointed across the bay, "so water can't run out of the lake. And when all this snow melts, and all the streams running to the lake bring more melted snow, this lake will be much bigger than it is now." He spread his arms, showing where the water would be. "At this end of the lake, logs will be crowding each other to find room to float." I didn't think there could be that many logs.

He turned to his work and put down two long logs pointing in a slant toward the lake, like rails of a track. He was making a skidway to hold the logs in a pile. Then he drove two stakes at the low end and laid the key log behind on the rails. That log would release all others when touched, if the stakes were removed. He patiently explained it all to me.

Each log had to be marked for ownership, like cattle are branded on the range. This he did before boosting them onto the skids. I liked to watch the process. He used a heavy iron mallet fastened to a long handle like an axe. It showed raised letters that would become pressed into the soft wood. Straddling a log, so the end was in front of him, he firmly gripped the handle with both hands and lifted the mallet high, then swung it down with might between his legs, against the flat, sawed end of the log. Walking to the other end he repeated the act.

I stooped to examine and there was the mark pressed into the wood. It was the company marker John Anderson used. All the logs would go along together and the money would be divided. The Minneapolis sawmill would take them from

Sure Enough The Mark Was There

the Mississippi with long iron poles and sort them.

Not all would get that far. Some would become caught in odd places and left behind, then get water soaked and sink out of sight. The men would share the loss. This shoreline would be filled with skidways before spring.

Together we all rode the empty runners back to Andersons'. And when the men started home for another load, we hied ourselves back to taste Bill's doughnuts. Teams were already being unhitched in the wide yard. The men quit work early; they had started early. From the west the lingering sun sifted blankets of gold over the camp, caressing the woodsmen's castle.

In the outside hallway, lumberjacks were leaning over washbasins, splashing their faces. Some, standing erect, had heads buried in towels, rubbing vigorously. We ventured inside where now the long tables were set for the evening meal. Tin cups, bottom side up next to tin plates, marched like tiny bright drums along the tables.

The foreman saw his guests and came at once, carrying a huge breadpan filled with the promised doughnuts. Bill was busy at the stove, but he called us to see the large kettles of bean soup he had cooked. He said, "I'm going to make flapjacks for the men." He urged us to stay saying, "Lots of these men have got children of their own and it'll do them good to have some women and children in the room."

Mrs. Anderson had come along, and it was decided we could stay. It was still early. So Bill dished soup and the foreman seated us at a separate smaller table along one wall.

The men began to filter in and settle at the tables. Bill placed large crocks of soup on the plain boards for them to ladle for themselves, and they buttered thick slices of bread Bill had baked.

While they were eating that, Bill became very busy at the square stove, trying to get enough flapjacks made to begin serving. We, too, were waiting for ours. I became curious and went to the stove and watched. I discovered that flapjacks were simple pancakes.

The top of the stove was completely covered with a square sheet of iron, onto which Bill poured batter from a pitcher in quick even slops, covering the pan with spreading circles. Then, grabbing a long-handled turner, he flipped the ones he had poured first. Those cakes danced. When he gave the finished ones a final leap to the serving pans at the back, I was ready to call them flapjacks: "Flapping, jumping jacks." And always he kept pouring, pitcher in left hand and turner in right, keeping every space filled.

The foreman rushed panfuls to the tables and ran back for more, carrying empty pans, while Bill stayed at his post waving his turner, and every now and then quickly poking a stick of wood into the front end of the stove with his left hand. The foreman helped him watch the fire. Two busy men!

We all thought the cakes were delicious. After that first visit, oftentimes when we rode past the camp, Bill called and gave Dubby and me cookies or doughnuts. We became friends.

9

Strange Woods Are Deep

Snow piled deeper, and days were gripping cold, but we never missed school. One morning I woke with a stiff neck, even though Aunt Carrie had tied my long black stocking around it the night before, foot-end under so the moist toe was next to me. I didn't like the idea. But it was supposed to help.

For the first time, Dubby started off alone in the half-darkness of early morning. I stood at the kitchen window and cried, watching her stride from the yard with swinging lunch box. But at ten o'clock, after coaxing constantly, I was allowed to wiggle happily into school clothes. Now, after all, I would eat lunch with the others and play Fox-and-Geese in the snow.

Only minutes later, while hurrying past Grahams' lane, more trouble came. A red cow seemed to be waiting in the road far ahead, and I was afraid to pass it, especially wearing my red coat. I moved forward slowly, hoping it would go away. After stopping a moment to consider whether to turn back, an idea grew. Farther on, the road turned sharply left and I was sure that by shortcutting through timber, I could reach it farther over and avoid the cow.

So, leaving behind smooth sled tracks, I waded into snowy, brush-filled woods, sort of sideways, to keep an eye on the danger lest it follow.

Forward progress was slow. The stiff neck was such a bother. It wasted time to halt and turn bodily each time to look back. I tried walking backward, but sat too suddenly over a fallen log, jerking my neck. Then I cried. The cow wasn't even looking, so I turned again toward school and tried to hurry on.

It was a struggle to walk in heavy buckled overshoes and not stumble on snow-hidden sticks and stones. After awhile, I wondered why the road wasn't where I expected it to be. My plan was to just cut off the sharp turn, and I couldn't miss the road. So, trudging on, I tried always to go to the right to reach it.

But no one could have walked a true line. Trees and bushes blocked the way. I thought I might get back close to where I had left the road, thinking I was now going to the right; but that didn't happen either. Hunger grabbed me after awhile, for it was long past noon, though I didn't know it. The food in my lunch box was to be eaten at school with others, not before.

It began to snow quietly; like tiny white messages the flakes filtered down. I stood still to look up at the dark sky. Soft bits touched my face so caressingly that when I waded ahead I didn't feel one bit alone. I wondered what time it was and hoped not to be late for the noon hour.

Later on, most surprisingly, a lake appeared on the left. I didn't know of a lake near the school. It was something to wonder about. After standing and looking, my legs felt almost too heavy to lift, so I rested awhile on a nearby stump, puzzling over where that lake had come from and why I hadn't reached the road. The cow was forgotten. I started on, and after awhile the sky grew darker, with lateness as well as snow- clouds.

Strangely, a long narrow clearing opened to the right and to the left in front of me, like a road never used. But it was a road — at last! - smooth and snow-filled and not at once familiar. Still thinking the school was to my left, I started in that direction. But there stood a house!

Stopping in the quiet empty space, I looked closely through pine trees and falling snow to the log buildings. How surprising to recognize the home of a schoolmate. Dubby and I had been there once. But that house was far beyond the school, and I just couldn't see how I had got to it, taking only a short-cut across a corner.

Here in the road, all tiredness forgotten, I was only ashamed to be so out of place, and afraid someone from that house might see me. So, turning quickly, I raced to get out of sight.

The way was now familiar, though it seemed queer to be going back in that direction. In the smooth pathway, even with loose snow swirling underfoot, I was on wings and wished all the children could see me — the fastest runner at school. They had never seen me run this fast I thought. The white flakes racing past my cheeks lent magical speed.

But on reaching school, I found everyone ready to start home. It all seemed wrong. Then they told me — it was four o'clock! I had left home hours before. Luckily, because of trying all the while to go to the right, I had managed to keep from circling left in the timber, as lost people always do.

My teacher, seeing the lunch box, knew I hadn't come just to meet Dubby, though I wouldn't admit I had been lost. I hadn't known I was lost. I just thought it had taken an extra long time to get there. I didn't want my school mates to know about the red cow. Not ever to know about that. The teacher and Dubby promised.

Dubby sat close while I ate from the lunch box and rested before starting home. It seemed unreal to be the only one eating in the quiet empty room. I had missed everything, even the afternoon recess. But the teacher now counted me "present" for the day, and that made up for a lot.

On arriving home, Dubby told Aunt Carrie and she cried. I fell asleep at the table and was put to bed, the red cow and stiff neck forgotten.

* * *

One day Uncle Ed came in laughing. He had been to Emily for groceries. "Fine neighbors we've got," he said. "Dumb as they come."

"Who do you mean?" Aunt Carrie asked. I was sure she almost knew he meant Searlys, who live along the way.

"Oh those nit-wits over the hill," he said nodding toward Searlys'. "She gave me a letter to mail with a stamp on it that she'd taken from an old letter."

"You mean one that had been cancelled?"

"Sure. I didn't even look at it until I put it down on the counter. The storekeeper noticed it first."

"Oh, what will they do to her?" Aunt Carrie asked.

Uncle Ed laughed. "Nothing. He wasn't surprised. He said he'd explain it again some day, and she'd pay him. He put a new stamp on."

"What a country," Uncle Ed groaned, and stooped to place a sack of flour near the cupboard.

Aunt Carrie had probably often thought, what a country, and I knew she was often lonely. But this had been a happy day. There was to be a dance that evening. Everyone from miles around would be there, including children, for dances were held in homes. Tonight they were taking Dubby and me along. What exciting preparations! Cake baking and getting best dresses ready.

A long ride in the bobsled brought us to a yard crowded with teams, and we entered a large room noisy with people. Children were gathered at the kitchen table admiring the beautiful cakes. I really beamed as Aunt Carrie put hers with the others. All were very high, so you knew many layers were under the frosting. Some were chocolate, my favorite kind.

Soon it was time to dance. A man with an accordion took a chair, along one wall. Another man stepped onto a box near him. The second man surveyed the room, then announced several times, "Everyone get your partner." He would "call" for the dancers, telling them what to do.

Four couples faced in a square and the caller chanted, "Choose your partner and promenade all." Immediately the couples were prancing and stomping and whirling, while the accordion player stretched the long wiggling box across his knees, making sweet jumping music come out. He stopped only long enough for a new group to take its turn.

The noise droned on — scraping feet matching the music mingled with laughter and buzzing talk. Aunt Carrie gave us our cake and guided us to the next room where beds were piled with coats and sleeping children. Somehow she made room.

But sleep wasn't easy. I sat up to look through the doorway and watch dancing heads move below the lighted lanterns hanging from the ceiling. The man on the box kept yelling silly funny things like, "High diddle diddle and there's one in the middle." And the dancers all sang along with him when he called, "Little red wagon painted blue, skip to Ma Lue my darling." The scratching and stomping and laughing continued.

We were sound asleep when time came to leave, and that part wasn't fun. It made stomachs squirm to sit up and get into coats and mittens. Chocolate cake wasn't wanted. Uncle Ed was good right then and carried me out to the bobsled and pulled heavy quilts around us for the cold ride home.

* * *

Christmas was coming. We watched the calendar, and had our tree chosen on the hillside long before time to cut it. Then, when it was all set up, there were no trinkets to put on it. Grandma Wright always had ideas. She fashioned fans and bows from color-striped candy sacks and popped corn for chains. Dubby and I spent hours stringing the fancy white bits onto cord with a darning needle. Aunt Carrie still had cranberries to make colorful red bead chains, very pretty with the white. She would unstring the berries and cook them afterward.

Grandma Wright enjoyed coming over to create trimmings, and one evening when we were all busy, Aunt Carrie said, "I'm going to leave all of you to your fun," and went upstairs to lie down and read. It was lonesome without her and as soon as Grandma Wright left, I climbed the stairs to see her. After cautiously drawing aside Aunt Carrie's curtain, I pulled back terrified and squealed, "Aunt Carrie — what's the matter?"

From her propped pillow she was facing me and looked like a being from another world. A narrow strip of cloth across her face was tied from the back of her head to hold up the tip of her nose; her nostrils stared out like a charging animal.

Dubby came fast, then gaped in amazement and demanded, "What are you doing to yourself?"

Seeing the horrified looks, and knowing what her mirror told her, Aunt Carrie broke into shaking laughter that bared her gleaming teeth, under two round holes. She looked like a grinning monkey in a zoo. Hiding behind her book, she laughed until the bed squeaked. On gaining her voice she explained, "I don't like my old hooked nose and I'm trying to make it straight so I will be pretty."

"But I don't like you that way," I pleaded, and began to cry.

"Oh darling," she giggled, "my nose won't stay up this way. Maybe this won't even help. But I'm going to try it," she said.

We had never noticed anything wrong with her nose and were so relieved the next morning when she looked familiar with her nostrils underneath where they belonged.

The Doll Was Still There

10

A Christmas To Forget

The tree stood ready and beautiful the day before Christmas, with snowy popcorn looping the branches like lovely lace. It was smaller than the tinsel-covered one at Aunt Nellie's in Minneapolis; that tree had glistened with expensive ornaments, and our mama and papa, neighbors, and a Santa had all been there. This one was special in another way — we had chosen it where it grew.

Aunt Carrie was glad when Uncle Ed came home that afternoon and said that DeLanos, who lived nearer Emily, were going to the Christmas program at the Emily schoolhouse that night and would take Dubby and me along if Wrights would bring us over. It would start early. We would have to hurry.

With tip-toe excitement we got ready and Uncle Ed took us. We would stay at DeLanos' all night.

It was Christmas Eve and we were so happy. At DeLanos' the team and low bobsled were waiting in the yard. Soon we were on our way. Mr. DeLano had fastened an extra string of sleighbells to the harness because it was Christmas Eve. The merry "ta-link ta-link ta-link" was the only sound on that white winter night as the horses followed the road through soft snow, between the tall dark pines. Overhead, a bright moon sent down sparkles to dance on the crystal-white ground and leave moon-shadows moving as the sled slipped by.

"On a night like this," observed Mrs. DeLano, "I don't think anyone will stay away. The room will be crowded." And Mr. DeLano said, "It will be an awful long program if every child takes part."

"They usually want to, you know," she reminded him.

The schoolhouse was lit brightly when we arrived. Teams crowded the yard. Surely, we thought, everyone from miles around must be here. People were still going in as we reached the door, where warm smells and humming talk floated out as it was held open.

In the room a center aisle led between rows of long desks set like church pews. Mrs. DeLano guided Dubby and me forward and took our coats so we could squeeze in with other children and see well.

Two most wonderful Christmas trees, loaded with gifts and sparkling with silver and gold tinsels, touched the ceiling at the front wall. The colored candles, pointing up from every branch, were not yet lighted.

Two men with stepladders stood waiting near the trees, and when time came to begin the program they climbed the ladders to light candles, stretching far over at times. From the top down, the trees came alive. Each man stationed himself to watch the flickering flames, and a minute later one scrambled up again to move a candle that was spitting and singeing green needles. It would be a terrible thing for the tree to burn with all the presents.

At the top of each tree a beautiful doll stood in an open box looking down, just the way a doll had done the year at Aunt Nellie's, all fluffy and lacy and blue, and it had been for me.

I liked sitting with children who squirmed from the seat to take part in the Christmas program, but the fluttering candles held my attention instead of the speakers. Several times the watchers were quick to smother small blazes that could have spread.

Finally, "The Night Before Christmas" was recited, and it

was time for presents to be passed out. Santa Claus stomped in with bells jingling, and everyone turned as he strode up the aisle in a red coat stretched over a pillowed stomach. His long white beard straggled wide across his chest. From over his shoulder he clung to a monstrous bag filled to the top.

On reaching the front he hopped around, shaking the bells and acting happy. Swinging his bag to the floor he shouted, "Ho - Ho - Ho. Hello everybody. Well, I got here, but I almost didn't make it with this big load. I'm sure glad I did though 'cause I see you're all nice people, and I know you've been good all year. Now let's see what I brought you." Everyone laughed loudly and clapped.

As soon as all gifts from the bag had been claimed, the ladder-men started taking presents from the trees, handing them to Santa and his helpers to call names and let the owners come forward.

They worked fast, and as the branches yielded gifts — so many of them — causing so much going and coming, Dubby and I sat very still, listening closely, so we wouldn't miss hearing our names. After each child near us had wiggled out and come back with still more presents, we became worried, and couldn't understand why we hadn't been called even once. The excitement increased as everyone showed their gifts around.

At the end of our bench, a boy, a little older than the rest, sat next to the aisle. He was a popular fellow and a pile of gifts lay in front of him. His name was called so many times that people began to notice and laugh as he dashed from the seat and back. Knowing he was watched, he started strutting, lifting one shoulder, then the other, as he came back to the seat grinning. He'd grab the corner and often not get seated before his name was called again, and he'd toss down his gift and start back swaggering, carrying his grey cap.

I wished so much that my name or Dubby's would be called just once, or if that fellow didn't need all his things that he'd give two to us. Because Dubby was almost two years older, she comforted me with enfolding arms and said, "Maybe ours are the last ones up there."

Now the trees were becoming bare. Only a few gifts remained near the top. Most of the sturdy candles had burned out, too, and the men blew, or smothered any remaining ones as they came to them. I whispered to Dubby, "Aren't we going to get anything?"

Dubby tried to keep me from crying and hugged me closer, and that helped to hide her own feelings, for she couldn't answer. One of the light blue dolls at the very top was still there, so there was hope. I had kept my eyes on it much of the time.

People were already putting on wraps when the doll was picked from the tree. The name was read. I couldn't believe the thing I heard. It wasn't for any little girl. It couldn't be true, but they called the name of the smarty fellow at the end of the seat. Surely he didn't want a doll! Someone had thought it funny to give him one. So it was he who swaggered up and claimed the beautiful thing, laughing heartily. Dubby and I could not talk for wanting to cry.

The crowd began moving from the seats, and the aisle soon filled with people standing and buttoning coats, and calling "Merry Christmas" across the room. It had ended.

We didn't move, although seats around us were now empty. Mrs. DeLano handed us our coats. But we hesitated. Such a thing had never happened before; there must be some mistake, we thought.

We had been so happy to come, and there had been so

many gifts, and the trees had been so beautiful. But now when I looked, they were dark, and empty, and very horrid.

The popular boy was standing, surrounded by laughing girls and boys, as we brushed past his pile of gifts. I looked longingly, but no one noticed I had none.

Mrs. DeLano urged us through the crowded aisle. She knew our names hadn't been called and felt so sorry. As we drew ever nearer the door, I held Dubby's hand, and my feet dragged. I could not believe we were going home. The crowd kept moving us along toward the door. At last I could not keep my tears back. But nobody saw me cry. I was hidden down between the overcoats and skirts of the happy people who were thinking only of getting outside.

Mr. DeLano was waiting beside the bobsled. When he saw us wiping our eyes he knew why, but didn't know what to say.

Soon we were tucked snuggly on the floor, and when Mr. and Mrs. DeLano were settle on the seat, she said to him, "I'd never have taken the girls if I had thought this would happen. We should have brought something from their Aunt Carrie or put it on ourselves. Even a sack of peanuts."

When we were well on our way, Mr. DeLano raised his voice above the sleighbells and called back, "Your father will feel awfully bad when he hears about this. He had no idea that you would be here tonight, or he'd have had something on that tree for you. You can be sure of that."

Somehow it all began to seem different: Papa would feel bad. That made a great deal of difference to me. And, of course, he had no way to know about the party. And Aunt Carrie would comfort us and make things right again. And tomorrow would be Christmas, and everything was ready at our house.

Within minutes I was sound asleep, dreaming of the morrow. And we were not to be disappointed on Christmas, for Aunt Carrie had sent for printed cloth dolls and had cut them out and sewed and stuffed them. She and Grandma had made new clothes for our older dolls, with the china heads and pink cheeks. Grandma had pieced small quilts for the dolls to be wrapped in. Candy and cookies and pies and nuts were waiting. Yes — tomorrow would be Christmas.

* * *

It was exciting fun to ride a load of logs to Crooked Lake and then visit Bill at the lumber camp. And now there was something else to see — winter fishing at Andersons'.

One day I followed Grandpa Wright to visit the men on the frozen lake, but first we looked inside the fishhouse, up in the yard, to check the number already caught. Many were hanging from spikes, in rows across the walls — that way they would freeze straight, and pack easier. Boxfuls were shipped every week to "The Twin Cities."

Out on the snow-covered ice, two tiny huts, like privies, sat separated quite a distance from shore. Others could be seen scattered around, far over, across the lake. The two closer ones were Andersons'.

I took off over the lake ahead of Grandpa, keeping in foot tracks that led to the nearest hut. Paths criss-crossed everywhere — old paths leading to where the little houses had stood at other times. Whenever a more promising spot was desired, a new hole was cut and the house moved over it and the old opening soon froze solid again.

We found John Anderson's helper inside the first hut where there was scarcely room for two others. But he said I could watch while Grandpa Wright went on to find his friend

Waiting For A Big One

John. The man, in heavy jacket and fur cap, was sitting on a short piece of log turned up for a stool. His spread knees almost straddled an open circle of water and his mittened fists gripped a heavy iron bar pointing straight down.

This was a spear, sharply pointed at the lower end. He held a long looped rope that was fastened to the top of the spear and to his wrist, enabling him to send the spear deep and draw it up again. A lighted lantern gleamed beside him, not just to light the dim interior, but to attract fish. Its bright rays glistened on the cut wall of ice, deep in the water. It was like walking on the floor of glass at DONALDSON'S GLASS BLOCK in Minneapolis.

I got down on my hands and knees, very carefully, and peeked into the cold deep wetness. Fish were swimming in all directions, slowly, gracefully, never knowing they were being watched. I felt guilty spying on them as they explored the light. Deep down some were darting in gay disregard, enjoying their hidden home, ceilinged with ice and carpeted with stones and weeds.

Suddenly there was action! A huge fish finned itself slowly into reach beneath the opening. I jerked back while the man measured quickly and dropped the spear. Only the rope remained in his hand. He drew it up at once, reaching to grasp the iron bar firmly and guide it through the ice, for a big fighting Northern was on the end. It could easily pull off, striking the wall, even though the hole was large.

He lifted the victim and smiled. It was a beauty and twisting fiercely. He had speared it in the center of its back, and it was whipping both ends of itself in a wild wiggle to get free.

After poking it safely into a gunny sack while still on the end of the spear, he pushed it off and closed the sack, and took his position for another one. By the time Grandpa Wright came, he had a sackful and was ready to quit.

While the men were handling the fish, Dubby came outside and we skipped to the logging camp and visited Bill. He greeted us warmly, as always, then gave us pie left from the noon meal.

This was the last time we would visit the camp for many weeks: We were to leave Aunt Carrie, but we didn't know it that day.

11

Changes Come

One bitter cold forenoon a knock sounded on the front door. I raced to open it. There stood a man so bundled, with wide ear-flaps pulled down, and sheepskin collar turned up, that I could see only his eyes, and they were smiling.

I answered his "Hello," and then he asked, "How are you?" While I studied him seriously, Uncle Ed reached the door, and the man leaned down quickly pleading, "Don't you know me?"

Suddenly, those dancing brown eyes were familiar, and I jumped with open arms, "Oh — Papa!" He grabbed me up in a tight hug and carried me inside.

He had received our letter about the Christmas program, and, as Dubby and I clung close to his chair, he told how lonesome he had been since hearing of that unhappy Christmas Eve. He had cried; and he said, "I would have walked twenty miles to put something on that tree, if it had been possible." He promised it would never happen again. For he would now be closer, living and working in a lumber camp only sixteen miles away, "Just to be near my girls." Later, while Uncle Ed was outside, Dubby told Papa she was unhappy and told him the "skin you alive" mean thing Uncle Ed had said. This made Papa Frank very angry.

Before the day was over, all wasn't pleasant. If Uncle Ed hadn't been home all afternoon everything might have been different. But his mean temper was loose, and he and Papa Frank said nasty words. So Papa didn't stay. He told Aunt Carrie he would be back, but left without waiting for supper. Aunt Carrie felt bad, for he had said he would find another place for Dubby and me. "My girls aren't going to take punishment from that man," he had told her, nodding toward Uncle Ed as he left. She probably wondered where he was going.

The next forenoon he returned to take us to Grahams'. He had stayed there all night. Aunt Carrie was glad we would be that near. She packed our clothes and told us good-by, knowing she could still watch over us.

At Grahams' we were welcomed. We would sleep upstairs in a bed close to Ollie's.

Soon it seemed like home, except for no piano. Papa Frank wasn't as far away now. That was better. Almost every evening Ollie joined in playing dominoes, and she helped us with lessons.

Our great attraction lay at the bottom of the hill behind the house. There the big pond was frozen solid, and Ollie had skates. She could glide over the ice in a gay manner and promised to teach us, if we could get skates.

Dubby wrote at once to Papa Frank. When he answered he said Aunt Nellie was sending skates from Minneapolis. The ones for Dubby were not new, but were better skates he said, than those she had bought for me. He hoped Dubby would not feel bad. Dubby did feel bad though, until the skates got there. Then she saw hers were nicer. They were nickel-plated. And very sharp! We were excited.

The problem of keeping snow cleared off the pond for skating was a big one. Ollie had worked out a plan. After shoveling a broad path straight out from shore, she widened it there so as to turn easily and skate back. It saved clearing a large area — a real task, for it snowed often.

Now we needed more room, with three of us on skates, so we added pathways, shoveling outward from the widened end, then connecting the paths with an outer circle. When we had finished, it looked exactly like a giant wheel with four spokes. It was a lot of work, but we could skate without running into each other.

The piled snow at the edges was as high as my shoulders. It was fun waving to one another from the different lanes, with only heads and shoulders seen moving above the heaped snow.

At the hub of the wheel, where the space was larger, Ollie showed us how to skate a figure eight and never run together, crossing over.

Afterward, on the way to the house, we stopped at the woodshed for armfuls of pine-knots and wood. Grahams burned many pine-knots: the hard tree joints of decayed trees, gathered from the floor of the timberland.

Ollie said it was dangerous to burn too many, for they formed an oily soot in the stovepipe. Later, the soot would catch fire and endanger the house with sparks on the roof from the red blazing pipe. That was why a ladder lay along the foundation of every house.

Ollie was the fireman, and she had shown us how fast she could scramble up the ladder. We were soon to see her climb again and not for fun. One day it was so crackling cold the stove was fed constantly to keep the house warm. The sun went down in yellow and red streaks, and the stars came out like thousands of candles in a black sky.

Ollie took us to bed early that night, much too early to sleep. She always liked to lie in bed and make shadow-animals on the walls, holding her hands in front of the lamp so all fingers formed the pointed nose of a fox, while thumbs stood up like ears. Ollie could wiggle her fingers to make her very real fox open and close its mouth. This night she did it alone, keeping the lamp close to her bed, while we stayed tucked.

After she blew out the light, instead of lying still and going to sleep, she got an idea and said, "I'm going down and get some cookies. I'm hungry."

But she didn't really go for cookies. She had a plan to scare us. We soon wondered why it was taking her so long and started to follow. Ollie urged her mother to order us back to bed.

In a few minutes, Ollie came up the steps wailing, "Woo — o, Woo — o," trying to sound like a spook. She came to our bed, where it was quite dark, and we saw her face! A strange creature! We screamed and ducked under the covers, and Ollie knew she had frightened us terribly.

Downstairs she had wet a match and rubbed it over her face, and it gleamed in the dark like bright green wiggling worms. She had circled her eyes and her mouth and put a line down her nose. She really looked like a storybook spook. Seeing how terrified we were, she begged, "It's me — it's Ollie — don't be afraid."

We took only quick peeks and ducked deeper, thinking she had, at the very least, turned savage. She lit the lamp; then the gleam was gone. We sat up and she showed the unlighted wet match, then rubbed the head of it on the back of our hands and told us to watch where she had rubbed.

Sure enough. With the light out, the wiggling gleam was on our own skin, shining in the dark. That fascinated us, and Ollie streaked our faces so we could laugh at each other. "You see," she explained, "it's the phosphorus on the head that does it."

She started down again for the cookies. I called after her, "I thought you'd gone wild, Ollie."

We settled down after eating.

In the kitchen below, Mr. Graham was filling the stove again. The wind was pressing against the house and the fire roared in the stovepipe, snapping and crackling the steel column that ran from floor to roof through our room.

Suddenly, downstairs, Mr. and Mrs. Graham began talking excitedly, and Mr. Graham came to the top of the steps and looked at the pipe. "Ollie! Ollie!" he called sharply. "You'd better get dressed!"

Ollie, who was almost asleep, raised herself, saw the pipe getting red and swung from the covers to grab her shoes. The glow of the blaze was creeping upward in the pipe like a thing alive. Nothing was stopping it. The chimney was burning out, roaring and threatening. Oily, hanging soot from the pine knots had filled it, and now on this windy night, flames from Mr. Graham's hot stove had sucked up and set it afire. It was the first time for Dubby and me to see it.

Ollie's mother came climbing fast, with the pail of water from the kitchen. Using the dipper she splashed water all around the pipe to cool it, and that also wet the floor to protect it from thered hot steel. Steam spit out when water touched the thin pipe.

Dubby and I jumped up and, as Ollie had done, buttoned the middle and top buttons of our shoes and dashed downstairs. Our coats would be enough over the flannel night-gowns, for we had left on our long winter underwear and stockings for that very cold night.

Ollie was pulling on her oldest heavy coat. Her father, already outside, was putting the ladder up against the house.

"Come on Mama — hurry!" Ollie called as she ran out. Her mother would pump the water for Ollie. Right then she was rattling around for small pails.

Soon Mr. Graham stormed in and grabbed the teakettle, steaming on the hot stove. "The pump's frozen!" he cried, alarm in his voice, and dashed out again.

What a time for the pump to be frozen!

Mrs. Graham flew out with two one gallon tin pails, the water pail and the milk pail. Dubby and I were close behind, buttoning our coats.

The yard was lit like day from the white-hot chimney, spouting up fire and sparks like a roman candle. In the lower air, burning bits, caught by the wild wind, were riding and swirling to the ground.

Ollie had climbed to the eaves-line and was turned, looking down, waiting for water. She made a queer fireman with a white nightgown hanging below her coat and black button shoes below the nightgown. She had pulled a knitted stocking cap well over ears and forehead, and the length of it, along with her heavy braid, was now dangling down in front of her.

Her father hitched himself up the ladder speedily, considering he could use but one hand to climb with. He raised the pail up to Ollie's reaching arm. She grasped the bail of it with mittened hands and boosted herself onto the roof, where short strips of wood were nailed like a flat ladder, and from there she splashed the water far over sideways, toward the pipe, hoping to keep it from running back to freeze on the steps or the ladder.

Her mother had rushed more water to Ollie's father, who stayed part way up the ladder and, changing pails with him, she ran back to the pump.

"I can help," Dubby cried. "So can I," I told her through teeth chattering with fright and cold.

"All right — pump some in that other pail," Mrs. Graham

instructed as she started toward the house. "But, Oh!" she called back, "don't touch that pump with your bare hands! They'll freeze to it!"

The command in her voice was enough. Dubby lifted the corner of her coat over the handle and soon told me, "Run in and get our mittens, quick!"

Dubby had filled the pail, but Mrs. Graham poured some out. "Ollie can't handle it if it's full," she explained.

When I came with the mittens Mrs. Graham asked, "Was everything all right upstairs?" I ran back — I hadn't looked upstairs. I found it steaming where Mrs. Graham had splashed water, but nothing was blazing. I looked closely to where the pipe went through the ceiling, but the roof boards were protected with extra tin. The pipe was pink.

Mrs. Graham was relieved when I reported. She asked me to run to the back of the house and see if any sparks had fallen on that side of the roof. None had.

Together Dubby and I worked the pump handle and kept both larger pails filled. From them, Mrs. Graham fixed the smaller ones and rushed them to her husband. They kept Ollie supplied.

Her job was most dangerous. The water froze everywhere, making it slippery, except right close to the chimney. After the flames died down, and the pipe had burned itself clean, she managed to climb to the very ridge of the roof and straddle it, tossing the remaining water from her pail directly into the pipe.

Her mother was screaming at her to come down and to be careful. Ollie's excuse was that she needed to see the other side of the roof, although I had continued to check that side from below. Her great joy was "high-perching," but that night she came down fast, out of the cringing cold.

Darkness again surrounded the house when the flame was gone. Now white steam was rising from the chimney and blowing swiftly away in streaks like running ghosts. And above, stars dotted the dark sky with fire, as if all those flaming sparks had been caught and held there.

Going back inside, chilled and shivering, we were thankful the protecting walls of the house were still there. We might have had to keep alive with the animals in the barn.

We three girls hastened to get warm in bed. There would be no trouble sleeping now. We could hear Mr. Graham working with the stove, shaking down wet ashes and building a new fire. No more danger, not for many weeks.

The next night it was still deep-cold and clear. On nights like this, it was frightening to hear the coyotes and wolves. That night they sounded so close, even Mrs. Graham shuddered.

"Now, Mother, you know they aren't as close as they sound," her husband assured her.

I tightened my shoulders each time they started their yipping wail. It sounded as if they might eat you alive. For long minutes all was quiet outside, then a low barking sound would commence, and jump to a high shriek and wail down again — "k-i-i-i-i YI yi-yi-yi-yi-yi - yi."

The howl ended mournfully at the bottom where it had begun, dying out to start all over again. One coyote could sound like several and there must have been more than several on this cold night for they howled like a pack of twenty.

"They have probably found that old carcass in the ravine and are feasting on it," Mr. Graham said. "You needn't worry about them bothering us." But the ravine was too close for comfort. We were glad to be inside that night.

Mrs. Graham popped corn to take away the lonely feeling. She set the pan of it on the table where we were playing dominoes. That game was fun, except my knees always hurt from kneeling on the hard chair and reaching so far to the center of the wide table.

So living at Grahams' was not unpleasant for us. Mrs. Graham baked pies and cookies just as Aunt Carrie had and it was nearer school.

* * *

Dubby and I had made friends with Chris Kling, who drove a tote-team that passed the school. He hauled supplies for a large logging camp — not the one near Andersons'. Chris worked for an even larger one. He drove the long miles to Brainerd and back every week for food and other supplies — lumberjacks ate heartily.

One day it was snowing as Chris came by on the bobsled pulled by six horses. He always stopped if he was going toward camp in the late afternoon, just to see if Dubby and I would come racing out to ride with him. The teacher allowed us to leave early if the day was snowy or very cold.

So this day we called, "Wait," and jerked on our wraps, grabbed our lunch boxes, and ran out. Chris sat low at the front of his load. Six fat, gray horses lined up like a parade, in pairs, ahead of him. They stood resting, seeming glad of the chance. Chris, as usual, was bundled all in fur, a high collared coat of it and a bulky deep cap. In heavily gloved hands he grasped six long leather lines, one from each horse, held separately between fingers. The ends of the flat black reins lay spread over the fur lap-robe that covered his knees, his filled fists reposing on top.

He smiled at us as we climbed behind him onto the piled

sled. Chris had a big load this day, but the bobsled was wide and long, so the load never needed to be real high. As always, boxes — dried fruit, canned tomatoes, and corn, bags of sugar covered with burlap and kegs of jelly — were on the load.

Over the top the meat lay. The quarters of beef looked like just what they were, the legs of an animal. These odd shaped humps were covered with muslin, stretched tightly and held with sharp wooden sticks that Chris called skewers. As the sled slipped along, he allowed us to climb around and pull a few skewers from the bone and meat. He stopped the team to pry a board on a box of dried peaches, so we could get a handful.

The ride was real fun because a fallen tree lay across the road, blocking it. There was a ravine beside the road, where teams had turned out and found their way around trees and back to the road beyond the blocked place. But the tote-team was three times the length of ordinary rigs.

When Chris was ready to take the plunge, he looked back quickly and called, "Hang on," as he turned the leading team to the left and down the bank. Dubby and I stretched flat on our stomachs and grabbed for the humps of butchered beef to hold to. I lifted my head to see the horses below. The leading two were in the snowy gully, far ahead and ready to turn to the right by the time all of the sled had tipped from the road. It slipped down slowly behind the squirming gray backs of the carefully stepping animals.

Chris was an expert driver. He sat stiffly straight now, and grasped the reins tightly, three in each hand, knowing exactly which line led to each horse. While the lead-horses were making that sharp turn in the gully, the reins looked all out of place as they slid sideways from the horses' backs till they stretched in space to Chris's hands.

The sled touched only one or two trees, and while it was still writhing and lurching through the ditch, the first two horses were furiously struggling up the farther bank, with their hind legs spread, and their buttocks flattened.

We clung desperately and dug our toes in. Sliding off would have been fun, but we had been told to hang on, so we stuck fast. So did all the beef quarters underneath us.

When the horses reached the road, and better footing, the sled jumped the last few feet up the bank, almost spilling everything. Then creaking and swinging around, it followed the tandem teams gaily down the road.

We were sorry to reach the turn so soon, and to say goodby to Chris. He drove straight on.

Arriving home, we saw a strange man in the yard talking to Mr. Graham. His heavy short coat, and ear-flapped cap, tagged him as a lumberjack.

Mrs. Graham greeted us, but kept watching the stranger as she held the door open. Seeing him follow Mr. Graham toward the barn, she knew he was going to stay overnight. He had asked to, and Mrs. Graham had told her husband he'd have to decide whether or not to "put him up."

"It looks as though we'll have to set the table for one more tonight," she remarked as she closed the kitchen door. We were already unbuckling our overshoes and Dubby asked, "Who is he?"

"Oh, I don't know. He says he's going over to the camp to look for work, and wants to stay till morning." She meant the camp near Andersons'.

Presently, Mr. Graham came in to say the stranger was staying, and to ask Mrs. Graham, "Shall I cut some frozen meat?"

"Yes, cut some steak slices for quick frying. I won't have time for anything else." Then she added, as she handed him a pan to carry the meat, "I'm not going to fuss a lot for him. He may be a Mr. Stanberry as he claims, but he looks like an ordinary tramp to me."

"Don't expect you to fuss," he said, "just cook a few extra potatoes."

The visitor gave unneeded help with the chores. We arranged plates a little differently on the table to include the extra one. We were having company and the table looked quite special.

After supper the stranger sat beside the kitchen stove with Mr. Graham and had very little to say. Mrs. Graham eyed the man.

That night Mr. Stanberry slept in the leanto. This was a small room opening from the kitchen. Grahams used it mostly for storing things, but they had built a bunk there to provide an extra bed when needed, which wasn't often.

There was cleaning to do next morning, and Ollie's task was to sweep. Everyone was busy. Breakfast was over, and Dubby and I were washing dishes. Mr. Stanberry had left before others were up. Grahams had decided he must have wanted to eat breakfast at camp. When Ollie opened the door to the lean-to she stopped, with broom in hand, and sniffed the air.

"Mother, are you using vanilla?" she asked, although she knew her mother hadn't started baking. "Something smells awfully good."

Mrs. Graham stepped close and said, "I think I smell it too. I wonder if my vanilla is leaking."

"The smell is coming from here," Ollie decided, her nose testing the lean-to.

Her mother turned to the pantry, a small open place with shelves. The vanilla bottle was there and not tipped over. But when she picked it up to examine the cork, she exclaimed, "Oh - Oh my goodness!" Lifting the other bottles, and becoming more alarmed over each one, she gasped, "Why - Why - where'd all my flavorings go to?"

All of the bottles were empty! The corks were in tight and no bottles tipped over. Mrs. Graham mumbled to herself - "What could have happened?" Then, the truth dawning, she spun around holding a large empty vanilla bottle forward in one hand, empty lemon extract and orange extract bottles in the other. Her eyes blazed.

"Why that dirty low-down scoundrel. He drank up all my extracts!" Her hands shook as she looked at the empty bottles.

We three girls stared at the clear glass, not knowing why anyone would drink flavorings. I asked, "Why did he do it?" And Ollie said, "Why would he drink it all, Mother?"

Mrs. Graham sat down at the table, and, looking sadly at the empty bottles before her, said in a bitter tone, "Why — he drank it for the alcohol that's in it. He's just an old soak. I'll bet he goes around the country doing that everywhere he stops. He was close enough to go on to camp last night if he'd wanted to."

I began to wonder if this was what "hit the bottle" meant. I remembered they said it about Papa Frank at Mama's funeral, and I was sure Papa had never drank our flavorings.

Mrs. Graham looked ready to cry, saying, "That's the thanks you get for being nice to tramps. I know now that's all he was. No wonder he left early. I hope it makes him just awful sick," she said. "Oh — what shall I do. He knew I couldn't run to a nearby store for more." We all felt bad. We knew she had planned to bake a cake for Sunday.

Holding her head, she tried to think. "I don't see when he had a chance to do it." They never did decide about that. But the pantry was without a door and close to the lean-to. It had been easy while everyone slept. Nothing else was missing.

Mrs. Graham used spices for the cake that day.

12

A Wild Storm Brings More Changes

On Monday, Mr. Graham drove to Emily, saying he needed harness parts, but first on his list was vanilla. And, of course, he brought the mail.

There was always a letter or two for Ollie. Dubby thought she must be a very important person and asked her, "Why is it you get so many letters?" Ollie said, "Oh, I just answer the advertisements. If you send them your name, you'll get mail too."

Dubby wanted mail, so Ollie showed her the back part of the magazines where pictures of magic-lanterns, watches on chains, and even violins were all marked "FREE!" Dubby was delighted — a violin would be a wonderful "gift."

The printing below "FREE" said "SEND NO MONEY, just your name and address, and we will mail you, for your inspection, this beautiful violin." Then in smaller print, "We will also send you fifty packets of our fragrant and exquisite Abrabian Perfume. The violin is yours, absolutely FREE for disposing of this perfume to your friends and neighbors, in your spare time, for 10¢ a packet."

It sounded very good, but the pages of jewelry looked tempting too: brooches with sparkling sets shaped like wishbones, horseshoes, and four-leaf clovers. Mrs. Graham said, "Don't write for more than one thing. Remember, you'll have to send them all the money you get from the perfume. They will expect $5.00." Dubby thought for a minute. Five dollars was an awful lot of money, but she did want mail.

Ollie said, "They pass your name around, and you'll get

mail from other companies too." Dubby decided on the violin. She wrote her name carefully on the clipped advertisement, and Mr. Graham mailed her letter at Emily.

Dubby watched for mail; Ollie still got letters, but nothing came for her and no letter had come from Papa Frank either, not since he wrote about the skates. Ollie told her it would take time for everyone to get her name and to be patient.

Then, one day, Mr. Graham brought a box addressed to Concetta L. Green. It was the violin! What excitement! It really had come! All carefully packed, too.

Ollie grabbed for the hammer and pried up the boards. The box was filled with splintery woodshavings that she called excelsior. Dubby began pulling it out, to reach the treasure. Then she held it up, all tightly wrapped in heavy tan paper, and looking like a violin even then.

But, oh — that queer odor! Mrs. Graham said, "That's the smell of cheap varnish."

The color was astonishing, much too red. And it was coated with a very shiny something.

Ollie dug through more excelsior and brought out the neatly wrapped bow. In a heavy envelope, she found the strings. Also a cake of rosin to coat them and a book of instructions. Dubby, meanwhile, held the reeking gift in her arms lovingly.

Putting the strings on correctly really took some doing, calling for much patience. Ollie was as anxious as Dubby. But then, after Ollie had tightened the strings and tried to tune it, somehow it didn't look right. Suddenly she remembered, "Why — it needs a bridge, under the strings."

That very small, fancy piece of wood, had remained overlooked in the envelope. I found it and Ollie got it under the strings, right side up, eventually. Then it looked really nice.

Picking up the bow, she tightened the little knob at the end and remarked, "These long hairs come from a horse's tail." She handed it to Dubby to try first, because it was hers. Dubby dragged the horse-hairs across the gut-strings, as she had seen it done. A shattering squawk erupted from the depths, rising to a squealing squeak, as if captured ducks had suddenly wakened.

Ollie tried it, pulling the bow more firmly, but still it protested. And louder. Mr. Graham took over, tuned it better and the sound was nicer, but he didn't like it.

Even so, Dubby adored her violin. She tried seriously to follow instructions in the book. "Easy Lessons For The Violin." Pictures showed how to hold the fingers, and there were notes and scales. At the back were songs. Singing was easier anyhow right then. "Oh look," Dubby laughed. "Here's 'Pop Goes The Weasel.' That's what they play at the dances."

But it would be a long time before she could play that, or any song.

The perfume to be sold lay in the box. Fifty packets of it! Dubby said she wished there were not so much. She didn't know that many people, but intended to try hard to sell it at school. I wondered if Papa would like the violin. We wished he would come. Some days were lonesome.

We hadn't seen Aunt Carrie for a long time. Uncle Ed had quarreled with Mr. Graham, as he did with most everyone, so the families didn't visit now. I wondered if Fanny's puppies had grown too big to please Uncle Ed, and if Aunt Carrie missed us. But we skated a lot, and school was fun. So the days passed.

Winter lingered, with snow banked high. We were soon to know it was far from over.

One day, while at school, it began blowing hard and
snowing before noon. The teacher couldn't tell how really
bad it was, so she didn't dismiss until mid-afternoon, and by
that time the whipping wind had drifted the road.

As Dubby and I waded by, Mrs. Steece called, motioning
us to come in. We could make our way but slowly, even that
short distance to the house. She pushed the snow from the
doorway and hurried us inside. The room smelled of doughnuts.

She said she was very worried, and had wondered if she
dared keep us all night. Mr. Steece said, "I think you'd be
making a mistake, Jane. Grahams might think they were lost
if they didn't come home." She hesitated, looking anxiously
through the glass at the whirling snow, and then at us, as we
sat eating doughnuts.

"My — I hate to let you go out in this awful storm. But I
don't think it's going to let up. It seems to be getting worse."
No one had passed all afternoon. Chris Kling's toteteam
wasn't due that day, either. The longer we waited, the worse
it would be.

With wraps still on, we now stood ready to go. Mrs.
Steece didn't open the door. She said, "If we only had some
way to let Grahams know we were keeping you here."

Her husband said he thought we shouldn't wait any
longer. She began a careful check, making sure we were
bundled well. "I think you will be warmer if I fold these up,"
she said, and removed our long stocking caps to skillfully
fold them back, so they were shorter, but doubled, and
warmer. And they wouldn't pull off so easily in the wind.
She found two scarves to tie around our upturned coat
collars, and she pulled our mittens up over our coat-cuffs.
Thus prepared, and with lunch boxes in hand, we pressed out

to face the storm.

Back in the outer road we turned into a white wall of stinging cutting snow that closed our eyes. Keeping in the road was difficult, but we pushed ahead, knowing we must get home.

In places, the wind had packed even the new snow so hard that by sliding cautiously I could move along over the top, while Dubby wallowed through. Once I did sink and was helpless until Dubby struggled over and pulled me out. We tried holding hands, but then couldn't swing our arms for balance. We knew we'd be late getting home.

At about halfway, a huge drift completely blocked the road. Wading in had proved it too deep to ever get through. We stood looking into the blinding whiteness, bewildered, knowing we must never leave the road. I especially knew that.

Over to one side, the smooth glassy top of an older drift was showing, where the wild wind was sweeping it clean. I knew older ice-crusted drifts were really solid for me, for on warmer days the bright sun melted the surface, and at night it froze again, forming a hard shell. One time Dubby had cracked through.

I worked my way over and found the crusted drift easy to walk on. It would carry us past the blocked place. Dubby had stayed in the road and was in the snow up to her waist, leaning back and resting, as if in deep white pillows, and could go no farther.

"Dubby, come on," I called. "It's just like a cement sidewalk in Minneapolis." And I ran in a circle and jumped to prove it.

Hopefully, Dubby pulled out to follow. She reached the top easily, the sun having melted that side oftener. But there, she broke through! I came back, so surprised, and reached to pull her up, but she was in too deep and could only wallow.

Then the edge under me cracked. I began to sink, but frantically managed to crawl away. Dubby's brown eyes grew wild. I began to think we wouldn't get home. I called, "We should have stayed at Steeces'." Dubby was puffing too hard to answer, but I knew she had wished so, even before that.

Fortunately, snow packs, and when the crusted top sank, it pressed on the softer underneath snow, and made a lowered platform. Dubby stopped sinking at her waistline. But there she stood, not knowing how to get out. More of the top broke when she grasped it.

After managing to crawl up enough to step on the newly broken piece, it, too, sank, but not as much as the first break. With supreme effort, she began swinging a leg high, to crack down a new piece with her heel, moving forward to repeat the process. All the while, her swinging arms waved the red lunch box above her head, and the driving, peltering snow plastered her face, melting there in little streamlets. But she made headway.

When again in the road, we stood a long time, considering whether to turn back. Deeper drifts might lie ahead, but we couldn't go through that one again, so we waded on and met no trouble the rest of the way, just deep snow.

Grahams were anxiously watching at a window. Mrs. Graham opened the door for us and said, so relieved, "Well, for goodness sake. Look at the snowmen! Come on, you can shake off inside."

We were dropping tired but not frostbitten as on some days when Mrs. Graham put our feet in water to thaw toes and heels. Dubby and I soon forgot the ordeal, but Mrs.

Graham didn't. That evening, talking to her husband, I heard her say, "I don't want to ever have another day like this and be worried to death. I think I'll write to Mr. Green and tell him. I know it will make it hard for him, but that's his problem. We just can't be responsible for the girls any longer."

Mr. Graham hesitated, then said, "Well, Mother, it's up to you. I know it's extra care for you, besides the worry. Go ahead and write him, so he can be thinking about it."

Only a week later, letters came from Papa Frank. Ours said the usual — "Are you being good girls?" and "Papa loves you very much." But Grahams' letter carried a plea to "Please reconsider so the girls can remain there until school is out." He promised to come and talk things over.

* * *

Soon it was April, but still wintry. In a sunny window in two shallow boxes, tomato and cabbage plants were grow-ing. Weeks before, I had helped sprinkle water and watch daily for first shoots. "You see," Mrs. Graham said, "by the time the ground outside is warm and ready, these plants will be big enough to set in the garden." We wouldn't be there.

13

Back To Aunt Carrie

The day Papa Frank came he was mistaken for a stranger: wearing unheard of dark glasses. The ground was glistening bright, and his eyes were inflamed from the reflecting whiteness. He said he was snow-blind, and we learned that such a queer thing could be true.

That rather spoiled things, for the sun was sharp again next day and his head ached. He needed a dark place, but didn't want to bother others by having shades drawn, so Mr. Graham covered the window in the lean-to where the tramp had slept. There, Papa Frank sat on the bunk in the dark like a prisoner.

Mrs. Graham sent Dubby and me outside, but we couldn't enjoy doing anything when we knew Papa Frank was sitting alone in that dark room. He, too, had wanted us to stay out in the sunshine, but we soon went inside to be with him.

Dubby brought the violin. Soon he begged her to stop. He thought she held the bow nicely, but didn't want her to sell all that perfume. He had told her so the night before. Now he said, "I think it would be better if we just packed it all up and sent it back."

"But I've already sold seven packages, and some of the others at school have promised."

"Yes, but, dear," he said, "you don't even see fifty people in months. And you'll get tired of asking everybody." Dubby really didn't care. She couldn't make the "free" treasure sound right anyhow.

I was sitting close beside him, and when I reached over to examine his high-laced leather boots, I remembered he had come without overshoes. "Papa, maybe your feet got wet and that's why your head aches," I said.

He smiled. "I can wade in water with these, and they won't leak. You see, we soak them in oil so they keep water out, and are warmer, too. All the men in camp do that. We keep them oiled." He wore heavy socks inside.

"I like your nice velvet pants," I said, running my hands evenly over his knee to feel the little ridges.

"That's corduroy — velvet corduroy," he explained. "It wears better than anything else I can buy."

"Do you wear them when you work, too?" Dubby asked.

"Oh yes. That's what they're for. All the men wear them."

He put an arm around each of us and nudged us closer. "You see," he said, "your dad is a fullfledged lumberjack now."

We talked about the chimney fire. And then about the tramp drinking all the flavorings. Papa thought that was a most inconsiderate thing to do.

During the two days that his eyes were getting better, he planned. "Some day we're going to be together," he promised, "and you girls can keep house for Papa. Just as soon as you're a little older, we'll have a home and stay together."

I think he wished right then that we were older. He told Mrs. Graham he would take us, and wished he hadn't quarreled with Ed Wright, so we could go back to Aunt Carrie. He said he thought she would be glad to have us. So did Mrs. Graham.

Only a few days before, Aunt Carrie had come to Grahams' lane and waited until someone saw her. Dubby and I had gone outside and we ran to her. It was my birthday, and she couldn't let the day pass, she said. She had told us she missed us and that she loved us.

Papa Frank explained to us why we would have to leave Grahams', and asked, "Which would you rather do — go to

Minneapolis to Aunt Nellie, or back to Aunt Carrie? You can do whichever you like."

We chose Aunt Carrie and the chance to keep on at the same school. We were sorry to leave Grahams. But now, if Uncle Ed would have us, it would be like going home.

On Sunday, right after dinner, we left with Papa Frank to go there. We didn't take belongings. "Because," Mrs. Graham said, "I don't want them to think we're kicking you out. You go by, every day, and you can take your things then, on your way home from school; and stop to see Ollie."

No good-bys were said, for we might come back if they should be away, or if Uncle Ed didn't want Dubby and me. It wasn't like leaving, but like going for a visit.

The road over to Aunt Carrie's was the narrow, pretty kind, with high brush hugging the edges. We walked slowly; it was so much fun being together again.

Rounding the first bend, Papa Frank grabbed our hands and we all stopped, surprised, and did not speak. A beautiful sleek deer with antlers was stepping toward us, nosing the wheeltracks as if following a scent. It kept coming, till suddenly it seemed to smell us, and looking up, stopped, but only an instant. The deer arched gracefully as it rose on hind legs, to take a flying leap over the bordering bushes. Like one of Santa's reindeer, it "flew out of sight." Papa Frank was so glad that we had seen it - a beautiful animal.

We needn't have worried about being wanted — Aunt Carrie hugged us warmly and we were asked to stay. "Dubby and Beeny Coony have come home," she said. Fanny showed her joy by rubbing us lovingly. Her puppy was almost as big as she. Grandma Wright had taken this one for her own. The other had been given away, we were told.

In a little while, Papa Frank said good-by, and returned to

Grahams' to report that all was well. Mrs. Graham told us, that when he left there the next morning, a box was under his arm, with Dubby's violin, rosin, directions and perfume, all going back to the advertiser. He had said, and laughed, "I'll send her a big mouth organ. She can play that a lot easier."

Dubby and I brought home every possession from Grahams'. Aunt Carrie warned us not to stay too long when stopping there and not to tell everything that she and Uncle Ed were doing.

When we had told about Grahams' chimney fire, Uncle Ed said, "That shows how dumb they are. I can burn pine knots and never have any trouble." He often pushed burning paper up into the pipe from the stove, and set the soot afire purposely. The burning stovepipe never stayed red long, nor caused much excitement. "If they'd keep the chimney burned out like I do, they wouldn't have to be climbing ladders at night," he said.

14

Spring Brings Sad Days And Glad Days

One day Uncle Ed came from Emily with a sad story.

"They've got the body of a young man over there, and no one knows who his relatives are. He died of pneumonia. They think that's what it was."

"How awful," Aunt Carrie said. "Don't they have any idea where he came from?"

"I guess not. He'd been working at a camp near Emily for a couple of years. But you know they don't always know things about a fellow."

"What are they going to do?" she asked.

"Well — they're going to bury him. There isn't anything else to do. They can't keep the body long enough to hunt his relatives. Fellows he'd worked with got some money together and two of them went to Brainerd for a casket. He died four days ago. They're going to have the funeral tomorrow. They'll get back with the casket today."

Aunt Carrie said, "I think we should go, don't you?"

"Yes, I half promised John we would. He's sort of taking charge of things."

It was the middle of April, with the road half-mud and half-snow. Uncle Ed decided the sledrunners would work better than wheels. Next morning, we were on our way by nine, Grandma Wright with us. Unless everyone who knew of it attended, there wouldn't be many there, so Uncle Ed gathered mourners. At our first stop, the lady whipped into best clothes and climbed into the sled. We stopped at DeLanos' and one other place, but found them already gone.

It didn't seem like a funeral day. The sky was so blue and

sunny. Once a bright yellow bird flashed in the bushes. "Oh look, a canary," I squealed in excitement, thinking it had escaped its cage. "That's a wild bird," Aunt Carrie said. "I've seen several like it."

The runners slid in mud much of the time, even while riding the edges for remaining snow. King and Lady pulled mightily. At the store we learned the funeral would be at one o'clock at the schoolhouse, so we waited at the store and ate our packed lunch. At the far edge of the schoolyard, a pile of earth-clods could be seen where the grave was. We joined others strolling over to look into the oblong hole. Several men, standing near who had dug it, said it had been difficult to chop the frozen ground. Picks and shovels lay nearby. The grave was all by itself. Emily had no cemetery.

John Anderson called from the school door and motioned Aunt Carrie to come. Dubby and I followed with a few of the women. He said he wanted Aunt Carrie to play the piano, and had been hoping she would get there. Handing her a hymnbook, he said, "Pick out whatever you think will be nice. Two or three that everyone can sing."

This was the room where Dubby and I had cried Christmas Eve. We sat now, only two rows ahead ofthat ugly seat. Up front, the casket rested on two sawhorses, draped with black cloth.

Gradually the mourners came in. We sat quietly while Aunt Carrie played slow, pretty hymns. When she stopped, John Anderson rose from the open front seat and turned, holding a soft hymnal like others placed on the desks. The books were used for church on Sundays. He said, "We are going to sing 'Jesus Lover of My Soul'," and told the page number. "Everybody sing, please." And they did.

I studied the casket, so close to us, and so different from

Mama's. Hers had had beautiful silver handles. This one was of smooth boards — varnished, but it did shine golden in the bright light from the window. And it was trimmed! Narrow painted bands of gold and green bordered it near the top and again near the bottom. The top sections boasted center designs, besides. The portion to cover the face was on the floor, leaning against the sawhorse at the head.

Not a fresh leaf or flower! I whispered to Dubby, "Where are the flowers?" She didn't answer, but looked puzzled. We were remembering the carnations and roses and even big white calla lilies at Mama's funeral.

Another song, "What A Friend We Have In Jesus," was well chosen. I thought: This young man had been just a friend, not a relative to people here. All verses were sung to properly make the service long enough.

John Anderson faced the few people and empty seats. There wasn't a lot he could say. So little was known about the young man, and John Anderson wasn't a preacher. He picked up the Bible and read the 23rd Psalm and the verses of "Let not your heart be troubled — —." He told the boy's name, and the little he knew about him, saying those who knew him had liked him. Now the Lord would take care of him.

Aunt Carrie played again. This was the saddest part for Dubby and me. "Nearer My God To Thee" had been sung at Mama's funeral while we were crowded in the back bedroom with all the relatives crying. I wanted to cry now, and I looked at Dubby and saw tears starting, so we both did cry.

To finish, John Anderson asked everyone to repeat The Lord's Prayer. All bowed their heads and prayed aloud, then rose and walked slowly past the casket. Last of all, one of the men put on the cover section that had rested on the floor, and four men lifted the casket and carried it out. Everyone followed over the rough ground.

It took some doing to get the casket safely onto ropes and lowered, but no one turned away until after it was down and enough dirt shoveled in to cover the casket. Only then, did Grandma Wright allow Dubby and me to look away. She had stood between us. People now visited while filling work continued.

The spot wasn't lonely. Beautiful whitepines grew near. Grandma Wright said school children could pick flowers to put on the grave, later on. When all was finished, the mound of mud looked dreary, even though tamped and correctly shaped. Aunt Carrie asked Uncle Ed to help her cut clusters from low branches of white-pine. As she held armfuls, he shoveled clean snow over the muddy oblong heap, and she arranged pine sprays over it. The green and white looked really pretty.

Everyone left. Their duty done.

* * *

There came a day a few weeks later, when Aunt Carrie said she wished more than ever they had never quarreled with Grahams, for a queer thing happened.

Chris Kling's tote-team now passed the school earlier, going toward camp. He no longer used a sled and, besides, hauled lighter loads. One afternoon, after he had gone by, Dubby and I found a wonderful surprise when walking home. A box lay in the road! A wooden box, about two feet long and a foot-and-a-half wide, light colored and new. It was tipped crazily on one of its edges. When we saw raisins spilling from a cracked-open corner, we knew it had fallen from Chris's load, and began eating.

These raisins were fresh and plump, not like the dry ones in the store. We were delighted at such good fortune, but didn't know how to get them all home. We couldn't carry or lift the box. Aunt Carrie needed raisins, too. Even after filling our lunch boxes and coat pockets, it seemed that none had been taken.

Dubby said, "I know — let's hide it." So we half lifted, half dragged the box into bordering brush, and covered it quickly with dead leaves. Then we started on a run for home — so afraid it might be discovered before we got back, although no house was near and few people used the road.

As we hurried along, Dubby worried that Grahams might get them. So on reaching their lane, she said, "I'm going to ask them not to take them. You wait here. I'll be right back." Putting down her lunch box, she started on a run down the lane. I thought maybe she shouldn't do that. It was wasting time, too.

But she came right back, puffing and smiling. "It's all fixed. I told them we'd found them first, and please not to take any, because Aunt Carrie needs them. And they said they wouldn't." I was glad; Dubby always knew what to do.

We reached home on a trot and spouted the news. Aunt Carrie grabbed her jacket. "How big is the box? — What size pails do we need?" It was almost a gold mine.

She snatched what would be easiest to carry — four half-gallon syrup pails. Moments later, we were sailing down the road, Aunt Carrie leading briskly. It was then she thought of the same thing Dubby had worried about. "We must hurry," she said. "Grahams might find them."

Dubby spoke up. "Oh, that's all fixed. I told them we had found them and ." Aunt Carrie stopped — struck with astonishment.

"You what!" she snapped, turning to face us.

Dubby braced herself, ready to defend — then tried to explain. "I asked them not to take any. And they said they wouldn't."

Aunt Carrie stood helplessly, her drooping arms dangling the empty pails. "Oh, there just isn't any use of even going," she said, and took a step toward home. "Of course they'll go and get them. I'll bet they're there right now." She looked toward Grahams', as though seeing it all — through the trees.

"Tell me," she demanded, "how did you think they would ever find out, if you didn't tell them? Especially if you hid them. They don't go that way once in a month."

Dubby hadn't thought of that.

We were wasting precious time. Aunt Carrie looked ready to cry. Dubby made a move to start on, saying, "Well, I'll go alone and get them." Her trust was very strong.

But Aunt Carrie couldn't let her do that. Half-heartedly she followed, shaking her head. Dubby was running. I meekly trailed Aunt Carrie, who was groaning, "Oh you dumb girls — Oh you dumb girls."

Suddenly, she took off, for there was need to hurry, if going at all. Dubby was far ahead. Aunt Carrie's long full skirt flared, whipping wide, while her swinging arms jerked the pails like pendulums, letting them play peek-a-boo, with me coming along behind. Every few minutes, she'd groan with disgust, "Oh you dumb girls."

Passing Grahams', she remarked bitterly, "I'll bet they're looking at us right now and laughing." But Dubby, whom we had overtaken, said, "I know they didn't take them. They said they wouldn't."

Farther on, around the turn, we finally spied the hiding

place. Dubby and I ran ahead, eagerly. There was the box, just as we had left it, covered with leaves. "See, here it is!" Dubby sang in triumph.

She looked into it — unbelieving — it was so nearly empty! I began to cry, thinking Aunt Carrie would. Dubby could only stare.

Aunt Carrie arrived and looked. Surprisingly, she seemed almost happy, saying, "Well — they had the decency to leave a few!" Dubby looked disturbed. Someone had taken a great many. The box had been pried open. She didn't want to believe Grahams had done it.

"Maybe someone else went by and got them," Aunt Carrie said to console her. But I knew that anyone else would have taken the box along and not covered it again.

She tenderly scooped the remaining raisins, partly filling two pails. That was quite a few. "Oh you dumb girls," she said again, but laughed a little this time. We didn't laugh. We felt bad and a little foolish, carrying our empty pails past Grahams'. Aunt Carrie wouldn't let Dubby stop to ask if they had taken them. We were wiser girls that night and very tired from so much hurrying.

15

Floating Logs Leave The Lake

Spring wormed in, as a tired winter bowed to the sun. On the greening hillside above the backyard, great masses of pink and lavender hepaticas bloomed, where human eye had never before seen them.

Grandma Wright found the loveliest flower, right in her yard, on the brown-needled shady ground, hugging the earth like a strawberry vine. She knew the trailing arbutus and told us not to pick any. "It will keep blooming if you leave it there." Every day I dropped on both knees, to bend low and draw its sweetness. And most every day I crossed the road to watch Grandpa's seedboxes in his window. His cabbage and tomato plants were already strong and waiting.

Busy, busy springtime. Grandpa Wright worked the garden every day. Uncle Ed worked the lakeshore. Over at Crooked Lake, the melted water of the bay was solid with floating logs. Uncle Ed and John Anderson had pried theirs from the skids and rolled them in, chaining a boom to keep them together. Uncle Ed talked of it at home until we all were impatient to go. When he took us, the surroundings were completely changed — no log piles — no snow. But so much water! The swelling, overflowing lake spread far up the sloping bank as he had said it would, even to where the skids had been. The logs had rolled in easily, floating almost where they were.

Our family stood marveling at the brimming bay, black with logs. The logging company's booms were there also, lying on the water like immense solid wheels, with only small spaces of water showing. "So that's what the booms are," Aunt Carrie said in awe.

I couldn't see how the logs could stay in a circle, and asked Uncle Ed. He took me by the hand and stepped closer, then pointed. "Do you see the row of logs all end to end around the outside of this boom right here?"

"Yes." I saw the logs within the circle lying in every direction, and those forming the rim lying in a curved line.

"Well, the logs on the outside are chained together," he explained, "and they hold the others, and that's what makes a boom." Looking closely, I saw the chains.

"Which one is ours?" I asked.

"This one, right in front of us," he said, pointing to the nearest wheel, floating, waiting for the two hundred mile ride to the mill.

"When do they take off the chains?" Aunt Carrie asked.

"They open up a boom over by the outlet to Crooked Creek," he explained, nodding toward the dam across the lake. All the water now held back, would flow through the outlet when boards of the dam were lifted. The rushing water would carry out the logs. We didn't know which day that would be. People from far around would come. Not just to see logs go out, but to get the great numbers of fish that would be trapped in the creek-bed when the water receded afterward. Men would bring team and wagon to haul them away. That would be worth seeing! John Anderson had told him all this.

The day came. Early morning saw Uncle Ed with Aunt Carrie, Dubby and me, rattling along with extra sideboards on the wagon. He hoped to be first and get the one choice spot closest to the creek. On reaching Andersons', he let us off and then rumbled down the rutted trail to the outlet. It wasn't far. Dubby and I raced to the logging camp. What a surprise! It was almost deserted! The men had broken camp. Most of the lumberjacks and all of the horses were gone.

We looked in the kitchen and Bill was not in sight. All the huge kettles were missing from the wall. Nothing was left on the cupboard shelves! The room was empty, except for bare tables and benches and the big black stove. They were to be left.

The foreman was alone. He took us outside and showed us where to find Bill. Bill had been moved, complete with the contents of his kitchen, to a houseboat, now floating out on the lake behind the camp.

The queer, flat-roofed, flat-bottomed, longish barge, painted white, was half a city block from shore, but only because trees prevented its getting closer. Small poplars grew thickly there, and this stretch of shore line was low, allowing the swollen lake to flood back to camp. So the trees now stood in water.

We explored the shore line and discovered a catwalk laid over the water to the houseboat. Only one board in width, it ran zigzag out through the trees, and we wondered if we dared go to Bill on such a doubtful track. It had been fashioned by nailing braces between two close growing trees, all the way out, regardless of angle, then laying longer connecting boards over them to walk on. They touched the water in places. This was the day for releasing the overflow and by night the walk would be useless, up in the trees.

Dubby tested it, leading the way, but it was for men's legs and the ends of the boards didn't always meet. We jumped the gaps and teetered our way, grabbing trees for balance, but they were mostly saplings, and as wobbly as the walk itself. It was quite a performance.

Bill was surely surprised and happy to see us when we

Balancing Out To Bill's Kitchen

came climbing onto the tiny porch-deck. He was aproned from neck to knees and quite at home in his kitchen. He had just taken three sheets of cookies from the oven. The huge tin pans had been thinly spread with dough and baked that way. We watched him whip a wide butcher knife over the tan crusty top in long even pulls, twirl the pan and cut crosswise. He handed us nice square cookies, and, afterward, piled the pans one over another, with the cookies still in, and slid them into a drawer.

He had put everything away. "Nothing can be left out to tip or slide around, because this kitchen is going over the dam behind the logs! And I'm going with it!," he told us.

We couldn't believe it. But he showed how the stove was fastened down, and how the cupboards, tables and benches were solidly nailed, so nothing could tip over. "A cook must follow the men as they work the logs downstream," he explained.

The lumberjacks were running on the lake at that moment. They would live in the houseboat. Bill pointed through a doorway, to the bunks at the rear. Then we believed it.

What a day of thrills! We couldn't wait to tell Aunt Carrie and hurried out after promising to wave to him at the dam. We stepped over the flimsy pathway, cautiously at first and then boldly swifter, and made it back.

Aunt Carrie was outside waiting when we came tearing down the road. "Girls, we must hurry," she called. "We have to get across the creek before they open the dam. There's more room there." Mrs. Anderson had warned her about that.

We blurted the startling story of Bill's intended ride over the dam. She could see the kitchen floating on the lake and had to believe it.

Dubby and I dashed on down the rutty road Uncle Ed had

Working Logs Toward The Dam

taken, and Aunt Carrie followed. Several wagons without horses were lined near the creekbed. The unhitched horses were tied safely to trees farther back — the roar and splash might frighten them when the dam was opened. Uncle Ed's wagon wasn't in the choice spot. He hadn't been first, after all. Looking far up, we saw him standing on the built-up shore where others were gathering. Aunt Carrie took the lunch basket from the wagon and we crossed to where we would stay till the dam was closed afterward. That would be long after dinnertime.

As we jumped our way over the rocky bottom, dry except for a trickle, we were directly below the dam. Boulders and stones rested in sand. It was wider than Bill's kitchen and would be deep enough when water filled it. When we reached Uncle Ed he said, "Do you know whose wagon that is in the front pew down there?"

Aunt Carrie saw Mr. Graham and guessed. "I suppose it's his." He nodded. "Yes, I think he came alone."

"I hope so," she said. "Visiting would be difficult."

The lake was brimful to running over, even where the shore line was built-up near the dam. The licking water was threatening and logs pushing. The dam itself was of heavy planks, held one above another horizontally by thick posts at the ends.

Some of the lumberjacks, in high leather boots, were running over floating logs, working them toward the dam with pike poles. Others, holding poles, stood on shore beside the neck of water leading to the drop-off, ready to go to work. Several waited beside the posts on either side for the signal to lift out the planks. Finally, orders were shouted and the top plank pulled up.

I dashed down the bank to see how it looked from below.

Not much water came at first, but when the second plank was lifted it rushed over, hiding the rest of the planks and splashing on rocks below. It streamed as a pretty waterfall until more planks were taken out and the creek became filled. Then the drop was shorter.

All women and children were watching patiently below. When still no logs came, I scrambled up the bank to take a look at things. Lumberjacks were holding the logs back with pike poles until enough water was in the creek. It was sucking strong toward the drop-off. At last came, "Leter-go!"

There was action! The waiting workmen with oiled boots leaped out over the floating floor of their winter's harvest — prodding, pulling and turning the logs into the neck of water, endfirst, to let them ride swiftly to the edge. Dubby and I wheeled, and half sliding, leaped to get back down before the first ones fell over. We didn't miss it as Aunt Carrie was sure we would.

The first log came, peeking like a nosing mouse on a shelf. Thrusting out, it overbalanced, diving end-first into the foaming creek. Logs following logs crowded over, three and four abreast, slipping easily and often up-ending and tipping a neat somersault, before riding along on the singing creek to another lake and other streams. If sometimes a diving log stayed on end too long and others piled around it, those above had to be held back, until the flowing water unloosed the jam.

Uncle Ed now walked down along the creek following it some distance, stooping now and then to peer deeply. Then he motioned excitedly to Aunt Carrie. The fish were coming! We ran to him and viewed it in amazement. Under the floating logs, rushing upstream, hordes were crowding —

not stopping for anything. All were big and looked dark in the water, but with light-reddish fins. So many fins! Everywhere! As they struggled against one another, flashes of light bellies showed.

Fish going one direction and logs the other!

"What kind are they?" I asked Uncle Ed.

"Oh, they're just a kind of sucker. They call them Red Horse."

"Well, Ed — tell me — why would they have to come in such droves as this?" Aunt Carrie asked.

"They come up to spawn. When they feel this new water, they come for a safe place to lay their eggs. They do it every time. It's a lot like the salmon runs."

What a shame they would be so fooled.

After several hours, the dam was still spitting logs and watching had become tiresome. Everyone waited now for Bill and his kitchen to plunge over. We wondered how it could squeeze between the posts. On the lake it was drifting slowly toward the dam with the receding waters, behind the remaining logs. Finally, when the last one was out, the big white barge came easing, ever so cautiously, up to the drop-off. From the creek below, the top could be seen riding into the narrow stretch through the bank. Workmen on shore guided it carefully between the uprights. The broad toboggan-front used every bit of space.

There was Bill, standing in the open doorway! Really going over! Just as he had said. His face beamed above the neck-to-knees white apron that almost filled the doorway. He had an audience and was enjoying it. Grasping each side of the doorframe, he braced himself firmly. As the porch extended out over the edge, he waved to the tense, watching group — like a real performer — then grabbed on again.

Bill Waves Before Plunging

The long house poked forward, much farther than had the
logs, before it overbalanced. Surprisingly, its front-end
plopped into the water with very little dipping, but making a
high splash that hid Bill for an instant. Then it leveled itself
on the churning water and rode away like a smarty.

Dubby and I ran along shore, waving good-by as we had
promised.

Workmen began closing the dam. This was the moment
we had come for. Those fish, racing upstream, would be
there flopping on the creekbed when water drained away
faster than they could find out it was leaving. Uncle Ed got
his shovel and stood ready, as did others. It took only a
couple of planks to stop the flow now. Soon the lowering
water came alive! As it drained further, it uncovered the
loads of fish we had heard about. Uncle Ed stepped down
into the squirming mess and began shoveling, but too many
flipped off. Others used pitchforks, so he got his pitchfork
and started stabbing, tossing fish far out into a flapping pile.

Dubby and I stepped in and grasped the fat, large-scaled,
bronzy things in our arms and tried to help, carrying one at a
time to shore. These fish weren't the kind anyone in that
lake-country would eat. Other uses were found. Many better
fish, escaping from the lake, and maybe some from downstream, were trapped with the others. Everyone watched for
that kind, along with grabbing, scooping and stabbing any
and all. Some had managed to wiggle with the receding
water and escape, but most were caught in water pockets that
would dry away in a few days.

Uncle Ed tossed the better ones, which Aunt Carrie might
cook, to the front-end of the wagon. She urged him to stop
when it wasn't half full. She said, "I never saw so many fish
in my whole life." Uncle Ed planned to cook them for the hogs.

When we were ready to go, fish were still hiding under rocks and would die there. Mr. Graham had gone; having his wagon closest had helped.

From the spring seat, Dubby and I braced our feet to the seat in front to avoid any possible contact with the gasping, dying and, occasionally, jumping livestock underneath.

Along the way home we beheld quite a sight: Standing in his wagon, as the horses moved it slowly over the field, Mr. Graham was tossing out fish — still alive and flopping — using a pitchfork, just as though spreading manure.

"Forever more! What is he doing that for? Doesn't that look perfectly crazy?" said Aunt Carrie.

Uncle Ed snorted. It did look silly, seeing fish jump on the ground. "I guess it makes a pretty good fertilizer, especially the bones," he told her. "He'll plow them under before they smell." Dubby and I wanted to wave, but Mr. Graham didn't look up.

For days Uncle Ed cooked fish in a wash boiler out in the back yard. He grew sick of the smell and the sight of fish. We moved our tettertotter after looking too long at red-mouthed creatures cooking in steaming water with open eyes — their heads, scales, and tails still on. When the remaining ones stank too horribly, Uncle Ed threw them on the garden and spaded them in. "I don't want to eat another fish the rest of my life," he told Aunt Carrie.

* * *

School was soon to close for the summer. With longer days, we stopped often to see Ollie. Mrs. Graham denied taking the raisins, but she told Dubby, "They didn't all belong to your aunt, either." We never lingered long. Piano lessons with Aunt Carrie waited. Dubby was happiest at the piano. Aunt Carrie assigned lessons to both of us and decided we must practice regularly. She had taught piano before coming north.

One day a letter came from Papa Frank. He was now living in Brainerd and working on trains from there. The logging camps were closed. He wanted us to come when school was out, to be near him during summer. His next letter asked that we be ready on Sunday, and someone would come for us.

We were happy, but Aunt Carrie cried. "If he takes you that far away I can't see you. And who knows, he may drag you to still another place in a month or two, and I won't know where you are," she said. She didn't know how well she was guessing.

16

A Trail Of New Homes

Sunday forenoon was warm with June sunshine. We played outside, wondering who would come. When a fast approaching team and buggy was spotted through the trees, we called Aunt Carrie, though it was too soon to expect anyone from Brainerd. The sleek brown horses trotted smartly into the yard, bringing Fanny to her feet, yelping. A young man sat with the top folded back, and he seemed to know exactly where he was. Stepping down, he asked Aunt Carrie if she were Mrs. Wright and handed her an envelope.

The note, from Papa Frank, said not to worry about letting us go with this stranger. "I've made careful inquiry about this young man, and he can be trusted to bring the girls to Brainerd."

Uncle Ed came from the garden. Neither he nor Aunt Carrie would at first believe that the stranger had come all the way from Brainerd since morning. He had left, he said, "Oh, a little before six." It was still harder to believe that he planned to start back right after dinner and drive all the way to Brainerd before night! Aunt Carrie wanted him to stay and go early in the morning. But he wouldn't consider it. "I promised to bring the girls today," he explained. "You'll kill your horses," she said.

He only smiled slowly, "No, they're used to it. They can start right out again after they rest an hour." But the animals did look sweaty. He unhooked the checkreins, letting their heads droop and relax. Uncle Ed helped him unhook the buggy. They started for the barn and Aunt Carrie hurried in to finish dinner, while Dubby and I put on our laid-out best dresses and shoes.

"It's a good thing you girls can comb and braid your own hair," she said, as she tied our ribbons. "I wonder what sort of place your father will find for you." The young man had said he was to take us to a hotel where arrangements had been made. Aunt Carrie said we wouldn't stay there long, for it would cost too much.

When ready to leave, the young man pulled up the buggy top for the sunny stretches. Grandpa and Grandma Wright brought cookies to lunch on. As Aunt Carrie hugged us tight, she murmered, "Good-by, my little sweethearts," and wiped her eyes.

The young driver stood by the buggy step, firmly clutching the reins of the ready-to-go team with one hand, and shaking hands all around. After assisting us to the padded leather seat, he quickly sat beside us. Instantly, the buggy was circled from the yard, with us waving till we were out of sight.

We passed Grahams' and saw no one. Soon the spot where the raisins had spilled was left behind. The slender brown steeds, curried and shining, sped so swiftly, with manes waving and heads high, that the road didn't seem the same.

No one was out at Steeces' to wave to.

We passed the schoolhouse — all closed and forgotten-looking. And I hoped we would play there again in the fall. But the schoolhouse could havetold us, "I won't see you again." I looked back a long time, remembering the fun in that yard.

The team held a steady trot, through timber and open places. "Don't the horses ever walk?" I asked.

"Not much. They're trained this way. It's easier for them to trot than walk," the young man explained. He never talked except to answer questions. Even Dubby grew tired of talking. We stopped at a farm house to stretch our legs and drink at the well. After that, the horses walked more. They looked sweaty. I remembered Aunt Carrie had said the trip might kill them. I wished the ride would end. My legs couldn't touch the floor.

Late in the afternoon, the young driver looked at his watch. "We may get there before your father's train leaves," he said quietly. "It's due to leave at six forty-five." The sun was still weaving red and yellow sky-streaks when we drove past the lumberyard at the outskirts. Ahead of us a train was pulling away, far over to the left, and gathering speed.

"I think that's your father's train," he said, pointing to the row of freight cars rolling behind a whistling engine. At the end a red caboose held gleams of the sun's rays as it wheeled away. "Yes," he said, checking his watch. "It's five minutes to seven, so that's it, all right." With a sinking feeling, we watched the departing train.

"What will we do now?" Dubby wailed, and started crying. I did too.

"Oh, he didn't plan on seeing you tonight," the young man quickly reassured us. "He didn't expect me to get back in time." That was better. Everything hadn't gone wrong; we hadn't come too late.

The team clattered to a stop in front of a nice hotel. As we entered and the young man put down our telescope bag, the man at the desk smiled, and said, "Yes, we're expecting them." He called his wife from the near-by dining room.

She welcomed us and took our bag. We trailed her up a long stairway and down a hall to the Ladies Parlor, where a guest sat reading. She looked up, and the hotel-lady said, "Here are the two little girls I told you about." And to us,

"This is Miss Wheeling. She is staying here, too. She does work for Jesus, and she has offered to look after you. I'm sure you will be well taken care of."

We bowed politely. Miss Wheeling looked older than Aunt Carrie. She put her Bible on the table and spoke to her bewildered visitors.

The parlor was quite elegant with red-velvet chairs and settee. A door stood open to a tiny balcony that overlooked the street. We felt very out of place here, having never been in a hotel. It was the beginning of two unpleasant days. There was a fancy square table in the room, piled with booklets, small Bibles and hymnals, all belonging to Miss Wheeling. She explained she was a missionary and worked in the north country. I thought it odd. We had given pennies at the Methodist Sunday School to send missionaries to China, and I supposed all of them were there.

She gleefully took charge, helping us wash face and hands at the marble basin in her bedroom — a large special room with two beds, opening from the parlor. It was planned that we would sleep in the extra bed. We were hungry. Though it was long past serving time, Miss Wheeling led us down to the deserted dining room where whiteclothed tables, hugged by empty chairs, waited for the next day.

Soon the hotel-lady brought two filled plates and everything seemed all right, almost fun. We would see Papa Frank in only two days. Miss Wheeling blessed the food and sat with us, waiting to take us back upstairs.

There, she asked us to listen while she read from the Bible. At bedtime she knelt with us, alongside our bed, for prayers spoken aloud. She was pleased to see that we knew prayers.

Next morning, Dubby and I proudly braided our own hair,

much to Miss Wheeling's surprise; and we went alone to breakfast. Afterward, back upstairs, Miss Wheeling, again, read from the Bible — and expected close attention. We wanted so much to go outside. We assured her we knew all about Jesus. She had told us her duty was to see that everyone knew about him. Dubby opened a hymnbook and started singing. Miss Wheeling chose songs and we sang, like a Sunday school class. She was delighted.

The sun was shining, and I edged over to peek out from the balcony door. Across the street, on the flat roof of a lower building, an animal walked back and forth under a wire clothesline. It was chained to the line, and paced from one end to the other, sliding the chain and turning each time without a struggle, always as though hoping for freedom.

It, too, was captured. Miss Wheeling said it was a coyote, although it seemed much like a dog, except for very pointed nose and ears. She said the owner had tamed it. It was like a dog to him. Dubby looked. We had never seen a coyote, but the howling was well remembered.

The Missionary started sorting papers, singing to herself. "He's the lily of the valley, the bright and morning star. Tadada - dada - dada - da of my soul."

She turned to us, "Girls, I have an idea. There's a saloon right next to this hotel, and I believe we can do some real missionary work." Her eyes danced as she spoke of Dubby and me singing to "glorify the Lord."

"I'm going to teach you a song, and perhaps we may sing it where it can be heard by men going in there. It might turn them from their evil ways."

We were very uncertain about it. "Will we have to go into the saloon?" Dubby wanted to know.

"I'm not sure how we'll do it - but here," she had found a

song. "See if you can sing this." She sang one verse. "Where is my wandering boy tonight? — Down in your licensed saloon. Down in a room — all cozy and bright — filled with the glare of many a light —" We liked the tune and began to study the words.

No other guests came to the parlor. Later on, when the hotel-lady looked in on the singing, the Missionary joyfully explained what we were doing. The lady agreed that to save the souls of men in a saloon was a fine thing to do. She was glad to help and felt very satisfied that we were in such good company.

The women planned. The hotel-lady led the Missionary, Dubby and me, down the hall to a room which had a window above the rear door of the saloon. "This will be fine," the Missionary said, after opening and looking out the screenless window. Dubby was so glad we wouldn't have to go closer to the saloon.

"When do you want to do this? I think their father is coming tomorrow," the hotel-lady asked. The two agreed it would have to be done that very evening.

The Missionary took the key, then hustled us back to the parlor to practice harder. We would have to know the words well to sing in darkness, when men would be gathering.

As evening drew near, anxiety increased. We choked down our supper. It all sounded so serious. I didn't know what to expect and felt wrong inside. Waiting in the parlor, trembling, we studied the verses. But the sky was still not dark when the Missionary said, "Now I think it's time."

We advanced soberly along the empty hall to the given room. Miss Wheeling unlocked the door, walked to the window, and raised it to look below. No one was in sight, but she decided to sing hymns while words could be read.

When it grew darker and lights were on in the saloon, she said, "Now we will sing our song."

All three of us were on knees before the low, open window. Miss Wheeling was behind, peeking over shoulders. We began, "Where is my wandering boy tonight ." Soon two men came outside. Miss Wheeling quickly pulled herself back and pushed us forward to be seen. We sang on, mightily.

As we paused to think of another verse, she begged, "Sing, sing," nudging eagerly. "Louder, louder, so the men inside can hear too!" She had great hopes of drawing all of them from the saloon. We, too, expected soon to have an audience. In the yard below, the two men faced each other as if arguing. After several minutes, they looked up at our window, but only for seconds, and turned to walk back inside — gesturing vigorously.

I turned to the Missionary in surprise. "They've gone back in!" She answered urgently, "Keep on! — They may come out again and bring others." So we kept singing. "Down in a room all cozy bright — filled with the glare of many a light —"

No one came, although we sang on and on. We were so disappointed, thinking all our day's work wasted. As we walked back to the parlor, the Missionary consoled us. "I think some of the men heard the words, and much good will come, at a later time."

All next day we watched hopefully for Papa Frank. Miss Wheeling was practicing other songs to sing that evening. Then he came! Right before supper! And we sat in the dining room with him instead of the Missionary. Everything was bright and right again. Although we were to stay at the hotel till morning, we wouldn't have to sing. Papa Frank

asked the Missionary to excuse us and we passed joyfully
out through the front office to where store windows waited.
Later we sat on wire chairs in a drugstore eating ice cream
and enjoying freedom.

We drove away proudly next day in a hired rig of fast-
trotting horses. "We'll get you moved first, then Papa will
take you for a nice ride," Papa Frank said. He had two places
in mind where we might room and board, but wanted us to
decide.

In no time, we jerked to a stop in front of a yard somewhat bare of grass, but filled with children. All of them
stopped playing and stared as we visitors advanced to the
porch. A redheaded boy of about ten, jumped away from the
others and bounded up the steps into the house to call his
mother. An older girl, with a pan in her lap, sat on the broad
rail-less porch shelling peas. This was the Heprun family:
Annie, on the porch, Willie, calling his mother, and Mable, a
girl of eleven, who wasn't in sight. Their mother kept
boarders; their father had died. All others in the yard were
there to play.

Mrs. Heprun came beaming; her blue eyes danced above
the checkered apron that covered her from neck to floor.
And, like Willie, she had fluffy red hair that you noticed
even before the smile. "Well, how do you do, Mr. Green,"
she welcomed, reaching to shake his hand. "And these are
the two little girls!" She patted us lovingly. Annie, too,
smiled eagerly, and kept dropping peas into the pan — never
speaking. Willie stayed within hearing, for he knew we
might be the new boarders.

We watched the whispering, glancing, playmates. Papa
Frank could tell we wanted to stay with other children, so he
told Mrs. Heprun we would be back.

The ride that day was special. Just being together made it so — it had been so long. Papa Frank held the horses to a walk on reaching a country road, and Dubby and I talked about the fish at the dam — and the funeral at Emily — and the raisins that fell from the tote-team. He laughed about that.

He told us how much he missed us. Then, smiling tenderly, said, "Do you know, I don't think it will be too long before you girls will be big enough to keep house for Papa. Then we can have a home together again." He had thought of it often, he said. "And now, when I see how you've grown in only a year, I think it won't be so long after all."

"I can sweep — and make beds — and comb my hair — and do lots of things," I said. We sang. It was much more fun than trying to get men out of a saloon.

In late afternoon, Papa Frank left us at Hepruns'. Mable, the eleven-year-old, had come home, and she took us up a steep stairway from the dining room. Annie, a year older than Mable, followed with the blue canvas bag. Annie smiled brightly, but didn't speak. Then Mable said, "She's deaf and dumb."

As though to show what she meant, she turned to Annie and made signs with her fingers. Annie nodded quickly and knowingly, put down the bag and raised her hands to answer, her fingers flying into all sorts of shapes. Mable could understand and they laughed, agreeing on something. That was why Annie hadn't spoken while sitting on the porch shelling peas — she was deaf and dumb! But Dubby and I didn't feel strange. Her eyes told us she liked us. Mable said, "Annie likes you." They helped us unpack.

* * *

A large table, under a checkered cloth, crowded the dining room. It was Mable's duty to set it. She did that now, and Annie took us on outside. There everyone was gone, even Willie, but he soon came, carrying packages for his mother — that being his job.

Suddenly, Annie ran back in the house, returning in a moment with a postal size cardboard. She motioned us to come to the porch. The badly worn card showed many pictures of hands, sometimes both hands together, one picture above each letter of the alphabet. Fingers were held differently for each letter. Annie wanted us to learn to talk with her! Pointing to the letter "A" she formed it with deft fingers. Then I tried. She laughed at my clumsiness and nodded happily when I did make it look right.

Mable came — releasing Annie for her duty in the kitchen. She invited us to her play house in the empty barn at the far rear. In the wide doorway, where carriages had gone in and out, a large wooden box stopped everyone. It was Mable's selling counter which held her handwork. There was a scrawled sign reading DOLL HATS FOR SALE 5¢.

They were tiny affairs with crowns and brims cleverly made of old straw braid and trimmed as any fine lady's hat should be — with flowers, ribbons and feathers.

"Did you ever sell any?" Dubby asked, picking one up to admire.

"Oh yes, I've sold four," Mable beamed.

I began sorting materials to make one. Too soon, Willie came to announce, "Ma says to come to supper."

Mable jumped. "Come on, hurry." Her mother's call meant — come now! There was no waiting for anyone when boarders were ready to eat. Dubby and I followed, and we all washed in the basin on the enclosed porch. Three men boarders were standing in the dining room. Annie carried in bowls of food. As soon as we were seated one of the men said, "How did you get along today, Bill? Earn any money?"

Willie was saving for fireworks, the Fourth being only three weeks away. "Well — I earned a nickel — but I spent it," he admitted.

One of the other boarders inquired, "Have you still got the fifteen cents you had?" Willie nodded. "Well, hang on to it, and add a little, and you'll be all right," he encouraged.

After supper, the yard filled. Willie showed Dubby and me how to play mumbletypeg so we could join the groups. He was an expert. Kneeling on the ground and opening his jackknife, he laid it on the palm of his hand, and flipped it in such a way that it came down blade first and stood in the ground. Then he did it from the back of his hand. He could toss it various ways and make it stand straight which was the object of the game. Circles of youngsters, sitting cross-legged or squatting, took turns with pocketknives till dark.

* * *

The next evening, Willie wanted to play Run Sheep Run when the usual gang gathered. Before anyone had even started to count, the beat of drums and call of trumpets in marching rhythm came from the direction of mainstreet.

"Oh — I forgot — it's Thursday," Willie yelped, and we all took off toward the sound of a parade.

While running, Mable called a breathless explanation — "That's the Salvation Army Band. We always go and watch. It's lots of fun." Hepruns lived but three blocks from where the Army would stop. We strung along — Willie in the lead

— running to "beat the band." By rounding corners and cutting across lots, we came dashing into the right street just as the marching men and women were swinging in, a block away.

Blue uniformed musicians, coming five abreast in striding step, pointed their trumpets high. Row after row followed them, and the ladies' long circular skirts kicked elegantly as they swept the corner. Some — playing banjos, mandolins, or guitars — were singing as well, though the booming drums and trumpets almost drowned their efforts. It all fit grandly and was exciting to hear. The drum boomed with the marching words:

> "There are souls to rescue
> (boom)(boom)(boom)
>
> There are souls to save
> (boom)(boom)(boom)
>
> Send the light
> (boom)(boom)(boom)
>
> Send the light
> (boom)(boom)(boom)"

. . . . And on they came — halting at the planned place, where the front row faced left briskly and began short-stepping into a single line. Followed by the other rows, they formed a huge, facing circle that filled the street, singing till the song was finished.

The younger girls, with shorter skirts that allowed a bit of black stocking to show above the high-top shoes, shook and

tapped tamborines before their faces. Sometimes they pulled
fingers round the rim to ripple the loose discs. The bonnets,
tied with a ribbon under the chin and big bow at the cheek,
boasted red bands across the top with the gold letters SAL-
VATION ARMY. Mable explained, "They do this real often
— every Tuesday, and Thursday, and Saturday."

And Willie added, "After awhile we pick up the money."
I demanded, "What?" to that strange announcement. "Yes,
lots of people throw money at the drum and miss. And some
bounces off. So we pick it up and put it on the drum." He
felt important.

The drummer laid the bass drum, skin side up, in the
center. The Captain, with Bible and hymnbook, led the
meeting. People listened — some from open windows
above. No teams came on the street. Many coins, tossed into
the circle, bounced off the drum. If they didn't roll too far,
they were left there. But when one rolled out toward Willie
— just as he had said — he snatched it up and ducked into
the ring with knees bent — as if not to be seen — and
quickly laid it on the drum and scurried out again.

The Captain, waving the hymnbook, sang lustily with the
others. Afterward, when he finished preaching and asked for
money, a rain of coins flew through the air over the heads of
the Army. The watchers in second story windows played a
game. Holding handfuls of pennies — throwing one at a time
— they gambled their luck on hitting the drum. When the
Captain started scooping coins, Wilie and other boys scooted
in to gather the scattered ones, placing them on the drum for
him.

As the uniformed circle unwound, stepping to the tap of
snare drums, the rows were formed for marching. With barely
a pause they swung forward, as trumpets blared, singing:

"Are - you ready? Are - you ready?
Are - you ready for the judg - ment - day."
boom boom boom boom boom boom

Children followed, and many others. Again, the long bell-skirts flared as the ladies whirled sharply at the corner, returning to the mission house.

Dubby, running beside them, called to me, "I'd like to play something like that," pointing to a shiny mandolin. "That's lots easier than a violin," I yelled back.

At the lighted Mission House, the band marched on in to where people were waiting. Others followed — the meeting would begin at once. Dubby and I reached the doorway, but our companions had stayed across the street. "Aren't we going in?" I called, wondering why the others had not come.

Mable called "Oh—No!" as if such a thing were unheard of. "We don't belong to that church!"

"Haven't you ever gone in?" Dubby asked, rejoining them. Willie said, "No—we just like to march with the parade. We're Catholics. We only come this far."

* * *

The next forenoon, Willie wasn't around, but he showed up at noon grinning happily. Putting a hand in his pocket, he jingled coins he had earned. Now he was ready for that question: "How much money did you earn today, Bill?" He had mowed a big lawn and earned fifteen cents. Just let them ask!

The boarder was right when he had said, "Keep what you've got and add a little." Thirty cents! Willie was proud. At the table all talk was about work. Willie didn't care, for he said he hoped to have even more by evening. His blue eyes danced above his freckles, just thinking about it. At suppertime, he did have another nickel in his "fund." Thirty-five cents! Thirty-five cents!! He could hardly wait for the questions. When they asked it, he grinned and pulled the coins from his pocket, spreading them on the tablecloth for all to see.

My place was next to Willie. This night, he sat very straight. He had combed his bushy red hair and even wet it, but from the side it looked as if a wind was forever blowing from behind.

* * *

All day long, but especially at evening, explosions allowed no one to forget that The Fourth was only two weeks away. It made Willie want to earn more money. Papa Frank came, whenever in town, and took us to look in store windows filled with fireworks: cannon-crackers, standing like tiny fence posts — torpedos wrapped in red-whiteand-blue paper. And stacks of small firecrackers in bright red paper. I wondered which things Willie would choose.

He spent much time looking and deciding, then changing his mind almost daily because his fund was growing. He hoped to buy a balloon, but unless he waited till the last day, when remaining fireworks were almost given away, he maybe couldn't afford it — and by then, none might be left.

A week before The Fourth, we learned we were to leave Hepruns. Papa Frank was living in Walker, a town sixty miles north, and he wanted us to come. We hoped to wait and see Willie shoot his fireworks. Whenever anyone asked him, "How much have you got now, Willie?" he'd pull his shoulders back and announce proudly, "Fifty-five cents!" — more money than he had ever possessed.

The days hurried by too fast, and our last evening came. In two days it would be The Fourth. Willie had bought his fireworks and now spent his spare time admiring and spreading them for all to see: pinwheels, pointed sky-rockets, and such. Each time, after everyone had exclaimed to his satisfaction, he carefully re-packed all of it in a box and carried it to his bedside.

On this last evening the whole town was exploding in noise, and Willie could wait no longer. He chose a few, but only a few, cannon-crackers and a package of firecrackers, to add his bangs to the rest of it. He was generous, too, and allowed others to explode several — passing them out proudly.

17

Living On The Shore Of Leech Lake

Annie and Mable took us to the train — We were proud to sit alone on red plush seats that faced, and watch pine trees race past the open windows. The conductor warned each time he swayed his way down the aisle, to not stick heads out of the windows. We delighted in watching the engine and the rest of the coaches, but we minded, except for quick peeks.

Sometimes black smoke from the engine darkened the air till it hid all trees. The gassy, smelly stuff sucked through open windows, dropping cinders on our hair and in our laps, but always it cleared again.

The engine galloped along, whistling mournfully now and then. After a ride of several ours the conductor said, "We're coming near to Walker now." We were crossing water — over a long, low, trestle that couldn't be seen, so it seemed like riding in a boat. This was one lagoon of a big lake, an angry lake we would know much too well later on.

As the gonging, whistling train pulled into the center of town, flags showed everywhere. Redwhite-and-blue bunting hung draped across the store-fronts in readiness for celebrating. Papa Frank was at the depot and hugged us happily.

Circling the back coach to go toward the stores, he said, "I especially wanted you girls to come for the Indian dance. Lots of Indians are already in town. So many live around here; and there's a reservation across the bay. They're the Chippewa Indians and I'll bet they'll really be dressed up tomorrow."

Then he asked, "Were you still getting along all right at Hepruns'?" We assured him we were and told him we had almost wished we could stay. "Because," I said, "Willie's got a whole box of fireworks. And he's even going to get a balloon, if they sell them cheap tomorrow morning."

He smiled down, "Don't worry, you'll see plenty of balloons going up around here." Shifting our bag to take me by the hand, he said, "I think we'll go right now and buy some firecrackers, before they're all gone." It was late afternoon.

We came out of the store with as many fireworks as Willie had worked so hard for. Papa Frank watched closely for runaways, as we crossed the street — exploding cannon crackers were frightening even those horses tied at the hitching posts.

The long summer evening was drawing celebrators. After checking in and dining at the redbrick hotel, we joined the crowds on the street, where squaws, with flowered full skirts sweeping the ground, mingled with others going in and out of stores that stood wide-open between overflowing saloons. Lumberjacks from far around were all in town.

Boys threw torpedoes on the sidewalk and laughed as people jumped away from the spitting, spattering, pellets. While women's skirts gave them protection, the pellets stung children's legs, even through heavy-ribbed stockings. Some of them flew in our faces. Papa Frank called a stop, so we could pass.

In a vacant lot across the street, a group was gathered and a little girl was calling, "They're going to send up a balloon." It was just how Papa Frank had said it would be, and we arrived there in a hurry. Several boys standing close, fenced a three foot balloon and were holding out the thin paper sides with finger-tips, so the inside flame wouldn't touch it. As it rounded out with heated air, the boys watched the sky for proper darkness, so it would show nicely as it floated.

When finally, the first stars gleamed faintly, it was time. The balloon was full, smooth and rounded — quivering with its lightness and trying to break free. Someone decided, "Let go!" Instantly, it started upward, passing the workers' faces. The flame showed bright and busy through the bottom opening.

It climbed straight and steady — even slowly — till caught by an upper breeze, where it shivered a moment, then took away northward, like a witch on a broom. Soon it was only a moving light in the sky that grew to a speck as we watched. It would fall over the wide waters of Leech Lake, where only loons and other water-dwellers could wonder what it was.

At dawn, booming cannon crackers welcomed "The Glorious Fourth," although anyone not sleeping soundly heard explosions all night long. By noon, Indians had arrived in greater number to dance. Crowds, even larger than the night before, jammed the walks. Because there were more saloons than stores and more men than women, many in the crowd weren't walking straight.

The Indians were most gaily rigged out — especially the chiefs, in bright colored beads and feathers — just as Papa Frank had said they would be. Dubby and I drank lemonade at a street stand, threw torpedoes and ate crackerjack. Papa Frank called us "the gimme girls." We had said, "Papa, 'gimme' a nickel," so often. We were celebrating.

Finally, the Indians gathered into a circle, over by the track, where there was room for wanted spectators. Squaws and young girls, and men, young and old, stood side by side facing center. Inside the ring, several young bucks knelt before an odd drum — a tom-tom — holding sticks, ready to pound. A glittering Indian Chief — colored feathers trailing down his back — stalked in the center as though deciding when to begin. The audience should be larger. Squaws nudged one another and giggled as they talked and waited. Gradually more dancers joined the circle, elbow to elbow.

I stood behind two fat squaws, peeking between their waistlines to see the drummers on the ground. Other watchers crowded so close I couldn't move, but I was in front to see when the time came. So was Dubby. Just as all was ready, Papa Frank pushed his way in and tapped Dubby on the shoulder saying, "You girls step back," then whispered, "Come here. I want to talk to you a minute." Out of hearing, he explained, "Those Indians will try to get money from everybody standing near. You'd better not stay that close."

Suddenly, the pounding started and the dancers began to "Hi-ya - Hi-ya - Hi-ya," hunching shoulders and lifting feet, wiggling and notching to the left. Slowly, the wheel turned, like a moving wall wherever the squaws' skirts joined. The feathered Chief went into action — bending chin to lifted knee — straightening — then twisting to look over his shoulder, as if something were biting at his heel. With each twist he took a peek, first over one shoulder, then the other, and snorted a word, "Buck! — Wah! - Yahee! - Ya-hah!" never stopping.

As the drummers beat harder, he pranced and whipped around, panting and sweating — his backfeathers swinging — while the squaws jerked shoulders smartly and the big ring moved faster. The dancers grinned. The Chief was doing very well. Another feathered warrior, sitting by the drum, leaped to take a turn prancing and twisting, but he wasn't as good.

Finally, the beating stopped and the wheel quit turning. Two Indians seated near the tomtom, jumped to squeeze through the ring to collect money, just as Papa Frank had said they would. Soon the first Chief, who had danced so furiously, came out to help, thrusting a cap in front of everyone. Then they danced again.

Afterward, Papa Frank said, "We'll go down to the dock now and see the lake. Maybe we can watch the steamer come in, if you don't get too hungry and tired. It comes in quite late."

Walking hand in hand, we paused at the top of the long slope to the water. "We can't see all the lake from here," he said. "This is only a bay. Most of the lake is behind that land." He pointed to the shore straight across. "I want to show you where you are going to live. You can see better from up here."

He had told us about the place he had found, near to where he would be working. We couldn't stay at the hotel alone. An elderly lady and her husband, both of whom like children, would give us room and board. Their home was on the lake shore. "You can't quite see it, but it's back of that first point over there," he said, trying to guide our searching eyes far over to the left. "You can look across the wide part of the lake from there."

A strange, lonesome feeling came to me as I thought of still another home and people I didn't know. Looking up and pleading a little, I asked, "Papa, can't you stay there too? Can't we have a home together like we talked about?"

"No — I have to stay in camp, and keep track of the men. But I'll be so close that I can come over every evening to see you." He smiled until I smiled back.

We continued on down to where the wide citydock

walked into the bay. People taking special boat rides busied the dock. Many would wait for the steamer. Venturing to the deep end, I hung from Papa Frank's strong grip, to watch the water gently slapping against the huge logs supporting the pier. Some of the merrymakers still had fireworks, so the time went fast. After quite a wait, we heard it. A long deep "Who-o-o-t - Who- o-o-t" told us the steamer was coming behind the strip of land that formed the bay.

In a few minutes, far out left at the point, it came in, sideview first, smoke spurting from its stack but drifting at once to nothing. A huge bustle of white splashing water trailed it. Swinging in a gradual turn, it came toward the dock — a wallowing mama duck — spreading a fan of rolling waves behind it.

Again it groaned, "Who-o-o-t - Who-o- o-t," (Hello-o-o-o - Hello-o-o-o).

It was white and flat-roofed — like Bill's houseboat, but four times as big. Papa Frank said it brought freight from Duluth and Lake Superior after trains had carried the freight to Leech Lake's eastern shore. There were passengers, too.

As it drew closer, the turning paddle-wheel showed plainly across the back — pushing and splashing — causing a wide roll of water to cross the bay. All little boats had pulled away before it came snorting and steaming in. Lettering on the sides announced that the "LILAH DEE" had arrived.

We were glad we had come. It had been a wonderful day.

* * *

Because the elderly couple on the lake shore wouldn't be home for another day, Papa Frank decided, after much worrying, to take us along to the men's camp rather than leave us at the hotel. He had to return to work.

It was glaring hot when we started out in early afternoon. The only way to reach the camp was by walking the railroad track. Where city streets ended, we cut over to the right-of-way. Dubby and I balanced along on polished rails, thinking it great fun, except that Papa Frank stepped too fast, even though he was carrying our heavy bag, and we had to jump off and run ahead every time he passed.

After about a mile, a path curved down from the roadbed to the right, leading to Snyders' where we were to live. But we didn't follow it — Snyders weren't home anyhow. Farther along, looking down to where a lagoon of the lake came close to the high brush-bordered track, a teepee of skins and sticks sat by itself on the wide, sandy shore. Two Indian children, standing like statues beside it, watched the strange sight of girls on the track where only men had been seen.

On reaching the camp, also on the lakeside, Papa Frank showed us one of the tents, filled with cots, where we would sleep. There were two large low tents and a kitchen on wheels, nestled in trees between the track and the lakeshore. After sliding our bag under his own cot, he hurried us out again, for it was breathless in the tent. Many of the men were still away celebrating, but would return by evening. Papa Frank kept track of the workers.

The little house on wheels seemed the center of things. Later, at suppertime, our curiosity was satisfied — though Papa had made us wait with him, so as not to use table places meant for others. Several steep narrow steps, near the front, called for climbing. Inside, turning left, Papa Frank guided us past the busy cook, through the narrow aisle between the stove and cupboards, and on to the other end where small tables with benches were in front of screened, open windows. Men, still eating, looked out past fluttering poplars to the rippling lake.

The cook was washing dishes when we brushed past him in leaving. He tossed and splashed tin plates and cups, in astonishing fashion, then stood them on edge in another huge dishpan. No towel for him! He swung the fat teakettle back and forth, dousing all with spouting steaming water. He assured us it was a much better way.

Down by the tents, and facing the lake, the men sat in groups relaxing before entering the hot canvas shelters. They sprawled against fallen logs, sat on stumps or squatted, all in rolledsleeve comfort, after two days of celebrating. With so many men around, Dubby and I could only wade, and wait for the morrow to bathe and splash. Papa Frank watched close by, at water's edge, and ended it all much too soon. Behind him the men had begun to sing and he wanted to join in. He was talking to a man as we reached him.

"Girls, this is Mr. Peterson," he said, looking highly pleased about something. "He is going to look after you tomorrow, while I'm gone. He will be here all day. He has little girls at home and I'm sure he'll take good care of you." Mr. Peterson smiled assuringly.

Strange songs were rolling over treetops. One seemed a favorite and Dubby and I soon learned it, for if a pause came, some voice was sure to start off, "Oh-, to be joined full and joyously:

"Oh the Jones'es boys — they built a mill.
They built it on a hill!
And they worked all night. And they worked all day.
To make that damned old saw — mill — pay."

The tune was catchy, except it ended most queerly, on the middle of a tone. Papa Frank thought we would forget it overnight.

Mosquitos began biting wickedly, and he showed us our cots and said prayers with us before the men came in. Two had changed cots, so we could sleep next to Papa.

The sun was up when we wakened to find ourselves alone in the tent filled with neatly-made cots. Dressing and venturing outside, we found a quiet, deserted yard, all sounds of the night before slept away. Only the lake and trees moved, with shining ripples and quivering leaves.

Up near the kitchen, Mr. Peterson and the cook were talking. We walked slowly toward them and the cook called, "Too late for breakfast," but laughed pleasantly and asked, "Can you eat oatmeal?" Knowing we were expected to, we nodded. "Good," he said, "I saved some for you."

We thought it fun, eating alone by the open window and looking through tree trunks to the wide water sparkling in the morning sunshine.

At noon, when Papa Frank came, be begged us to keep our dresses clean. "I don't want to take two dirty girls to Mrs. Snyder," he said, reminding us that right after supper we would walk to our new home.

In the tent he unpacked two old play dresses we could wear in the water. As he left he pleaded again, "Be good girls. Stay close to Mr. Peterson. And do what you are told to do." Dubby liked so much to talk to everyone, but she promised.

Later, we waited at the shore till busy Mr. Peterson finally came. He sat on the sandy beach, puffing his pipe, and called us back to shallow water several times. We didn't know what bloodsuckers were. The night before we had seen none in the water. Today would be different.

It seemed such a short time, but an hour had passed when he called us to come. We had planned to stay in all afternoon. "It's enough for the first time," he yelled. "You're going to live by the lake. You can go in every day."

We waded, very slowly, toward shore to use as much time as possible. Dubby was watching her wiggling feet. The water was still to her knees, when she saw the long black thing hanging on her leg and reached over to brush it off. It wouldn't let go!

She let out a yelp and tried to kick it off. With knees pumping high, she attempted to run for shore, splashing water into her gasping mouth with every leap. Mr. Peterson sprang forward alarmed, "What's the matter?"

Dubby could only scream and point down, as she splashed wildly through the shallow water to meet him. "Oh that's only a leech," he said with relief. "Here, stand still, I'll take it off." With thumb and a finger, he pinched its sucking head away and threw it down.

I had stood watching, but then began to look myself over. Yes, there were two on the back of one leg. Mr. Peterson reached quickly to remove them before I had time to become frightened. "You'll have to get used to those things here in this lake," he told us. "It's full of them. That's what gives the lake its name. Some people call them bloodsuckers, but they're only leeches." It didn't seem so bad, explained that way. Leech was the name of the lake, of course.

We ate supper ahead of the others and prepared to leave. Papa chose the dresses he wanted us to wear, and just before we stepped from the tent, he smiled down and said, "I'm proud of my girls."

We said good-by to the cook and Mr. Peterson, waved to

the others and climbed to the track to walk back to our new "for awhile" home.

The Indian children, again, looked up to watch us pass. A trail of smoke was rising from the campfire in front of the queer little home. "I'll bet the Indians are having fish for their supper," Papa Frank said.

The track curved on through high brush, and Dubby began to sing, "Oh-the Jones-es boys they built a mill-" I hopped from a rail and joined in, smiling at Dubby as we skipped farther ahead and sang, "They built it on a hill. And they worked all night, and they worked all day, to make that damned old saw - mill - pay."

"Girls! Girls! Girls!" Papa Frank called sharply. We halted and turned. He soon caught up, plunked down the heavy case and faced us, exploding, "You don't know how terrible that sounds. I don't want you ever to sing that song again, or any of the songs you heard last night. Do you understand?" His shocked concern was so real, we didn't argue but meekly agreed.

"If you want to sing, I'll teach you some nice songs," he promised, now walking close. "Papa knows lots of good songs. Don't you remember some of your Sunday school songs?" We did, but the new one was so much fun to sing.

After crossing a trestle, we left the track for a short cut to the left through trees, to Snyders' little farm. Coming first to a small low-roofed barn, we were met by a barking shepherd dog racing out from the house. A path led from here to the kitchen door. The house faced the lake, and unless people came in a boat they didn't see the front.

A kitten moved from beside a bench, and seemed on good terms with the dog, whose bark was half friendly even to strangers. Mr. Snyder, in blue overalls, was hoeing the

garden close by, and Mrs. Snyder, a short plump lady, came
from inside to greet us, smiling kindly.

When Papa Frank started introductions, she said, "Just
call me 'Grandma Snyder.' That's what others call me. And
call him 'Grandpa'." She nodded toward her husband, a tall
slender man, who had joined us. "We're used to that. We've
had children stay with us before."

She placed the canvas case inside the back door and we
all walked around the house to look across the water. As
Papa Frank had said, the main part of the lake showed from
here. Looking straight across, we could see no end to it.

Moving ahead through a bright flower garden that covered
all ground between the house and the drop-off to the lake, we
came to the edge of the high bank. Steps led down to where
Snyders' narrow board dock ran out over the water. "It's
nice sandy bottom down there," Grandpa Snyder said, "nice
for wading and swimming."

"Yes, this whole point is sandy," Grandma Snyder added.
"Why, the bank is so sandy that the lake just keeps eating it
up." She pointed out into air beyond the bank, and told us,
"Our house used to stand right there. We've moved it back
twice and I guess, if we live much longer, we'll have to
move it again."

I looked down at the quiet water and to the high solid
earth where we were standing, and wondered how such a
thing could be. Papa Frank said, "It doesn't seem possible
that water can do that much damage to such high ground."

"Oh, you should see those waves when it storms!"
Grandma Snyder said, shaking her head woefully.

We followed one another down the steep wooden steps to
the dock. Papa Frank held my hand while I looked every
place except where I was stepping. Snyders' rowboat was

tied there, and Mr. Snyder told Papa Frank he was welcome to use it anytime to take us for rides.

Although the bottom here was sandy, there wasn't a beach, and water pushed against the bank — but not deeply. Looking behind us at the steep-rising earth, we could see where high waves had cut into it, leaving the steps to stand like a ladder with space behind. At the very top, the ground had sagged over in places, sifting good soil into the sand along with seeds from Grandma Snyder's flowers, so that now her red poppies and blue bachelor-buttons bloomed like hanging flower baskets down the sandy wall.

Up in the path again, we looked closer at the beds of poppies. Some of the double, ruffled ones were sweet as roses, and some sat on long stiff stems, like tiny bowls with rolled edges. The fluffy, fringed, white ones were my favorite — a white-silk flower!

Later, when Papa Frank said goodnight, he promised to come again very soon — and he did. The very next evening he came and took us in the boat, rowing far out so we could view the shore. Again and again he asked us to look at Snyders' little low house sitting high on the bank — tucked into green trees that framed it at the back and sides. Brilliant flowers aproned it down the front. From the water, people could only guess what made all the color, but we knew it was the red and white poppies and pink and blue bachelor buttons spilling down the bank.

He dipped the oars slowly. "Your mama would want you to remember this," he said. "She liked trees and flowers so much. She would have enjoyed this." We continued on, singing church songs, and having a wonderful ride.

Grandma Snyder's Surprised Visitors

18

A Canoe Ride With The Indian

The Indians, paddling by, stopped often to see Grandma Snyder. They'd leave their canoes floating beside the dock and come up the steps.

One bright forenoon, Dubby and I were out front picking flowers. We looked up to see two squaws at the top of the bank, stopping as if frozen at the sight of us. One had reached ground and her companion, still on the steps, peeked from behind her. They were ready to run back, but Grandma Snyder called, "Come on."

They thought she had company and didn't move till she walked out to meet them. Then, one behind the other, they moved slowly into the path, guiding their full skirts past the arching flowerheads and stopping to touch and admire them.

Grandma Snyder settled on a bench beside the house and motioned them to sit with her. Both were young squaws, with smooth skin. Their shiny hair was combed back tightly. They understood all that Grandma Snyder said but seldom tried to answer. Much of the time the three sat gazing across the water, visiting Indian fashion — silently.

The squaws smiled warmly at us, having learned we were here to live for awhile because we had no mother. As the Indian women were leaving, Grandma Snyder began picking and handing them flowers, till they tried to stop her. "I have to pick them anyhow, to keep them blooming," she explained, and they understood. All the while, they kept bending over other blooms to reach the fragrance.

Grandma Snyder pointed to the low green mignonette edging the path. The squaws frowned, thinking it dull. But when she picked a sprig and smelled it, and handed it over for them to do the same, they nodded quickly — Yes, Yes — and smiled. They knew the white sweet alyssum. One of the squaws now plucked a spray and sniffed it, but they puzzled over it, having forgotten the name. Grandma Snyder said, "Sweet alyssum." They nodded happily and laughed at themselves for not remembering. These Indian friends were nice.

One day, I came upon a curious thing while playing not far from the house: On the ground, under some scrubby jack pine that edged the high bank, I found an oblong wooden box, like a dog house, but tiny and with no doors or windows. It was almost falling apart and looked black and old, with dirt of many years piled around it.

I ran to tell Grandma Snyder. She said it was an Indian grave and that many others had been there at one time. She said not to move it. I went back and lay on my stomach to peek into the wide cracks, but saw only sifted dust.

The next time the squaws came, I asked one of them if her family was buried there. She laughed aloud and shook her head saying, "No—No," and patted my head understandingly.

* * *

Grandma Snyder had the firm belief that all children should be kept busy and learn to work. She taught us to dust and sweep and help in the kitchen. And Grandpa Snyder wanted weeds pulled in his garden — and he wanted every handful carried to the end of the row! It did, then, look very clean and worth the doing.

Grandma Snyder also thought all girls should use a needle and sit quietly for an hour each day. So she bought cloth, gingham with half inch checks, for sofa-pillow tops. We liked this different way of sewing, where little wooden rings were needed to stretch the cloth tight. Heavy cord-like thread was caught from check to check and more of the same thread then woven across to form keystones. It was like weaving on little looms in school in Minneapolis.

Just as Mr. Peterson had predicted, we were in the water almost every day. Grandma Snyder knew how to make floaters out of pillowcases by wetting the case and whirling it full of air and gathering the open end tightly in one fist.

One afternoon we were splashing and floating, air-pillows under our chests, when two birch bark canoes came gliding around the point, side by side. Each was paddled by a kneeling squaw who knew us. They were visiting just as if walking together.

They nodded, smiling, and rested their paddles to watch a few minutes, amused at the awkward method of swimming. They tried to tell us something — motioning vigorously, but without being understood.

Suddenly, one of the squaws decided to do something about it. With a deft stroke, she pointed her white craft toward us, and laying the paddle on the bottom as it glided in, she ever so easily rolled herself over the side, right into the water more than waist deep. Giving the empty shell a thrust shoreward, she waded toward us, pushing the dark circle of her floating skirts down into the water as she came. Like a swooping eagle she reached me first and jerked the airfilled pillowcase away to send it floating, quite flat, to shore.

I sank, neck deep, and swallowed water, but the squaw grabbed the back of my dress and lifted me off my feet. Then I understood — she wanted to teach me to swim. I tried hard, paddling and kicking as she was showing me. I began to sink every time the strong hand let go. Her companion, in the other canoe, looked on and they both laughed trying hard to tell me how to swim. Dubby couldn't do it either, but made a great effort.

All the strange words and motions and smiles held a meaning — encouragement. We knew we must learn, for the squaws would stop other times. Indians thought everyone should swim. It was part of their life, and we were being shown.

Afterward, the squaw waded to her floating canoe. Reaching out, she drew it along to the dock, for there was no dry shoreline. There, she pulled herself onto the boards. Then, standing, she wrung the water from her long skirts — which took some doing — they being so wide and gathered and clinging to her body. She seemed not to mind wetness and stepped skillfully down into her canoe, lifted the paddle and slipped the craft forward to join her companion.

When the squaws were well out of sight, we recovered our flat, floating pillowcases, wrung them, and whirled them full again, for our heads went under otherwise and I'd already drunk enough of the lake. We practiced kicking while floating.

Later, when the twin canoes passed again — going home with piled packages — we were dressed and on the high bank watching for the LILAH DEE to come into sight on the far horizon. We waved to the squaws as to old friends — for they really were — having taught us several Indian words and also how to swim - maybe.

It was part of our day to watch for a column of black smoke to rise out of the water on the horizon, then see a boat come up underneath. We always tried to wait and play till it came close enough to Walker Bay to whistle its long low greeting: "Who-o-o-o-o-t - Who-o-o-o-o-t." It was home for the night.

Papa Frank came the next evening and greeted us with a great idea, "How would you both like to go for a ride in a birch bark canoe and have a real Indian paddling it?"

He had come early and there would be time. It was a wonderful thought. We walked through the wooded area to the track and over the trestle, the way we had come the first evening. Now we were on our way to the Indian teepee, on the shore, where the children had stood watching.

Coming within sight of it — sticks pointing out of the tip, and smoke coiling near it as before — we looked for a way to get down. The high-built bank of the track was brushy and steep, but Papa Frank took me pickaback and broke a path for Dubby, following close behind. We reached the beach at a spot quite a distance from the teepee. That was as Papa Frank had intended.

He put me down, then began walking very slowly along the wide pebbly shore — and we followed, though fearfully. We were approaching from the rear. Before getting even close, the father, in blue overalls, appeared at the side of the teepee and stood watching us sharply as we moved timidly closer. His alert ears had heard the strange footsteps, or our brushy descent from the track.

Papa Frank knew we shouldn't go too near. Pretty soon, he took each of us by the hand and stopped to allow the Indian to come forward, if he desired to meet us. And he did. Papa Frank spoke a greeting, and the Indian answered. Then they shook hands and stood still.

A fire was burning under a kettle in front of the teepee, but the children and the mother weren't in sight. Papa Frank told the Indian what he wanted and was sure that he understood. But the Indian thought we wanted to borrow his canoe, and he shook his head — NO.

Papa Frank explained that he wanted him to do the paddling, and he pointed at him and then to Dubby and me, trying to tell him he wanted his girls to have a ride with him in his canoe. The man looked at us and said, "No," again and shook his head definitely. He would not have strangers in his canoe.

Papa Frank reached in his pocket and showed the Indian a silver half dollar. The Indian changed his mind and started toward the canoe, motioning us to follow. Halfway down to the water's edge he stopped, as though remembering, and looked back to his teepee. A squaw pushed aside the skin flap of the opening and stepped out far enough to stir what was cooking in the kettle. It was their suppertime, and Papa Frank told the Indian to go and eat; we would wait.

The Indian strode to the teepee and ducked inside. He came out again in a moment and stepped quickly down to where Dubby and I were looking at the canoe. Quietly, Papa Frank said to us, "Stand back — don't go close to it." It was made of heavy birch-bark, sealed well on all seams with dark pitch, though a little smeary in places.

The Indian was ready to go. We would go right then. He made us understand that.

Back at the teepee, the flap was now tossed back and the two children, a girl of perhaps five and a boy of eight stood in the opening, eating food they held in their fingers. They had been sent out of sight when strangers approached.

The canoe was lying on sand, and the barefoot Indian carried it right into the water knee deep. Then, holding it as it floated, he looked at his guests, deciding how to place us. Papa Frank stepped away showing that he didn't plan to go.

The man should take only the girls, as the canoe looked a bit small and fragile.

The Indian laughed pleasantly now and said many queer words. He wanted the father to go, too. The canoe was strong. He had made it himself. His motions told everything and directed Papa Frank to get in first. To help things, he pushed one end to the dry sand. His first passenger climbed in and balanced his way to the front where a pointing finger told him to go; there Papa Frank turned to face us and sat on the bottom at the very tip.

The canoe steadied and the Indian continued holding it firmly, while Dubby climbed over to sit at the opposite end. Then, stepping from the water, he picked me up in one arm and grasped the canoe as he waded out again pulling the shell farther out to float freely. He placed me in the center, solidly on the bottom, and stood back in deep water to study the load for balance. He made Dubby and me understand we shouldn't move.

It satisfied him. He climbed in with dripping pantlegs and kneeled behind me. He asked me to move a bit forward; he moved a notch ahead, then back a little, until the craft balanced perfectly.

Holding the paddle in strong hands, he looked around to see if all was as it should be. Then, without a sound, we glided forward. Papa Frank smiled, then said to us, "You must sit very still. Don't move at all, or it might not balance right." Sitting so close in front of the Indian, I knew I would never move.

I saw now that the little slats running across like seats were not to sit on, but to make the canoe stronger, or to lean against. People sat flat on the bottom or kneeled.

As we crossed the small bay to reach the outer water, no

one ever rode through greater glory. The sunset sky was blazed with gold and streaked through with red and yellow and vivid blue-greens. All of it reflected in the mirror of quiet glassy liquid that surrounded us. The loaded white shell cut through, leaving scarcely a ripple, as if sliding over a giant glistening soap bubble whose mixed colors flowed deep.

At one place, the Indian stroked deftly between floating logs lying dead-still on the water. Papa Frank asked where they had come from, but the Indian didn't know. I remembered when Uncle Ed's logs went to a mill months before. Papa Frank thought these must have come from a broken boom in the spring.

Looking at the brilliant sky, Papa Frank said to the Indian, "That little girl right there," pointing to me, "can paint a picture of that. She can make it look just like that on paper." In Minneapolis I had brought watercolor sunsets from school, and he had remembered. The Indian laughed. He didn't believe it. Papa kept saying, "Yes, she can."

I wished he wouldn't think so. I wasn't at all sure I could. Those amazing colors couldn't be caught by anybody's brush, but I would long remember them.

Out in the main body of the lake, the Indian showed us that a canoe was faster than a boat and could be turned much easier. He handled it skillfully, but little drips of water fell on me when he passed the paddle overhead. The beautiful reflections were lost out here where the water was touched by a breeze so that soft lacy ripples replaced the mirror. The canoe hung so deep that I, sitting low, felt sunk in acres of surrounding water.

We rode past Snyders' point with all the flowers and followed the shore for a long wonderful ride. When we got

back to the bay, the squaw and the children were outside.
The boy and girl stood beside their father, as Papa Frank
paid him and thanked him. Even the mother ventured near to
smile good-by with the others.

As we walked back along the track, Papa was satisfied.
We had ridden with an Indian in a canoe he himself had
made. It might never happen again. It was something to
remember; and the sky had been so beautiful. "Your mama
would have liked that ride. I wish she could have been with
us tonight," he said.

Because it was getting late, he bid us goodby in the
wooded pasture and we hurried on alone. After that, whenever he came, we walked with him to that spot to say good
night, friendly Shep always following along.

* * *

One evening a train passing Snyders' pasture whistled ten
short, loud toots. Something was wrong. Papa Frank, listening with the others, said it meant an animal was on the track.
It sounded really scary. Dubby and I wanted to go at once to
see, although Snyders' cows were safe near the barn; but
Papa Frank wouldn't take us beyond the usual parting place
when he left, soon after.

He came back the next evening, describing a bloody
scene. A cow had been on the track, and by the time he had
got there, he saw Indians carrying the carcass away. It
looked as if they had butchered it on the spot. "I'll bet those
Indians drove that cow onto the track so they could get meat
without really stealing it," he said.

Snyders were sure their Indian friends hadn't done it;
there were so many other Indians living nearby.

19

The Housekeeping Experiment

A week passed, and Papa Frank didn't come. We watched every evening, even going to the pasture-place, hoping to meet him. The men's camp was gone — the work there was finished, but we didn't know that.

Then he came from town, saying he could no longer come every day. He told Snyders, "I've contracted with a dealer in Walker to cut cordwood and I'll be several miles away all winter. I know I should send the girls to Minneapolis, to my sister, but I want them with me. I like living here in the timber. Besides, the girls seem much healthier up here." But 'several miles' meant he couldn't be reached easily should we need him, especially when snow was deep.

During the week, he had tried to find a place for us nearer to where he would be. Now he had a plan, but was quite unsure of it. In the deep woods there was a large log building, the only one remaining of an old deserted logging camp. He had wondered if he dared bring us there and try to keep house. We had learned so many things lately.

He asked Snyders what they thought of it. If they had any doubts, they didn't get a chance to discourage him. Dubby and I were determined. We hugged him, happy and excited. "We can keep house," Dubby begged. "We know how to do everything now. Please, Papa."

"I can peel potatoes," I announced, "and we even know how to cook things too." I was sure it wasn't hard. "You just pour water over vegetables in a kettle and put them on the stove."

Grandma Snyder beamed with satisfaction for having taught us, and nodding approval, said, "The girls can look

after themselves well enough." She had faith! So Papa
Frank decided to take us. No more lonely days.

The log building was three miles the other side of Walker.
Getting there on foot called for planning. He had talked to a
lady, living a mile from the old camp, who would be our
neighbor. We could stay with her and her husband a day or
so, till our own place was cleaned and ready. "If you decide,
just come ahead," she had told him.

Mr. Snyder suggested we all stay till morning and start
early. That would give Grandma Snyder a little time to pack
everything clean, the way she wanted to. So Papa Frank stayed.

Arriving in town early the next day, we visited the hardware store first. Papa Frank had looked for an axe there the
day before and had left his suitcase to pick up later. Now,
more than an axe would be bought.

Most important was a cookstove. We chose a little square
one of black iron with four round lids covering holes where
kettles would be set. It stood on four short curving legs and
had a small oven. I opened and closed the swinging door of
it, down below, and felt like a real Missus, even more than
when playing house with Donald. Papa Frank guessed at the
amount of chimney-pipe needed.

The store owner was most interested, helping us choose
all the other things we would need to set up housekeeping: a
tin dishpan, a blue steel frying pan, a kettle for soup, besides
a couple of smaller pans — shiny new. A tin pail and dipper,
for drinking-water, and another pail for scrubbing. We chose
tin plates and cups, like those in the men's camp, wooden-
handle knives and forks, and crockery bowls for soup.

Papa Frank looked at guns on the rack, admiring and
handling several, but didn't buy any that day. He did decide
on an axe, trying the feel and the weight of it while gripping

the handle and making several airy swings.

Because all this would have to be delivered with team and wagon, Mr. White, the store owner, told us he would gladly haul along anything else. That was a lucky chance, so we happy homemakers hurried out to buy groceries and bedding, making many trips with bundles and sacks and becoming really acquainted at the hardware store. Mr. White would bring it all the next day. Papa Frank described a certain place in the road where he would watch for him. The old camp was back in the trees and couldn't be seen.

After putting all overnight needs into his own case, as it was flatter and easy to carry, we looked for a place to eat before starting our long trek to the home of new neighbors where we would stay that night. A cafe sign read "SQUARE MEALS - 25¢" and we settled in at a table for three. When the waitress loaded it with food, Papa Frank looked at the three platters of steak and all the side dishes and said, "Well, this certainly is a square meal."

"Why do they call it a square meal?" Dubby asked.

"I think, perhaps, it may be because there are always four main things in a square meal — meat, potatoes, vegetables, and pie or something sweet. Maybe those four things stand for the corners of a square," said Papa Frank. Dubby, busily rounding the edges, didn't question further.

We passed a white church marked "Methodist," on the way out of town. We would know it better another day and not too pleasantly.

Scuffing down the dusty road, with the town well behind, we passed a large building called a boarding house. It stood alone on our right. On the left, farther on, houses showed around a bend. Papa Frank called, "Girls, come back here a minute. I want to talk to you."

He set the case down, waited, and spoke sternly. "Now, when we pass these houses, I want you to keep your eyes straight ahead. The people living here are not the kind of people I want you to know. I don't want them to know who we are or where we live." Dubby got acquainted so easily.

Preparing us to walk the stretch, he said, "If children call to you, don't say anything. Just keep walking unless they only say 'Hello,' then you may answer 'Hello.' But don't say anything more." The children had rudely thrown sticks when he had passed before, we learned later.

We started on, staying strictly in the middle of the road. The seven or eight houses, strung along on either side, were all alike, plain and small and painted brown, with only platforms for porches. Children in the yards stopped playing to stare, and I felt silly walking with head up and eyes front. It was hard to do, but we didn't look, only peeked.

Someone called, "Who are they?" Others hooted and laughed, but said nothing. So our haughty, parading three-some got safely by.

Around another turn, and still within sight of the houses, Dubby and I spied a queer looking heap of boxes and papers a little way off the road. While Papa Frank marched on, unaware of everything, all dignity deserted us and we ran to explore.

A clean new box, half-filled with oranges, lay on top of the pile. It surprised and delighted us, and we hastily gathered armfuls. The oranges were spoiled, and this was the city dump! But we didn't know that. And the fruit didn't look spoiled.

From far up the road, our proud papa looked back. He halted, horrified, and shouted, "Girls! Get away from that place!" When we started running toward him, loaded with oranges, he waved wildly, yelling, "Drop those! Drop those!!" We paused, looked at our loot, and wondered why.

He plunked the suitcase in the road and leaped into a stalking run, commanding, "Drop those, I say." We quickly piled them on the ground, close to the road, "Why, that's the city dump!" he thundered, coming closer. "There might be poison on that stuff. Rats run all over a place like that. If you want oranges, I'll buy you oranges."

"But Papa," I argued, "these were in a nice clean box right on top."

He was already at work, stooping for oranges and winding up like a pitcher, heaving them far over to the pile, one at a time, like yellow baseballs. What humiliation! He looked down the road, groaning, "What if those people saw you! What would they think!" We had passed so regally, moments before.

When we started on, I walked behind and peeled a nice orange I managed to hide. I tasted it. Papa Frank was right. It was bitter. I spit it out and threw the rest away, hoping I wasn't poisoned.

"There are lots of wild raspberries along the road, farther on," he consoled us. "You can eat all you want of those."

We were soon dashing off the road to examine every bush. "Oh come," he said, after patiently stopping several times. "We can't waste time this way. You can find them without hunting like that. Come on. There's something interesting farther along here I want you to see." We began leaving red berries to keep up with him, and it was hot running in the narrow sandy road.

When he called back, "We're coming to it now — look closely and see if you can notice anything," we could see nothing unusual — only brushy ground and scattered trees under a blue sky. He set his load down and pointed to a ridge of ground, flat on top, and running very straight. "That's an old railroad right-of-way," he said. Because we were so close, we walked over to climb it.

At the top he said, "This must have been a road for logging trains." The iron rails were gone, but the ties lay there, spaced evenly and rotting on the ground. Wood was plentiful. If this built-up stretch hadn't been there, the old road-bed would have been completely forgotten, for as we followed it to level ground, the rotting ties became lost in long grasses and growing saplings.

As we stopped, Papa Frank looked at us thoughtfully and said, "You know, the country around here wasn't like this a few years ago, and you should know about this. You should always be interested in your surroundings. Then you can find something to enjoy every day, right where you are."

Gazing skyward, he continued, "There used to be many tall pines, but loggers took all the big ones to make boards. That's how our cities get built." We knew that. We had seen logs sent to the sawmill for that purpose.

"These tracks were here for logging trains to haul the logs out," he explained, "and after they had cleared this area, they moved the iron rails to a different location. They cost money." We were surprised to learn that trains carried logs, as well as did the Mississippi River.

Back in the road again, Papa Frank gripped the tan case and we trudged on, Dubby and I snatching berries here and there and racing to catch up.

Finally, a grassy trail, led away to where we would stay overnight. Mrs. Prodock invited us into the cool inside of a one-room log house. Two iron beds showed at one end, separated by a curtain. At the other end, newspapers covered the walls behind a cookstove, and there hung pots and pans. It was nice to find rest here, and food.

Next morning, the dark air was sharp when we left very early. Papa Frank wanted to get the bunkhouse cleaned before the hardware man arrived.

We carried broom and pails loaned by Mrs. Prodock. Two small tin pails, tightly lidded, held drinking water. I was carrying a huge loaf of bread from Mrs. Prodock and swinging the broom. She called from the doorway, "I'll be down in a few days to visit you," and you could tell by her laugh that she didn't think two small girls could do much housekeeping.

There was a short-cut path to the road we had left the day before. It led through a back-pasture where a crowning dome of dense fog sat over a sleeping pond, completely hiding it. We knew water was there, and frogs, too, for as we circled the edge, a steady ringing, "Yeep-Yeep-Yeep-Yeep," mingled with cronking thumps of bullfrogs, kept us company. All nature was awake! Welcoming us.

The outer road hunted its way between and around wooded rolling hills. Progress was slow. Dubby, carrying one pail of water, changed hands often, for the wire-handle hurt. The walk seemed longer than the one mile. Again, the road was ours alone, just as it had been the day before.

When Papa Frank set his pail of water and luggage down, we thought it just another rest, and stared, unbelieving, when he said with a sly smile, "Well, this is where we bunk in."

Nothing but wilderness surrounded us. No path or road led from the one we were standing on. Our bewilderment pleased him. He said, "I don't believe strangers will ever find their way to our place from here. You girls will really be safe when I get you tucked in. Now, you try to see where our road is."

We started hunting on both sides with no success. "Papa, how could you tell where to stop?" Dubby asked.

But he wasn't listening. Looking into our faces tenderly, he spoke his thoughts, "I wish you girls would call me 'Dad'. I like the sound of 'Dad'. Do you think you could do that?" We weren't ready to answer. It was such a new idea. To us he had always been Papa. I wasn't sure I wanted him to be anything else.

"I don't know — maybe," Dubby said finally.

He looked through the trees on the right side of the road and said, "Don't you see our road right here?" He swung both arms forward, indicating a road running in. But the trees were growing there! We could see no open lane like a road. He stooped to show us an unnoticed leaf-filled wheel track, completely lost in brush and long grass — though running straight in, to somewhere. A few feet over, he found the mate to it and kicked away dry leaves to probe its depth — dug with steel-rimmed wheels.

These were the tracks of the old road where heavy tote-teams had gone in, years before. Unless people knew of it, they would never find it. No teams could use it now, with young trees growing there.

We loaded up again and started in, Papa Frank walking ahead. Following him more slowly, I kept thinking, "He's Papa. I want him to stay Papa."

The timber was heavier here, but soon a queer log struc-ture showed, in a clearing ahead. "Is that it, Papa?" I called. I couldn't say Dad.

"That's the camp," he called back. "This first building that you see used to be the barn." He didn't ask me again to say Dad.

The barn was roofless. Its long, massive, round ridgepole, supported by several log-beams, rose like the skeleton of a deserted ship — in a sea of weeds. Another building showed, around to the left, but we stopped first to have a closer look at the old barn. High weeds surrounded it, very high weeds, and all of one kind, as if planted there. Some were gray and dry and many seasons old.

Papa Frank started pushing aside the towering spikes and they cracked over easily, showing their hollow stems. Dubby and I followed, and we all stood in the gapping doorway. Inside, almost hidden in growth, the stalls and feed bins remained, looking solid. Overhead, the log ridgepole now loomed huge, while the rising sun calmly peeked in over the east wall to nurse the wild growth in the long-forgotten room.

Finding our way out again, we walked on toward the other building, where bushes and long grass grew. It faced away from the barn, so we passed along its side to reach the door at the front end.

"This is our home," Papa Frank said. "This used to be the bunkhouse where the men slept."

It, too, was a long building and made of huge logs, left round. But it had a roof! The door, of planks, opened hard on its hinges. We stepped inside and looked around.

There was a double bunk at the end in the right-hand corner. Behind the door that opened to the right, stood a long table with two equally long benches. All the rest was space, lots of it, with heaps of leaves and layers of dirt covering the floor. Oblong open places in the walls, on either side of the room, where window frames belonged, had allowed all the outside to blow in. At the south opening, vines were climbing over the edge.

Papa Frank walked to a box nailed shoulder high on the opposite wall and said, "Someone has lived here since the camp was abandoned." The box had one shelf and was nearer the front where there was space for a stove. Overhead a round hole in the roof waited for pipe. Touching the wooden box, he said, "This was their cupboard."

Turning to survey the room thoughtfully, he went on, "They must have torn out all the other bunks. Probably sawed them up for stove wood. This room was full of bunks once because this was the bunkhouse. I know that."

I crossed to the window, where the vine was trailing in, and peered over the sill and squealed, "Oh look!" Red raspberries were within reach, and we hadn't wanted to leave any! Now we could pick them from our own room. It delighted me. From this window I could look down to the nearby marshy pond with water at the center and grassy humps sticking up across it. These were muskrat houses.

Straight across on the far side, a short section of road could be seen at the top of the high bank. "That's the road from Walker," Papa Frank said. "That's the one we just left. It goes on to Akeley. When water freezes in winter, we can go right across the ice that way, instead of the way we came today." So the house did show from that spot in the road, though it sat safely back. The marsh was almost a city block wide.

He strolled around the room, looking up at the ceiling. I looked, too. The roof had many holes where bits of sky showed. Between the logs of the sidewalls, cracks of light peeked everywhere.

"There's a lot to be done here," he said.

We went outside to take a quick look around. There was a wide, deep hole a little distance up from the door. Papa Frank knew at once it had been the well. Dubby and I were overjoyed to find it, knowing how much one was needed.

But he looked into it, saw the rotted leaves and wood, and said it couldn't be used.

"Can't you clean it out, Papa?" Dubby asked.

He was already poking down with a long stick. "No, I'd be afraid to risk it. Dead things may be in there," he said. "You girls stay away from here until I have time to take care of it." He laid the stick across and warned us to leave it.

There was a large hump of ground not far from the door. We walked to the lower end that faced the pond and saw that it had a door where the hill seemed cut away. It was a cave dug into the hill.

The door of rough boards was closed, but Papa Frank pushed it in and it worked all right. I started in. He grabbed my shoulder, pulling me back and pushed Dubby back, commanding, "Stay out of there! Don't ever go in there! That roof might cave in on you and bury you alive."

We leaned from the rotting doorway frame to look inside. Poles showed at the ceiling. Papa Frank said, "I'll put some new timber-supports in there, and then I think it will be safe. Don't go in until I have time to do it."

"Will we put vegetables in it?" Dubby asked.

"Yes, we'll put everthing we need in there," he said.

The pond was on down the slope, but from here a larger marsh showed, joining it behind the cave hill. It held more water and was surrounded by a wide cranberry bog.

We happy explorers picked our way along the edge and examined the mossy vines, finding berries, not yet ripened, deep in the spongy growth. We couldn't linger. Important work was waiting. Hurrying back to the house, Papa Frank said, "You girls stay outside and listen for a team. I'll get this place swept out before Mr. White comes."

We roamed around inspecting while trying to listen, so

Papa Frank could hurry to the road and show Mr. White
where to turn in. Before any wagon-rattle was heard, whistling came from across the pond. It was Mr. White with all
our things. Papa Frank ran outside and called over, telling
him to turn around and go back, and he would meet him.
While the man did this, Papa and Dubby and I started from
the house — following the overgown trail to the road.

Mr. White drove in, around trees, but still could come
only part way. He tied the team to a tree, and he and Papa
Frank carried the stove from the wagon to the bunkhouse.
Dubby and I began lugging things to grassy ground near the
door. There was quite a pile — a roll of wire-screen for the
windows and a roll of black tarpaper for roof repairs, as well
as big bundles of bedding, and boxes and sacks of all sizes.

Mr. White helped set up the stove and pipe. When he had
gone, Papa Frank went back to pushing out leaves. He was
finding it a heavy task, for the walls needed sweeping, too.
Dust and sand, from old chinking, lay thick on every log and
more loose clay dropped out too easily when touched.
Clouds of heavy dust floated out the windows and the open
door and cracks. Finally, he grabbed two pails and strode
down to dip water from the pond for scrubbing.

When he struggled back to the door with overflowing
pails and saw us peering into sacks on the ground, he cautioned, "You girls stay out of those things. Papa will hurry
and get this place scrubbed out. Then we'll find something to
eat."

He made many trips with both pails. A river of mud
flowed from the doorway, but afterward, the clean floor
dried quickly and we carried everything in, piling it on the
scrubbed benches and table.

The room looked more like a home now, with the stove

set, and new pipe filling the round hole in the roof. It stood in the corner on the left, just inside the door, all polished, efficient and ready.

Packages were undone fast. Dubby spread the knives and forks in a neat row on the table, and she and I ran admiring fingers over the shiny blades. The red wooden handles looked ever so new and pretty. Papa Frank unpacked the lamp of heavy glass, then found the chimney, packed in cardboard, its thin glass flared at the top to a crinkled edge. A slip of paper tucked into it told of a lady in Vermont who had used one like it for twenty years without it ever cracking. He suggested we be as careful as that lady.

It was past dinnertime and he punched holes in a small can of milk, which was something we had never seen. It flowed slowly into a spoon. I would have eaten all of that sweet stuff, but he took it saying it should be mixed with water and drunk as regular milk. He pried the cover from a little wooden bucket of pink apple jelly, and though it tasted queer, because of the wood, we spread it on Mrs. Prodock's bread.

Afterward, Dubby and I kept house by arranging things in the box cupboard. Papa Frank unrolled screen to nail over the open holes and said he wished he had bought windows, for now he knew that an ordinary window, laid on its side, would fit the space quite well.

I climbed to the top bunk and wanted to put on the bedding, but Papa Frank said, "Wait till I can help." He said no when I asked if ours could be the top bunk, remembering Dubby's fall. But he stopped nailing long enough to make up the beds the way he wanted them, and we tested our lower one and almost fell asleep.

That evening we stood on the gentle hillside and watched

the muskrats criss-crossing the surface of the pond like rolling balls, cracking the sky-reflecting waters into fan-shaped trailings. A beautiful quietness enfolded the camp, but at water's edge everything sang. It had been a happy day - moving into a home where we could be together - even with so much still to be done.

* * *

The urgent need was drinking-water. Papa Frank dipped some from the pond, strained it, and put it on to boil. While it was heating, he looked again at the gaps in the roof. "I don't know which to do first," he said. "We need a well, and we need this roof fixed." He walked around counting holes. The larger ones were above the stove. "I think I'll have to fix the roof first," he said, "before the equinoctial rains come. When they start, it rains for days and I don't want rain like that coming in on us."

I asked, "What are equinoctial rains?" It sounded fearful. Eager to inform, he fastened a scholarly gaze on us and asked, "Do you know what the equinox is?" We didn't. "Do you know what the equator is?" We had an idea of that.

"Well," he explained, cupping his hands and shaping the air to a ball, "the earth spins around, making a complete turn each day. You know that. That gives us our days and nights. Then it passes, once a year, in a path around the sun." He swung his imaginary earth in a wide circle around an imaginary sun and went on explaining, "It does that while it's turning daily. That gives us our seasons."

"That's how we get winter and summer. When the sun is north of the equator, we have summer, because we live north of the equator. And when it goes south of it, we get winter. Usually, when the seasons change, it rains a lot."

"Will it rain and make a flood?" I was eager to know, remembering the Sunday School story.

"Oh — no, no. It just rains steady and more than usual. It's sometimes rather nice. In fall, they're called the autumnal rains. In the spring, it's the vernal equinox."

I thought him very wise to know all that. I was proud of Papa.

During the next two days, he repaired the roof, climbing up at the corners where ends of he logs crossed.

Mrs. Prodock came to visit, being curious to see how we were making out. She brought us more drinking-water. She had a woman friend with her who had driven out from town. Each carried a kitten—Mrs. Prodock had promised to bring them.

We both wanted the yellow one with a white belly. The other one, with stripes, looked wild. Mrs. Prodock called it a Maltese. I felt sorry for the little blue-gray, unwanted one, and took it for my own.

Dubby named hers Ruby, but I wanted no ordinary name. Besides, none seemed to fit — mine wasn't an ordinary cat. I called it Tridget. Dubby said that was no name at all. But I liked it. I had made it up.

Our visitors were surprised to find the house so clean and said a woman could do no better. Papa Frank told them, "We'll have it fixed much nicer later on. I'm going to make one of these long benches into several short ones for chairs. Then I'll get a heating stove for this end." He indicated the area near the bunks.

While the kittens stepped gingerly around, nosing the floor, cat-curious, Mrs. Prodock, with the friend, took her leave, saying, "Come and see me soon. If there's anything you need, I'll be glad to lend it, if I have it."

Although cracks in the walls weren't filled, Papa Frank decided to dig the well. "I can chink those walls even when it's raining, easier than I can dig a well in the rain," he reasoned.

We hiked to Prodocks' one day and borrowed a spade. Right after breakfast next morning, carrying the narrow tool, and followed by Dubby and me, Papa Frank took exploring steps down near the pond.

"Aren't you going to have it up by the other well?" Dubby asked, thinking that must be where wells belonged.

I'd have to dig too deep to strike water there. I know water isn't too far down right here, because it's close to this water. But it will be pure this far back."

He rested his spade on end, saying, "What do you think of this spot?" The ground was level but covered with dry leaves. After thinking a moment, he stepped over a few feet to get out of the pathway from the house to the pond. After scraping an area clean and getting our pleased consent, he started digging.

A circular space of opened earth soon showed, with a pile of dirt beside it.

"Are we going to have a pump?" I asked, and was disappointed when he said we would have to dip water with the pail on a rope.

Dubby and I stayed nearby and built playhouses, clearing out areas with the new butcher knife and piling the cut brush into outlining walls. We each had our own house and tried to heap the walls like real ones.

Papa Frank laughed, "You're funny girls. You have a real house to play in and then you come out here and work making playhouses." But at mealtime, he brought the food outside and ate with us in our "dining rooms," visiting first one "home" and then the other.

After two days of digging, his head no longer showed above ground. That was why a worrisome thing happened. It was midafternoon and we saw two men stopping in the road across the pond, and in a few minutes we saw them put their packages on the bank and begin climbing down to come across.

We raced to the well, blurting, "Two men are coming across the pond."

Papa Frank looked up from the slippery hole, his face sweating and his forehead smeared with clay. "Are you sure? Where are they?" he asked.

"They're still on the other side, but they've put down their bundles and they're coming."

"Don't look over there," he commanded. "You girls go up to the house, and don't look across there. Do you hear? They can't get through it. Don't pay any attention to them. I'll take care of it."

Trying to act unconcerned, we walked slowly to the house, but didn't go inside, sitting, instead, on the split log before the doorway, trying not to look. But we couldn't help seeing. The men had reached deep center and were wading in water to their underarms.

Papa Frank had stopped throwing out clay, but was still down out of sight. We got panicky and raced to warn him. He was provoked that we hadn't obeyed and stayed at the house, for he had looked and was ready to climb up quickly when the proper time came. He could step on the large stone in the side of the well, which he'd found too big to remove.

Urgently he demanded, "You step back, and don't stand there looking down at me."

The men really struggled at the boggy border, but kept

coming. When they reached the bank and started up the slope, I bolted to the well and breathed frantically: "Papa, they're here!"

He leaped onto the stone, grabbed for the rim of the hole, and shouldered himself out. The men stood still and stared at the sudden sight of him. They stammered in confusion, "We - we - we thought the girls were lost. We didn't think anyone was living here."

They didn't wait to get acquainted! Turning, they spun away like startled deer, down the slope in leaping strides. Then splashing, they highstepped the bog much faster than when they came. Snatching up bundles, they took off down the road.

Papa Frank climbed back into the well to throw out more clay. That evening he knew he wouldn't have to dig deeper. Water was coming in at the bottom. At the table after supper, weary and discouraged, he held his bowed head, disturbed in thought, knowing Dubby and I wouldn't be safe alone.

He said, "I think we'll try to get a dog for you girls. Maybe we'll get a gun, too. I can't take you with me every day."

Next morning, the well was half full of roily, milky, clay-water. It would take several days for it to clear. Papa Frank worked that day chinking walls on the outside, using clay taken from the well. "I think we'll go to Walker tomorrow. I'm going to buy boys' overalls for both of you. I can't wash dresses all the time," he said. He would also look at guns.

We left early, after filling a small box with sand so Ruby and Tridget could stay inside. Hiking along the road, Papa Frank said, "Isn't it nice. In a few weeks we won't have to go to Walker for groceries." Prodocks were planning to build a new house and would have a store in it.

Passing their land, he said, "I think it will be right about here somewhere, close to the road. That will be nice, won't it! We'd have a hard time getting to town in winter."

At the hardware store, he lifted rifles from the rack, trying different sizes, for weight, as we stood close. He had Dubby try holding them, then bought a large revolver because she could manage it easier — a second-hand Colt's Navy.

I saw a small-sized rifle that I liked so much, but little girls didn't shoot rifles. I knew that. Besides, it cost too much. Papa Frank told me I could fire the Colt's Navy, once in a while.

But he did buy me the little axe I wanted. The handle and head were shaped exactly like his own axe, and I adored it. It was just my size.

Mr. White told us where we might get a dog, and Dubby and I stayed at the store while Papa Frank looked several places.

While selecting overalls and blue shirts at another store, we saw checked gingham cloth and wanted to make sofa cushion covers, like at Grandma Snyder's. Papa Frank bought the materials, embroidery-hoops and all, and Dubby explained to the lady clerk, "Maybe we can sell them, if we make them real nice." The lady encouraged us to try, saying everyone liked keystone cushions.

Starting for home, Papa Frank carried a full bag of purchases over his shoulder. He put it down after a few blocks and left us guarding it at a corner, while he quickened his step to go after the dog he had decided on. The owner lived several streets away.

He came back leading a brown, curly-haired dog with long floppy ears and rather short legs. He said it was a water spaniel, and a very good breed of dog, although he didn't know if it would make a good watchdog.

Dubby led the spaniel and carried a package of bread. I hugged my axe and also carried bread. As Papa Frank shouldered his sack, he warned, "Watch where you're going now, and don't stumble with that axe."

The children of the forbidden neighborhood beyond the outskirts called, "Hello," and ran out to the road, curious to see the dog. Papa Frank hurried along and no one got acquainted. On the final stretch of road, less than a mile from the bunkhouse, we saw a team coming slowly. The driver, sitting on a spring seat at the front of a low wagon, was not alone. As he drew closer, we could see the head of a huge dog, standing behind him and looking over the seat.

The man stopped his team when he reached us. He and Papa Frank said, "How do you do?"

"Nice dog you got there," the man said. Papa Frank agreed, "Yes, I think she's a nice one."

"Spaniel, isn't it?" the man asked.

"Yes, a water spaniel."

The man kept looking down at the light-brown curly haired dog, then said, "How'd you like to trade?" As he spoke, he turned to the big dog behind him, saying, as he patted its head, "This is a Newfoundland and St. Bernard mixed. And there's some bulldog in him, too."

It was a fierce looking animal. Papa Frank, thinking of the size of its stomach and its appetite, shook his head no. Besides, we already liked our little floppy-eared dog.

The man made no move to start his team but kept visiting, and when he guessed we really needed a watch dog, he became eager.

"This is the dog you need, right here," he urged. "He's used to children. He likes children. I'll guarantee no one would ever get near those girls with him around. He'll knock a man right over. He lunges at a stranger. And his name sure fits. His name's Bounce."

"No — I don't believe I want to trade," Papa Frank decided.

But the man wanted the spaniel and kept talking. He hadn't had Bounce long, he explained. The former owner could no longer keep him in town, in Akeley, because he frightened people. He had chewed so many little dogs that the police had filed his teeth. After that, he had used his weight to win battles.

The man assured us that only the points were off and no one would ever know it. He lifted the overhanging lip of the dog so we could see for ourselves. Huge teeth grinned wickedly.

"He'd be fine protection. And that's what you need," he suggested. "That little girl there could ride him like a pony."

Papa Frank still held back, saying he had paid three dollars for the spaniel.

"Tell you what," the man persisted, "I'll give you three dollars to boot. I've always wanted a dog like that. They're a good hunting dog."

So Papa Frank agreed and took the money held out to him. The man crawled over the seat and coaxed Bounce to the back end, "Come on, Bounce — come on, boy." When he swung himself to the ground, Bounce slowly and clumsily jumped after him.

In the road the dog's eyes reached my shoulder, a frightening thing. We had never seen a dog that large, except in picture books. His huge head turned slowly, as he surveyed us with brown eyes that seemed kind and sad, even in a savage face. A somewhat stubby nose separated his heavy hanging jowls.

"He's a queer looking beast," Papa Frank observed. "A St. Bernard with a bulldog face! Well, the very sight of him should keep anyone away."

The man lifted the spaniel to the wagon seat and settled beside him, then untied its rope to hand to Papa Frank, who started fastening it around Bounce's thick neck. Bounce leaped into the wagon, and the man, again, had to coax him out. This time, he tied the rope himself.

We talked soothingly as we started away, Dubby pulling the rope cautiously, while the man watched from the seat and held his team. From far down the road, when the wagon moved, Bounce broke away and raced back to go along, the loose rope trailing behind.

Bringing him back for Papa Frank to lead, the man said, "I'll wait till you are out of sight before I start this time."

At Papa Frank's suggestion, I tossed chunks of bread to the unwilling newcomer. In that way, we got home. Inside the bunkhouse, Bounce padded around slowly, looking more bear than dog, although he swung his heavy fringed tail in a friendly manner. He finished one loaf of bread and looked for more.

"That dog will eat more food than all three of us," Papa Frank remarked uneasily. "I wish I could bake our own bread somehow."

"Papa, I can bake the bread," I quickly assured him. "I watched Grandma Snyder make it. If you get the flour, I know I can."

"We'll see," he said. "He'll have to eat other things, too."

In no time, Dubby and I were buttoning on blue chambray boy-shirts; and Papa Frank was adjusting shoulder straps on the denim overalls while we stood proudly, feeling in all the pockets. He smiled, "Now Papa's got two little lumber-jacks."

When I picked up my axe and left the room, I did look exactly that, except for parted hair and looped pigtails. Hurrying to the woodpile, I swung the axe straight down, and it cut and wedged into the log everytime. There was much to learn. An axe must be slanted in, to cut a chip.

Papa Frank was just as anxious to try out the revolver. Standing outside the door, he fitted bullets into the little keg-shaped chamber and, holding it at arm's length, pulled the trigger. Its power jerked his arm, as a sharp crack echoed from the hill beyond the marsh. He fired several times at a tree some feet away. We found the holes in its bark.

After making sure the revolver was empty, he handed it to Dubby to practice holding it steady. She needed both hands for the heavy old weapon, and, as she held it straight out at eye level, he helped her to place right-hand ahead of left, and then guided her fingers to the trigger. It took the strength of two fingers to snap it.

"When you learn to hold it well, I'll put in a bullet. Maybe tomorrow. We're going to have target practice every day — until you can hit anything you look at."

In the night, Bounce growled at the kittens and woke Papa Frank several times. The next day Papa cut a small square section from the door, at the bottom, and nailed leather strips to hang it so the kittens could get outside and back by themselves.

Also, the next day, I let Bounce's leash slip from my hand. He was free! I ran begging, "Come Bounce. Come Bounce." But he had no thought of leaving. Papa Frank said, "I think he likes you girls pretty well." He was never tied again and remained our close companion.

Riding The Ridgepole

20

Getting Tucked In

With boys' overalls for climbing, and the fat ridgepole of the skeletal barn beckoning, Dubby and I scrambled up to perch at the highest point. Papa Frank stopped chinking the bunkhouse and found us walking the pole, tight-rope fashion — performing. He shouted his command, "Either sit down or come down."

We sat down, straddling, at midsection, then boosted along, leapfrog style. Later, we turned it into a game, starting from opposite ends and hitching forward in a race to the center. Laughing and rocking in this unladylike posture, the urge to sing swept over us. Only the sawmill song could fit this situation.

We sang it gustily, but dropped voices on the "damned." Over and over, meeting at center, we let it enfold the countryside, except for the whispered swear-word. Papa Frank scolded when we got to the house. He had listened from where he was working and had guessed why we seemed to be leaving out a word.

"Papa, it's so much fun to sing that song." I pleaded. Dubby asked, "Wouldn't it be all right to say 'darned' instead of — you know?"

He explained patiently: "But 'darned' is slang. That's not much different. 'Blamed' would be a better word. But I'd rather you didn't sing it at all." Seeing our disappointment, he relented. "Well, perhaps you may sing it — if you just say 'blamed'."

Two weeks later, all tucked in, we could look out from neatly-framed glass windows, sit on benches made from one of the long ones, and hunt for holes without finding any. A round heating stove was set, ready for colder days, and rutabagas and potatoes were in the cave.

Papa Frank had worked for hours one day, cutting a heavy oak bar for inside the door and fitting it into brackets. He showed us how to slide it across, and said, "Now, when I'm gone, I want you girls to keep this bar over, like that, and no one can ever open this door." We worked it back and forth easily.

With that all done, and Bounce showing loyalty, things were looking up.

* * *

We pigtailed lumberjacks weren't yet ready to be left alone, and supplies were needed from town. One day, with Bounce locked in — he couldn't meet other dogs — our family started out.

Coming in sight of Prodocks' ground, we spied the new building taking shape with walls outlined by two-by-fours standing on end, promising a place of shelter along the way when winter would close in.

We stopped by. Mrs. Prodock, right there on the job, said, "Let the girls stay, and I'll give them a lunch at noon." Papa Frank hastened on alone.

Up above, workmen were nailing on roof-boards and scolded when I appeared beside them, then saw I could help — carrying nails and picking up dropped ones. This would be a house, and store, and barn, all under one roof. It seemed a most unusual arrangement!

Later, Papa Frank came stepping along with a fifty pound white clothsack of flour, balancing on his shoulder, and a bright tin breadpan tied dangling at his side. Both arms clutched bags of groceries. I dashed out to meet him and reached for the deep pan, then carried it, planning happily, all the way home. He had bought Yeast Foam, too, with directions for bread on the small package. I studied the words. Dubby wasn't at all interested.

Knowing Bounce would eat whatever turned out, Papa Frank said to go ahead and try. He watched with amused interest that evening as, feeling very important, I made the sponge with flour, potato water, and yeast, just as I had read. The next morning — what excitement! The sponge was full of bubbles! Papa Frank said, "Maybe this won't be Bounce's bread, after all."

I began slowly adding the right amount of flour and the dough worked easily at first, then stiffened too much for me to handle. I struggled to find a way. The jiggling pan shuffled on the bench, so I boosted it to the wide table and kneeled on the bench to reach it.

Though the container was awkwardly deep for my short arms, I kept folding and turning and punching with all my might, pressing one hand over the other to combine the strength of both wrists. Then, again studying directions, I left it to rise.

Later, three wonderful crusty loaves came from the oven in the long pan Papa Frank used for Johnny Cake. He beamed his satisfaction and said, "Now I won't have to make so many soda biscuits and pancakes."

Dubby wanted to try — and be praised — so she baked the next batch. But after punishing the dough so furiously, trying to outdo me, it didn't rise at all. The loaves were hard and small, with a hole in each center. Bounce ate it.

* * *

"I've got to get on the job tomorrow," Papa Frank said one evening. "I'm going to take you girls along in the morning so you'll know where I'm working. Then, if you need me, you'll know where to come."

The morning was bright for playing outside, and after following Papa Frank, and learning where he was, we became self-confident and returned to begin our first day alone. We had promised, over and over, to run in and bar the door if anyone was seen coming.

Now I brought out my axe and began cutting away brush from the far end of the house, a job waiting to be done. When Dubby climbed a nearby tree and became a lumberjack in her boy-clothes, I followed.

Clamping legs around branches, we sang "The Joneses Boys," loudly and lustily, and soon decided that, if we were to be lumberjacks, we needed men's names. Dubby became Charlie, and I chose Fred. Gazing at each other in the lofty manner of grown-ups, we talked of imagined families, the way men in a camp talk of home and children. Suddenly, Dubby said, "Men don't sit in trees. Let's make a men's camp."

Scrambling down, we started whacking brush vigorously. The axe and the butcherknife worked well, and after awhile, Fred and Charlie were settled in "camp" on "chairs" fashioned of brush, properly piled.

I found a hollow-stemmed weed and broke it into cigarsizes, and Dubby ran for matches. Leaning back in the "chairs," puffing at "cigars" that smouldered at the lighted ends, we looked at each other and laughed. The smoke trailed up, just as we wanted it to, but choked us with stinging bitterness if breathed in.

Bounce watched all this closely and seemed to be trying to tell us he didn't approve. His stern drooping expression spoke a threat.

When Papa Frank came at dinnertime, all signs of mischief were out of sight. Fred and Charlie had schemed not to tell. Even so, he scolded when he saw uncombed hair, always having to remind us: "Your mama wouldn't want you to look like that."

As he trailed us into the house, Tridget and Ruby, on their way out, sailed past his legs with tails high. "Mercy," he groaned. But going about preparing food, he remarked, "I guess you haven't been lonely. Maybe everything will work out all right." It was well for him to think so.

Afterward, the dishes washed, and Papa Frank on his way to the timber, we returned to make believe. No loneliness here, under comforting, motherly trees and sky.

Later, having had enough of Fred and Charlie, we discovered a new world out front on the knoll over the cave. Here "Mrs. Peterson" and "Mrs. Smith" visited each other's "homes," and Dubby brought some of the white string bought for the Keystone cushions and strung a "telephone line," by way of trees, between the "houses." The air rang with "ding-a-ling-alings," and Mrs. Peterson and Mrs. Smith stood at a "telephone" in front of the tree most of the time, visiting.

Papa Frank moved things in a hurry when he arrived and saw we were on the roof of the cave. "You could break through and be buried alive," he explained and went about restringing the line on safer ground.

Evening Song Time At The Bunkhouse

* * *

We waited for the after-supper-hour, when evening-light was slowly leaving the sky, and muskrats swam criss-cross trails on the pond, and crickets thrummed a lullaby in nearby grasses. Then we three bunkhouse woodsmen, with Bounce at our feet, sat outside on the hewed-log doorstep to sing.

Papa Frank knew many songs - those learned in a church choir, and others too. As words rolled to the hillside beyond the marsh, echoes began, till it seemed the clustered pines, growing there, were people singing back. One favored ballad was about the old preacher, told to resign because he was "Just Behind The Times."

Another had these words:

> "Dear wife, I found the model church, and
> worshipped there today. It made me think of
> good old times, before my hair was gray.
> The meetinghouse was finer built, than they
> were years ago. But when I got inside I
> found, it was not built for show."

When Papa Frank threw his voice out on the high notes of "The meetinghouse was finer built -" the trees rose taller and every hiding animal must have listened.

As the night-shadows folded down, and we moved inside to light the lamp, tears often fell if "Just Behind The Times" had been sung last. One night I said: "I suppose the new minister talked of puffs on the sleeves and ruffles on the skirts."

Papa Frank, tucking an arm around me, said, "Don't take it so seriously dear. It's only a story."

With darkness now coming earlier, target practice was

before supper. Dubby had learned well. With determined stance, she'd lean back, both arms extended and feet spread, then fire away and most always hit the mark.

I didn't ask to try. Touching Dubby's jerking arm was enough. Dubby beamed when praised. No need for her to bake bread. Proudly she carried the big silvery revolver to the rear wall, holding it just as taught. There it remained, on pegs, loaded and ready, a reminder to all, and providing a comforting feeling to Papa Frank. He felt prepared.

On days when we three were weathered in, there were magazines to read. The Argosy and The Red Book provided poems we could turn into songs with made-up tunes. This was a favorite:

> "When automobiling my woes confine,
> And the fuel gives out on my road machine,
> And it's sixteen miles to that home of mine,
> Then Oh for a gallon of gasoline."

Although no automobiles were seen in Walker, in Minneapolis people had sometimes laughed at the horseless affairs, for often owners did have to walk home.

As Dubby thumbed the pages, she remarked, "We won't use the ones about love." She explained, "I'm not ever going to love a husband and get married, because if he'd die I'd be sad and have to cry a lot." And Dubby had already cried a lot.

Days became long and lonesome, even with following along to the timbering lot, for we were sent home away from falling trees. But one morning, after extra pleading, we stayed, with the warning, "You'll have to stand where I tell you to."

Papa Frank was cutting poplars, used for stovewood. Staked piles of it stood at all angles in oblong solidness. When ready to fell another tree, he called us down from climbing the piles.

"Come here — —. This is a good thing for you to know. First, I want you to stay behind me. Don't run around so I'll have to watch you. you're safe as long as you're behind me."

He stood back, studying the height of his chosen tree, to decide where it could drop and not hang on others. "I can make this tree fall wherever I want it to," he said. "It's all according to where I start cutting. I'm going to drop it right between those trees, there." He pointed ahead where it seemed that surely there wasn't room.

With axe in hand, he stepped close and measured with his eye for position, moving a bit forward, then a step back, so as to start exactly opposite the line of fall. Then, raising the tool high, he whipped a downward swing that slanted low and bit deep in the smooth trunk. Then a level swing sent a big chip flying. We took Bounce and kept edging back as chips danced out. "Papa, that's going to fall on us, isn't it?" I called.

"Stay right where you are," he instructed over his shoulder. Resting a moment, he repeated, "You are safe as long as you stay behind me. Except," he added, "for the last minute, when I cut it away on the other side. Then I don't want you behind me. You stand still. That's all you have to do. I'll tell you when it's ready to fall."

Finally, the tree seemed standing on air, and he called, "Now it's ready. Stay where you are." It was difficult to stand still when he went behind. We moved farther back and so did Bounce.

Suddenly, with a snapping crack, the tall poplar leaned

stiffly away from the stump, and ripping its way down, fell shuddering right where he wanted it — then lay, like a giant killed, its silvery leaves quivering.

We raced forward to walk the trunk and climb on leafy, springy branches — extending up, spreading out, and holding it up underneath. The tree jerked and settled excitingly as Papa Frank began trimming. He ordered us tomboys down.

The next day I brought my axe, planning to fell a tree. It was easy to tell the gray-green poplars, smooth like a birch, with small leaves — round and shiny. Papa Frank showed me which to take - those just large enough to use unsplit. But the chips didn't fly as I expected. My axe wasn't heavy like Papa Frank's and could only chew. When he came to deliver the last blow and see it fall safely, I stood breathless as it shook itself over.

Dubby brought the measuring stick, and we marked and sawed the lengths. Not wanting to put mine with the others, I asked help to begin a new cord that would be mine alone. Dubby thought it a silly idea. She was playing Jump and Spring, straddling the cut-away branches lying on the ground.

As we trudged home carrying saw and axes, Papa Frank looked down fondly and spoke, "Papa's got real helpers."

I felt proud, "Do you think my cord will be good enough to sell?"

"If you pack it full of the right size pieces, I'll check it in 'O.K.' along with my own," he promised.

It would take many trees, of my kind, to fill the stakes. And I couldn't go every day; there was bread to bake, and often, for the oven was small.

Bounce was a devoted companion, even sleeping beside

our bunk at night. I had tried to ride him, but it didn't work. Although he stood patiently while I climbed on, it was difficult to stay there. Even with a thick harness rope around his neck, it wasn't like riding a pony; there was nothing in front — he kept his head down so much, nosing the ground. So it was more fun to run beside him.

Bounce was a good worker, too. When he first saw stove-wood being carried from the pile, he opened his large jaws and picked a piece up easily, then trotted inside and put it down in the corner behind the stove as he saw us doing.

Soon he was carrying all our wood. Each time, after dropping a piece, he'd switch around before the door could be closed and hurry out for another. I hugged his huge neck and praised, "Nice Bounce. Thank you, Bounce." He understood and carried till sometimes we had to stop him. He never came empty-jawed.

21

Treasure Waits Everywhere

Cranberries were ripe in the bog. Over the countryside, colored leaves and vines hung in mellow quietness under a sharp blue sky. One day, taking small pans, Dubby and I, with Papa Frank, knelt in the delicate springy vines of our own marsh and pulled apart the spongy moss. Red berries rolled from the hairlike stems. It was wet work, and not half of them could be reached. Working only around the edge, a bushel and a half was gathered after several days.

"You know," Papa Frank said, "we'll have enough to sell. And if we can find more somewhere, we can earn quite a few dollars to buy things."

"Now, let's see," he went on, "first we'll get some new shoes for you girls. And, maybe, new coats later on." He looked at our badly-scratched shoes and said, "You need some good calfskins." Cranberries would be easy to find.

* * *

Papa Frank was disappointed with the muskrat business, having learned that each skin was worth such a few cents. One evening as we washed dishes, he sat on a bench, holding his raised knee with clasped hands, and talked, "It wouldn't be worth messing with them at all. Besides, I'd need a boat to get out there and go after them right."

"How would you catch them from a boat?" I wondered. "Could you hit them?"

He laughed, "Well, almost, I guess, with so many out there. But I mean I'd need a boat to get around to their houses. I'd have to set the traps right on their doorsteps and underwater. It would be a lot of work. And not worth it."

"What happens when the pond freezes?" Dubby asked.

"They live in their houses and swim under the ice from house to house. I could get out there then, but it still wouldn't be worth it." He paused, letting his thoughts wander. "We're going to get about three rabbit traps though, and catch rabbits. That will give us meat all winter." We liked rabbit.

He planned. With dishes finished, I, too, sat down, but Dubby decided to scrape the dried dough from the breadpan - that being easier than soaking. She toted the drum-sized pan outside, along with the wide butcherknife, and started scraping.

The short heavy strokes had a rhythm that drew her into song, and she bore down, pounding a louder bang- bang-bang to cover the words. The cat's door flew up and Tridget headed into the room with Ruby squeezing beside her. Wild animals must have dived for deeper timber at the same time.

I was amazed that Dubby's voice sounded so clear. The whanging didn't hide it. And she was singing the sawmill song! I jumped to warn her, but Papa Frank was alert and rose at the same time and ordered me, "Stay right where you are."

While we looked at each other, I sharing the guilt, Dubby reached the last line, along with a volley of tin clangs, and finished strong: "to make that damned old sawmill pay."

Heavy boots clacked bare boards as Papa Frank strode to the door. As he jerked it open, Dubby turned, showing the queerest expression. She thought she was smiling, but the question in her eyes killed the smile.

"What's the matter?" she asked in innocent wonder, seeing sober faces.

"I think you know what's the matter," he said.

She looked at me, her eyes asking, "Could you really

hear that?"

I said, "We could hear you singing as plain as if there wasn't any noise at all."

Papa Frank took Dubby by the shoulder, saying, "Come here." And, handing the pan and knife to me, said, "You pound and sing," and he marched Dubby inside with him to listen. She wouldn't believe anyone else had heard, when even she couldn't hear herself.

But the truth was soon proven. Then Papa Frank became so interested — explaining the mysteries of sound — that he no longer felt any desire to scold about the swear-word.

* * *

Prodocks' building was finished — house, barn and store under one roof. Two doors faced the road. One led into the barn; the other led to the store, with living area back of it. A solid center wall from front to rear separated animals from people and held away smells and some of the noise. An upper floor had bedrooms on the house side and a haymow in the barn area. That haymow would one day become a haven.

The most important part to us was the store. One day I took a loaf of my bread to Mrs. Prodock and a lumberjack customer was there. When he saw the big crusty loaf he whispered to Papa Frank. He wanted to buy my bread, for he thought it looked better than Mrs. Prodock's, whose bread he'd been buying.

On the way home my proud papa said, "Beeny Coony, how would you like to earn some money?" He told me what the man had said and I was delighted. We decided to charge 8¢ a loaf. And we planned not to talk about it, so there would be no hurt feelings.

This day, Papa Frank had gone into town while we waited at the new store. So there were special packages to open. He had used the cranberry money for new calfskin shoes. Along with overalls, which were always the same, there was something quite different to be tried for size, as well as the shoes: he had bought the fleece-lined underwear he'd talked about— with white soft fuzz on the inside - the very warmest, for a frigid country. Later, after baths, I stood on a bench to show him how mine fit—snug at the wrists and ankles, and very warm. He decided he'd made a good purchase.

We were happy and cozy that night with the round heater warming the room, and the glass lamp glowing cheerfully on the table. Our lower bunk was curtained. Papa Frank had moved down to one he'd built at the foot of ours. The huge revolver spoke a threat from the wall above his bunk, and with a vicious-looking monster lying on the floor, we were prepared.

Winter came striding in, heaping the ground with snow. Dubby and I didn't go to the timberlot every day and never as early as Papa Frank.

One morning it was crackling cold. When we stepped outside, air froze in our nostrils. Papa Frank ordered, "You girls stay inside and keep the fires going. Maybe by noon it will warm up and you can go back with me." He built roaring fires in both stoves and waded off with bucksaw and axe.

I mixed flour into the bread-sponge, and in a little while, the sun looked ever so bright, even warm, leaving no reason for waiting till after dinner, when there would be bread to bake. So, bundling well, we followed Papa's snow-tracks, I with my axe, and Bounce, shoving slowly along beside Dubby and jumping fallen logs clumsily.

Soon sharp echoing clips told us exactly where he was, and when Bounce raced ahead, Papa Frank turned, saw us coming, and dropped his arms, provoked, then scolded, "Didn't I tell you not to come!"

I called, "But Papa, I've got to get my cord finished." It had seemed, at times, my spindly tree-poles would never reach the top of those stakes.

"It's too bitter-cold for you to be out here," he insisted. But we stayed anyhow, and Dubby found new fun.

Many of the big stumps Papa Frank left standing had splinters pointing up where the trees had split away in falling. To her they looked like pipe organs. She knelt to "play" the "keyboard" formed by the axe-marks, and began "Who-o-o-"ing loudly with musical sound, trying to imitate a church organ.

I quit work and joined the "whoo-whoo-ing" that soon changed to song. When a new tree dropped, our black-overshoed legs raced to watch sap ooze from the freshly-cut stump, and to be first to play the newest organ. The nice high-splintered ones caused arguments.

That spot in the timber rang joyously with axe-clips and shouted songs.

Going home at noon a different way and cutting through timber, we waded deep snow to find locations for the rabbit traps. Many criss-crossing tracks patterned the clean snow, for there were as many rabbits in the woods as muskrats in the pond. With the snow so deep, the little white-furred animals now stayed in packed-down paths while racing along. Though Papa Frank, so far, had shot them with the Colt's Navy, it would now be easier to catch them in traps set in the deep runs. He saw several that looked well traveled.

After dinner, and after promising, "You can go with me

Pipe Organ Stumps Call For Singing

tonight to see if we've caught any," he left for the timberlot with the traps dangling at his side. He buried them in the snow at separate places, marking each with a short stick to which the hidden chain and trap were fastened.

We watched at the window most of the afternoon for his coming; and he did come early. He used the older path so as not to see the traps: We would make the discovery together.

The bread was baked and under a cloth on the table. "We just may have some nice browned rabbit with that fresh bread," he hinted, whetting our appetites as we started after our quarry. The days were shorter and we needed to hurry.

Coming to the first run, he ordered, "You keep Bounce back now."

The stick was easily found, near his earlier foot-tracks. But, peering expectantly into the packed-down trail, we could see only an empty path.

"Where is the trap?" Dubby asked and I knew she expected it to be right there on the snow with a rabbit.

"It's buried in the snow," he explained. Only a few inches of chain were showing near the stake outside of the run. Papa Frank pulled the trap out to make certain it was still set. Then he covered it again and we waded on to another trap.

Here a dead rabbit lay, its front feet clamped in the trap lying uncovered beside it. It had been there for hours. Bounce was much too curious, and I hung hard on his neck while Papa Frank released the frozen meal and re-set the trap so another victim might unknowingly jump into it.

The third trap was empty, but we were satisfied with one rabbit. It didn't take Papa Frank long to get it ready for the pan. He nailed it by its hind feet to the outside of the house where crossing logs extended at a corner. With a sharp pocket knife, he quickly cut the skin from around the nailed feet; then began peeling the hide down, inside out, snipping and jerking till a naked body of flesh hung there, all the skin down over its head, and sagging almost to the ground.

The belly bulged, and Papa slit it from top to bottom and pulled the entrails out, letting them string to the ground; Bounce took care of most of it. A deft chop with the axe left the feet nailed to the house, and he carried the body to the woodpile, severed the neck, and let the hide, with the head and front feet inside of it, lie there.

While it browned in the pan he cooked rutabagas from the cave. We ate a fine meal.

* * *

Another Christmas was near. We wrote to Aunt Carrie to let her know where we were — she might want to send gifts. Mrs. Prodock told everyone that she was planning a party, with a tree, and all were invited to come Christmas Eve. There would be many lumberjacks — customers who often sat by the stove.

One day, two weeks before Christmas, when we Greens had gone to the store, a young man wearing heavy work clothes was there. He stood alone at the window. Prodocks' wondered about the stranger's quietness.

Bounce had come along that day. Prodocks had brought their dog to the bunkhouse and there hadn't been a fight. Even so, I kept watch from the window as Bounce and the shepherd dog played.

The stranger asked me about the huge dog, and then said, "And what do you want for Christmas?"

I looked up and smiled. He was the only person who had asked that question. Thinking a moment, I answered politely, "A gun."

"A gun!" he repeated. "Don't you want a doll?"

I shook my head slowly, "No," for I hadn't thought of a doll.

"What kind of a gun? A toy gun?"

I turned quickly. "Oh no. I want a real gun, to shoot - like one I saw in the store at Walker."

"What would you do with a gun?"

"Oh — shoot rabbits, or squirrels. I'd just go hunting."

He smiled, and seemed amused at the thought, and asked, "What does your mother think of it?"

"My mother is dead," I stated. I had said it so many times to so many people that it was a common statement now.

"Oh, I see," he said. Then noticing Papa Frank he asked, "Does your father want you to have a gun?"

I thought a moment. "Well, he wouldn't care, because my sister shoots our revolver, and the only reason I can't shoot it is because it kicks."

He stood silently, then after awhile he said, "Maybe your father will get you a gun. What kind did you see in the store?"

"A rifle. And I could hold it! But it cost too much. So Papa bought me an axe." I smiled again, knowing that a gun was only a wish. At Christmas you ask for lots of things you never really expect to get. Wishing, and thinking about it, is almost like having it. I promptly forgot what I had told him. But it seemed the young stranger went home that day with a secret idea brewing in his head.

Now that winter controlled the north and cold blue shadows closed the day too soon, long evenings in the bunkhouse saw programs carried out with each performer taking his turn, walking to the end of the room, bowing, and reciting poetry or singing. An imagined audience filled the room.

Blindfolded for "Hide the Thimble," we hunted the cork that served for the thimble we didn't have. There was singing, too, though it wasn't the fun it had been outdoors, where echoes were companions and trees were an audience. Often, just as in a schoolroom, spelling and arithmetic lessons were recited for Papa Frank.

Neither were days ever lonely, with life showing everywhere. The snowy hillside beyond the marsh forever carried foot-marks of large animals, mostly deer. Even after new snow smoothed it for a day, the following morning fresh tracks showed. Papa Frank would look out and say, "A — ha! We had visitors again last night."

But trouble visited, too. One day my throat was sore, and my shivering frightened Papa Frank. I knew he remembered when Mama sat long nights and days seeing me through pneumonia and that he was probably wondering what he could do, if I'd be that sick again.

He stayed home, but I wouldn't go to bed. I was sewing a waist for Dubby. There was a large square of cloth that had been a flour sack, and the red letters had faded so evenly that the entire sack was a pretty pink. I thought it very beautiful. It would make a lovely dress, but there was enough for only a waist. I laid the pink square against Dubby, this way and that, planning and measuring, but getting no co-operation. After cutting a hole for the head, it looked more promising.

Dubby squirmed and wiggled impatiently, and said, "Oh, why don't you let it be? I don't need a waist." It was most discouraging and added a headache.

I was firmly put to bed, after Papa Frank felt my forehead for the teenth time. Later, leaning over the bunk, he pressed his ear to my chest — the wheezing and rasping rattle terrified him. He began pacing between the bunk and the heater. "If we only had some turpentine," he said to Dubby, "I could put turpentine and lard on her chest." He didn't want to leave now, even to go to Prodocks' for help.

"Let me go get some Papa, please," Dubby begged. But he was afraid to have her go, for it would be dark before she could get back, although he knew she had no fear of darkness — neither of us had. We had been taught never to fear being alone.

The next time he listened, the rattling wheeze was worse. In desperation he decided to send Dubby, saying he wished he had done so sooner. He told her to get her coat; no daylight could be wasted now.

"I'll take Bounce along, won't I?" she asked, buckling her overshoes. He thought a minute, then said, "I believe you'll be better off alone. He might attract other animals. But they won't pay any attention to you."

She showed him she could hurry. He watched from the window as she ran down the slope and out over the frozen pond to the road. Then he stepped back to me and said, "Sister is hurrying."

The room became very quiet. Bounce lay near the round heater, dozing, with head on forepaws. He'd open his eyes to watch the man sitting beside the bunk, then slowly close them, seeming to know something was wrong. I fell asleep.

The room was dark when I opened my eyes and, for a moment, I couldn't remember where I was. When I stirred, Papa Frank moved at the window. He had been peering into the darkened outside, looking for Dubby coming across the pond. He walked quickly to the bunk, asking, "How do you feel, darling?" Putting his hand to my forehead, he said softly, "Lie still and keep warm."

Then I remembered — Dubby had gone to Prodocks' for

turpentine. "Isn't Dubby back yet?" I asked. It seemed like
the next day.

"No, but she'll come pretty soon," he said. It helped to
hear him say the words. Again he flattened his ear on my
chest. It might have been better had he left us with Grandma
Snyder, for he couldn't do things a woman could do.

He moved back to the window, then lit the lamp and put
more wood in both stoves. Minutes grew longer as Dubby
didn't come. He began walking the length of the room,
turning and walking back again, hands clasped behind him,
each time starting out a little faster, stalking the bare boards.

Then, in anquish, he began to talk, low and half groaning,
to himself or to nobody at all, "What shall I do - don't know
what to do - shouldn't have moved out here - never should
have tried it - (his heavy shoes rapped the hard wood) —
should have left the girls with a woman - can't have a doctor
- be ashamed to have a doctor -."

I was listening from the bunk and said, "Papa, why would
you be ashamed to have a doctor?"

He stopped short, seeming surprised that I had heard. "Oh
darling," he implored, stepping to the bunk, "I only mean I'd
be ashamed to have a doctor see this place. I'd hate to have
any of my folks know we lived this way. It isn't the way
things should be. Mama wouldn't want us to live like this."

His English pride was bleeding.

Then he turned to watch again. "Sister should be here
pretty soon," he said.

I lay thinking of all he had said. I didn't want to be the
cause of trouble. And I didn't want to miss the Christmas
party at Prodocks'.

After what seemed like forever, Bounce gave a deep soft
"woof" over by the stove. Dubby was coming! Papa Frank

jumped to the door and unbolted it.

"How is she?" Dubby asked, even before reaching the doorway. She was breathless from hurrying so, through the cold air and up the hill.

"She's been asleep most of the time. She isn't any worse, I guess." He spoke with relief for Dubby was safely home. She had the turpentine and a piece of flannel Mrs. Prodock had sent along.

"It got almost dark, didn't it?" Dubby said when she noticed the lighted lamp on the table and saw how black it now looked outside the window.

"It's been dark for quite a while," he told her.

"It didn't look dark to me. I could see everything."

"That was because your eyes were used to it. And the snow and the moonlight made it lighter, too." Dubby went to the window-pane and looked out. It certainly hadn't seemed like night to her, walking alone on the road.

The lard, in a small tin lid, was hot and waiting on the stove. Papa Frank added drops of turpentine and put the flannel in the oven. Dubby leaned over and comforted me as we waited. The hot mixture burned as he patted it on my bare chest. Dubby brought the flannel from the oven, but he took it back and laid it directly on the lids for a minute — to get it really hot — then hurrying with it tight between his palms, he tried to lay it on, but I grabbed it and held it away from my skin until it cooled a bit.

He felt better after doing this and cooked a late supper. Dubby was so hungry. I didn't get pneumonia and was better the next day. He thought the turpentine and lard had helped. The flannel was left on. "I'll be afraid to take it off before next summer," Papa Frank said.

* * *

One day a package came from Aunt Carrie, along with a letter which made us cry. Grandpa Wright had died. They had buried him beside the young man — near the schoolhouse in Emily.

There were cookies in the box and plaid taffeta hair-ribbons, besides stockings and mittens, and something very special — a cake of bitter chocolate. Aunt Carrie had remembered! I loved to nibble it at the corners and eat it with sugar from a teaspoon.

How we wished we had finished the keystone cushion-covers to give to her and to Mrs. Prodock. We got busy now. Although the checked cloth was so dirty and wrinkled that Papa Frank laughed, he thought maybe they could be washed. But Christmas came and no covers were finished. They never did get finished.

It was snowing softly on the day of Christmas Eve. We had been invited to eat supper at Prodocks', so were leaving in midafternoon. Bounce watched sad-eyed. He always looked sad-eyed, but we thought he must really feel bad to be left home on this special day. Strange dogs might be there, though, and he couldn't be trusted to not fight.

Papa Frank took the lead across the pond, kicking a path, while overhead, cotton flakes floated lazily by. The snow was too deep for me, so on reaching the road above the bank, he squatted for me to ride pickaback. Down the trail we sallied, Dubby following in his foot-tracks.

The snow-filled, untouched road stretched ahead through white wilderness, and at our feet sparkles swirled with every step. Tonight would be different from the last Christmas Eve — Papa Frank had told us so. There would be gifts. He had seen to that.

But as we shoved along, Dubby saw that Papa Frank had no packages and asked, "Are you sure you didn't forget to buy something for us, Papa?"

He turned to give her a sly glance. "Now — don't you do any worrying about that. Santa has that all taken care of." That brought smiles.

Dubby struggled to keep up, even though he walked slowly. With me clinging to his back, he leaned forward for balance while holding my legs firmly against his sides. Lying with my head on his shoulders, I could feel the muscles of his back moving, and hear the whit-whit-whit-whit of his corduroy pants rubbing between his thighs with every step. I thought he was being very good and hugged him tighter.

Up on the left, a wooded hillside tilted to the road. Every branch of bush and tree held heaps of whiteness. Only the trunks stood dark and orderly. Suddenly, Dubby shrieked, "Papa! Papa!" He turned quickly to see her stopping and pointing wild-eyed at the hillside. "What's that thing?" A huge cow-like creature was looking at us from a short distance away.

"Well, for goodness sake! That's a moose. If we only had our gun, we could have meat the rest of the winter." Its longnosed face and spreading antlers marked it plainly. It watched us steadily.

Papa Frank started on, but I clutched him, and Dubby let out a screech and stayed where she was, feeling sure that it would attack if we moved any closer.

Papa Frank sounded very brave. "That animal won't hurt you. He's more afraid of you than you are of him." But the moose didn't look afraid, and it didn't leap away as the wild deer had done. It looked ugly, even mean. Dubby ran to the safe side of Papa Frank, just in case it should start to come. As we drew closer, it turned abruptly with an awkward swing, and stalked, stiff-legged, up the hill, an easy target for a hunter.

We were first to arrive at Prodocks'. The Christmas tree hailed us, all set up and ready on the counter, and reaching for the ceiling. Sparkling silver tinsel-rope coiled it lovingly with looping spirals as it waited only for its candles and the gifts.

Mr. Prodock began putting the candles on. I climbed on a chair to help: Unpinching the little clamp-holders to straighten the candles and rearrange the twisted colored wax sticks so the prettiest would be in front.

After supper, as people arrived, Mrs. Prodock was gay, offering each a drink from the wooden keg at one end of the counter. With every extended cup, she sang, "Here's your luck to cider, drink'er down." Everyone laughed loudly.

The guests laid gifts on the counter and tucked some on the tree branches. There was only one other lady there. A little boy leaned over her knees continually as she sat. The rest were lumberjacks. The young stranger who had talked with me about Christmas was standing with hands in pockets, watching everyone and saying nothing. When I looked at him, he brightened, and smiled.

Candy and cookies were passed. It seemed the time would never come for presents to be given out. Mrs. Prodock asked Dubby and me to sing "Two Little Girls In Blue." She said a program would make things right; and we really were two little girls in blue — overalls.

Finally, the waiting was over, and as Mr. Prodock held a match to each candle, everyone in the room stood quieter, watching the colored twists pluck a flame from the match and hold it with steady glow. The tree came alive, from the top down, the candles tossing sparkles on the tinsel.

Stepping behind the counter, Mr. Prodock reached down, then held up a sled. I thought it was the little boy's, but he read the tag "For two nice girls — from Papa." We hadn't been kept waiting this time. Now we could coast, and maybe Bounce could be hitched for rides, and things could be hauled from town. Papa Frank wouldn't have to carry heavy sacks of flour on his back, even from Prodocks'. We hugged him.

When all gifts had been given out and the room was buzzing with talk, the quiet young stranger stepped unnoticed, except by me, to a corner where he had tucked his coat and parcels on arriving. Leaning over, he drew a long package, wrapped in heavy tan paper, from under the coat and walked over to where I was sitting with Dubby, on the sled.

"That's a pretty nice sled you got," he said, smiling down.

"We're going to fix a harness and have our big dog pull it," Dubby chattered.

He handed the heavy package down to me saying "Here — Merry Christmas," but not letting go until I held it firmly with both hands. I looked at him intently while clutching it in great wonderment. Then I remembered the day he had asked me what I wanted for Christmas. But it was unbelievable that he had bought a gun for me.

He took it again and unrolled the heavy paper. It was a rifle! Handing it back he said, "That's for you. Is that what you wanted?"

A gun. A rifle! A real one! With a shiny blue-steel barrel. And a polished wooden stock to place against my shoulder. I hugged it — speechless.

Dubby moved away to bring Papa Frank. He crossed the room gaping at the sight of me holding a rifle, not knowing of my earlier conversation with the young man. I had never expected to get any kind of gift from someone I didn't know.

Papa Frank could see it was new, even the wrappings. When I announced, "It's my Christmas present!" he corrected me, "No, No," and reached for it.

But I held tight saying, "Yes, it is!"

"I gave it to her. It's all right," the man said.

Papa Frank turned to the stranger. "You don't mean you are giving it to her to keep?"

He nodded yes. "I bought it for her. She wanted a gun. It's hers to keep—sure."

Others in the room were now looking. Papa Frank took the rifle. "Why - this is a Winchester!" he marveled. A rifle like that cost money, more money than anyone there would spend, even on their own families. And this rash young man had spent it on a nine-year-old whom he barely knew. It was difficult to understand.

All eyes seemed to wonder who the Santa Claus stranger was. Papa Frank asked his name, and he said, "Johnson." He explained quietly to Papa Frank that he had ordered the rifle from a catalog two weeks before. "I just wanted to celebrate Christmas with the rest of you and I had no one else to buy for," he said, seeming pleased with the outcome.

I opened the small box of bullets he had taken from his pocket and rubbed my fingers admiringly over the waxy ends of lead that extended from the tiny brass cases. As Papa Frank handed the rifle back to me, he beamed, "That's the finest rifle that can be bought." He was almost as happy as I was.

Standing straight, I put it to my shoulder and aimed. The

young man showed me how to sight the tiny bead at the end of the barrel into the notch nearer my eye. We pointed it to a corner, and I snapped the trigger, practicing. Then "Santa Claus" loaded it, pulling a side-bolt up and back, inserting one bullet, and pushing the bolt forward again and down. Then he and Papa Frank went outside with me.

It had stopped snowing and a glorious starfilled sky smiled down. The young man fired high into the darkness, and the little rifle "cracked" as a rifle should. He put in another bullet and handed it to me. Papa Frank knew I could manage.

I was shaking with delicious excitement as I aimed at a star in the dark-blue cold sky. This was the real thing — a loaded gun. I wondered whether to pull the trigger slowly or jerk. Suddenly, in spite of caution, it snapped. A happy squeal escaped me. It hadn't kicked at all! And it was mine to keep! A 22 Winchester!

That night we Greens stayed at Prodocks', and after others had gone, Mrs. Prodock, said, "That young fella must not have any folks, or he wouldn't spend his money so easy. But maybe he just wanted to make someone happy." Mr. Prodock said he thought the man was young and foolish. But I thought he was wonderful.

22

Alone And Frightened At Midnight

Bitter weather followed Christmas. The new sled soon had the hill packed slick from the bunkhouse door to the pond. Papa Frank fashioned a rope-harness for Bounce to pull it, but he didn't care to be a horse and kept turning around. We tried taking turns leading him, but too much of the time Dubby walked because Bounce could pull me more easily.

Although it was too cold to go hunting, I practiced firing my rifle, and I learned to handle it properly, carrying it pointed down. And always, before putting it away, I polished the woodstock and the blue steel barrel. Papa Frank had pounded two more pegs back of his bunk, below the Colt's Navy. I placed it there carefully.

One forenoon, when Dubby and I were alone in the bunkhouse, Bounce, who was outside, suddenly gave a warning growl, then began to bellow angrily. Skipping to the window, we saw two men coming across the pond. Dubby hurried to the door to make sure the bolt was over tightly. That bar was there for this very purpose, and Papa Frank had warned us to keep the door bolted.

Bounce advanced part way down the hill, barking fiercely to keep the strangers far from the door. We ducked back from the window, wondering what to do.

Soon the men began calling, "Hey there — anyone home?" They could see smoke coming from the chimney. They called again and again and talked to Bounce as he held them off.

Finally, we became so curious to see what was happening,

Dubby pushed back the bar and opened the door, just a crack, to peek. Bounce was lunging whenever the men stepped nearer, and they begged, "Call off your dog — please."

"What do you want?" Dubby ordered, sounding quite grownup.

"We want to get warm and get a drink of water. Can't you make that dog leave us alone? Call him inside."

They were young men, dressed in fur-collared jackets, and they sounded so demanding that we couldn't decide what to do. "We shouldn't refuse them a drink of water," Dubby said.

I reminded, "You know, Papa told us never to open the door to strangers."

The men pleaded, "We're cold — we're almost frozen. We only want to get warm and get a drink of water." Then, being sure that we were alone, they begged, "You wouldn't refuse to give us water, would you?" They moved closer, in spite of Bounce.

Dubby pulled back inside and closed the door against the cold while we tried to decide. We would never be cruel to anyone, and hearing the constant calling, she opened the door again.

Then one fellow said, "You needn't be afraid we'll hurt you — not with that dog around."

We felt ready to agree, seeing Bounce's determination. "All right," Dubby called, "but just wait a minute." She ran to the back of the room, crawled up on Papa Frank's bunk and took the loaded Colt's Navy from the wall.

"This is why we got this," she reminded me on returning and reaching for the door latch.

At the sight of the gun the men drew back in horror,

"What have you got there?"

"A Colt's Navy," Dubby informed them. She called to Bounce, who wouldn't listen, or couldn't hear above his own barking. Then, stepping out to tell him to let the men pass, she patted his head with her free hand while leveling the revolver with the other. I shivered close behind. We were without coats.

The bold intruders suddenly became uncertain whether to enter or run. Using great caution, they sidled through the doorway keeping an eye on the gun. We followed. Dubby had command. Inside, she told me, "You go ahead and finish the dishes. I'll take care of this."

The strangers walked to opposite sides of the round heating stove and stood with extended palms, silent and sober. Dubby dragged a short bench to a good place for aiming, half way across the room, and sat down, holding the revolver pointed at them from her knees, and gripping it in both hands with forefingers on the trigger.

Bounce stood close to her, unable to quiet down. His low warning growls put meaning into his fierce glaring, riveted on those beings who didn't belong there.

One of them asked, "Have you ever fired that gun?" They hadn't taken their eyes from it.

"Oh yes," Dubby answered. "I practice target shooting all the time. I can hit a mark fifty feet away now."

"Have you got that thing loaded?" the other asked.

"Oh, it's always loaded."

Then, because Dubby liked so well to talk, she explained why we needed the gun, that we lived with Papa Frank and were alone while he worked, and he had told us never to let any strangers in, and to shoot if we had to.

"Well, I don't think he needs to worry with that beast and

Point It Down — Point It Down

that gun around," she was told.

"Stop pointing that thing at us," one pleaded. "Point it down — point it down," they begged, motioning downward. Dubby did, but kept forgetting and lifting it, and was constantly reminded.

No one ever got warm so fast. They moved to leave in such a few minutes that Dubby told them they could stay longer, that they hadn't had time to get warm. As they started for the door, she reminded them they were forgetting their drink of water.

Without taking eyes from the gun, they reached for the dipper in the pail and drank quickly, looking over the rim. They assured us they were very warm and thanked us in a manner subdued and polite.

Strangers never again stopped at the bunkhouse. The word was spread — "Stay away from that place if you want to stay alive." They had gone on to Prodocks' store and told of their terrifying moments.

Prodocks' were secretly amused, and when they told Papa Frank, he laughed with them and was glad it had happened. He wondered if the young strangers might have been the same two who had waded the pond that day when he was digging the well. Now they would never come again. He praised Dubby.

* * *

One day a few weeks after Christmas, when we girls and Papa Frank were at Prodocks' store, the young lumberjack who had given me the rifle was also there. He was pleased that I had learned to hit a mark and he encouraged me. "Now you can shoot a wild animal. Maybe a rabbit or squirrel."

That afternoon he told Mrs. Prodock he was going away

but didn't say where. Before he left, he took three rings from his pocket and handed them to me saying, "Here, you can have these." Two were gold, the other silver, and all too large, although the silver one held quite well on my first finger and I put it there.

Papa Frank had gone on to town, and Mrs. Prodock and Dubby and I were alone after the young man left. We examined the rings with curious surprise and Mrs. Prodock said, "Maybe he's planning to do away with himself and wants to get rid of everything. Maybe he's been disappointed in love." His actions were hard for her to understand.

She took the rings and admired them on her own fingers. "You will only lose these," she said. "You can't wear them for years. I don't see why he wanted to give all of them to you."

She put the gold ones away. When Papa Frank came, she told him she'd make dresses for Dubby and me in exchange for the two gold rings. He agreed, for dresses were needed.

I wore the silver ring and didn't lose it for a long time.

Hauling supplies home on the sled was easy, and fun too. But that evening everything went wrong. It was late when we sat down to eat. It had taken Papa Frank so long to cook the meat he had brought. And he laughed and talked a lot.

At first, we thought it was fun to have him so jolly, but at the table we thought he was acting very queer, and couldn't understand it. He dropped a piece of bread and laughed hard, saying, "It always fell butterside down! I was in a class play in high school and that was what I said in that play. Those were my lines - - - - This - is - how -- I said it." He sat a bit straighter and lifted his chin as he slowly and awkwardly recited, "And it always fell -- but-ter-side ----------- down."

I was sitting between him and Dubby on the bench, but I

nudged a little closer to Dubby. Papa Frank's eyes were so red he didn't look like Papa. Then, when he used his fork to stir the sugar in his cup of coffee, I was amazed, for he was always careful about table manners. He began to laugh as he stirred, saying, "This --- is - the --- way --- we - used to do ----- in camp." His words came clumsily.

I turned to Dubby and thought she looked scared. Dubby leaned and whispered, "Papa's drunk."

I knew what that was, but had never seen my own Papa drunk, just other men; and I always ran from them. I was beginning to remember what they had said about Papa at Mama's funeral and I wondered if now maybe he had done what they said about hitting the bottle: If he had been drinking alcohol like the tramp at Grahams'. I couldn't eat and after awhile he noticed and asked what was wrong. I was afraid to answer.

It seemed so terrible not to talk to him. It was as though he had become someone else. I couldn't swallow my food. My tears ran over, and he said, "Wha's the matter with my lil' girl?"

I could hold the sobs no longer, and turning to him, wailed, "Oh, Papa — you're drunk!"

It shocked him, and he at once turned sober and serious. Then he said slowly, "Why no — I'm not." He looked at Dubby and said, "You know Papa isn't drunk, don't you?"

Dubby was afraid to disagree, so said nothing. He didn't talk after that. As soon as we left the table he told us to go to bed. It was late anyhow, and dishes could be done the next day.

We were glad to crawl into the curtained bunk, but we peeked, and saw him sitting before the stove — head in hands — for a long time. Then he went to his own bunk and to bed.

We couldn't sleep. Dubby whispered that she thought he had bought what he was drinking, in town, and that maybe he had it in his pocket. We felt very much alone that night. Only it was worse than being alone. We had always been afraid of a drunk man.

Later we heard him getting up, and peering from behind the curtain, we saw him weave slowly across the floor, guided by the moonlight from the windows. He moved to the cupboard on the wall, and reaching far into the top shelf, lifted out a bottle and drank from it, replaced it, and carefully found his way again to the bunk. We snuggled back under the covers, wide awake and very still.

Dubby whispered, "We've got to get that away from him. That's liquor. That's what he's getting drunk from."

It wasn't long before heavy breathing signaled that sleep would make it safe to move. We crawled out, ever so carefully, patting Bounce when he got to his feet beside our bunk. Sneaking across the floor, listening to every gutteral breath, we found a short bench and quietly lifted it over to the cupboard. I held it firmly as Dubby climbed up and reached far back. When she was safely down, the bottle in hand, we didn't know what to do with it.

"He'll know we took it, and he might get mad," Dubby whispered.

"Can't we tell him we're just keeping it?" I suggested under my breath.

"I know — come on," Dubby whispered, starting for the door, coatless. We pushed the oak-bar back making no noise at all, working very slowly; but then, the rusty door-hinges creaked with every inch. We had never before noticed the creaking. Bounce followed, squeezing through the narrowest of space, but he made no noise and now only watched.

Dubby pulled the cork from the bottle and began to carefully pour the clear stuff onto the ground, but only part of it. Several times she held the bottle high against the white moonlight, looking closely to see how much was left.

"I'm going to leave some and put the bottle back, so he'll think he drank it," she explained, whispering even though outside.

I was shaking violently with fright and cold as Dubby took too long to decide. "Hurry up," I urged through chattering teeth, "he might wake up."

We got back inside safely and closed the squeaky door. There was still the task of getting onto the bench again and replacing the bottle. It was harder this time as we were so chilled and shivering. The breathing of deep sleep continued and we were able to do it all, even carry the bench back to where it belonged, before climbing cautiously into bed. We trembled for many long minutes until the warmth of our bodies, close together, brought sleep.

The next day nothing was said of the night before. And, although we watched, we didn't see him look at the bottle. He couldn't deny that he was drunk after drinking that amount. I'm sure he didn't know we had taken it, or even that we knew he had it.

* * *

Happier days came. On February 2nd we waited with keen interest and much hope for the sun not to shine, so the groundhog wouldn't see his shadow and go back to sleep. When it did grow bright outside, as we watched from the window, Papa Frank comforted, saying he felt quite sure the little sleepy animal had taken an early look before the sun was up. Winter wouldn't be too long.

The rabbit runs were deep, and so full of racing cottontails that just one trap was used, and not every day. We couldn't eat so much rabbit, even with Bounce's help.

In the weeks that followed, the wood-cutting job was completed. I struggled to fill my cord stakes. Dubby helped at the last, to boost the long sticks to the top. Papa Frank tossed on a few of his own, finally saying it would check "O.K." I was proud and very glad to be through with it.

Early one morning, all of us, including Bounce, started for Walker. Bounce had met other dogs at Prodocks' without fighting, so he was being taken all the way. Passing Prodocks' we stop ped for just a minute, and suddenly, Prodocks' dog and Bounce tore at each other's throats. No one knew which dog started it, but Bounce was blamed.

Although the shepherd dog was smaller, he was still a good sized dog and had sharp teeth. As they snarled and fought, poor Bounce couldn't get a grip on him with the points gone on his own teeth. They rolled, paying no attention to all the frantic calls. Papa Frank thrust a stick between them. Mrs. Prodock got a bigger one and tried beating them, but that only made them fight harder.

Soon blood was spreading over Bounce's face and mixing into the snow. The shepherd dog had sunk his teeth into the Newfoundland's hanging lip and when Bounce tried to shake him loose by tossing him overhead through the air, it only tore his own flesh more. One eye seemed hanging out of his own cheek, and blood was running thick, but still they fought.

Then Mrs. Prodock remembered how to separate fighting dogs. She ran for a bucket of water and splashed part of it over them. They didn't like that. She drenched them with the rest of it, and the shepherd dog let go. Mrs. Prodock chased it into the house, and the fight was over.

Bounce was hurt the most. He looked pitiful. Papa Frank pushed the skin up around his eyes as well as he could, and Mrs. Prodock brought rags to wash the blood from his head. The trip to town was spoiled.

I'll tell you what we'll do," Papa said. "You girls go back home with Bounce. I'll hurry on to town and get our things, and I'll bring medicine for those cuts."

Though we wanted him to help with Bounce, he explained he could go very fast when alone, and that medicine was needed. He urged, "You girls go home, like nice girls, and soak some beans, and Papa will come by dinnertime," and he hastened off.

All the way back we comforted Bounce. Once inside, he lay down. I dropped to the floor beside him to try to hold the torn lip in place. He looked so sad, as though unable to understand how it could have happened. He'd growl when doctored too eagerly, but liked the soothing murmurs, "poor Bounce — too bad — too bad — Papa is getting medicine to fix it — poor Bounce — poor Bounce." We patted and stroked, thinking our nearness eased his pain.

Noon came, and Papa Frank wasn't there. We ate what we could find and kept the fires going, as always, when alone. Later on, Dubby cooked the beans, and when at suppertime he still hadn't come, we ate alone and watched and wished he would get there.

Bounce had lain through the long hours with his great head on both forepaws; the cuts seemed to stay closed and feel better that way. He'd open his eyes when we knelt near, then slowly close them again.

It grew dark, and Dubby lit the lamp. It seemed scary to be alone now. Papa Frank had never stayed away after dark.

Now he had been gone for hours, all day.

Bedtime came and we worried most for Bounce. It was too cold to leave him suffering on the floor alone. I wanted to put the quilts down and sleep beside him, but Dubby said, "I know, we'll take him in our bunk."

So we coaxed, and boosted, and pulled, until we got him up, suffering and protesting, into the low cubicle. No undressing was done, so it wasn't like going to bed, even though we were so tired after such a day. The lamp on the long table was burning, waiting for Papa Frank. We didn't plan to sleep.

"What if something has happened to Papa?" I said again, and tears came in spite of all my efforts. "Maybe a wild animal got him."

Because Dubby was eleven, she tried to comfort, "He'll come pretty soon, you go to sleep."

We both fell asleep, but I wakened later and shook Dubby. "I heard a noise outside," I whispered.

Dubby said, "Oh, maybe it's a deer walking around." The light would attract them.

Dubby lifted our curtain and looked at the alarm clock on the table beside the lamp. It was twelve o'clock! I looked and knew it was midnight, when things were ghostly and unreal. Ruby and Tridget had cuddled together on their gunnysack on the floor. The lighted glass lamp burned steadily, and the room was very cold.

The door had been bolted tight, so we dropped the curtain and found warmth and protection with Bounce, who filled most of the space. Deep weariness again brought slumber, and we might have slept till daylight had nothing wakened us. But hours later Bounce gave a low growl. Someone was outside the door. A voice called, "Concetta." We woke

instantly and listened as it called again. "Concetta —
Dubby." No one knocked — that would have frightened us.

Dubby said, "It's Papa!"

We jumped from the bunk and hurried to unbolt the door,
and there stood Papa Frank, with bandages showing below
his cap. Mr. White, the hardware man from whom we had
bought our stove and other things, stood holding him by the
arm. They came inside, and Mr. White helped his pale weak
patient to a bench.

"What's the matter — Where have you been — Why
didn't you come home?" We crowded our questions,
distressed but relieved to have him there.

Papa Frank didn't answer. He could scarcely talk — Mr.
White had called Dubby's name loudly for him.

Mr. White spoke kindly, "Your papa has had an accident.
He was in a run away. He was on his way home riding with
another man when it happened. He got a big cut on his
head."

"Is he all right now?" Dubby asked.

Mr. White thought so, and that he would get along fine.
He explained that no bones were broken, and the doctor
would come in a day or so to take care of the wound. He
carefully lifted the tight cap from the bandaged head.

Papa Frank thanked him warmly for all his help and
assured him he could get into bed by himself. The Good
Samaritan left to drive home in the cold night. By the clock
on the table it was after three in the morning.

Papa Frank didn't move on the bench, seeming not able to
think. Then he began to cry, and murmured in weak, slowly-
spoken words: "What he said — about an accident — isn't
the — truth. I wasn't — in a runaway at all. ---- Now, Papa
doesn't want to — lie to his girls. ---- I want you — to know

the truth."

He forced painful words, "I owe my life — to that man. He's the most wonderful man — in the world. ---- He found me — where they'd left me — to die." Stopping to cough, and sob, he gathered strength to go on. "He saved my life — I was in a saloon — but I wasn't drunk — I was only trying to see — that another man there — got his rights. ---- The bartender was cheating him — and I was standing with my back turned — when the bartender reached — for a club. ---- He struck me — across the head — before I could stop him."

We hugged him, feeling great pity. He kept talking, "Mr. White found me — and got a doctor — or I would have bled to death. ---- He's a wonderful man."

Mr. White really had saved his life we learned later. He had been left on the floor of the locked saloon, unconscious and bleeding. No one had bothered about the stranger. Mr. White, after working late at his own store, passed the saloon on his way home and saw blood running from under the door. Through the window he could see someone on the floor and sought the town marshall. They went inside.

Mr. White knew Papa Frank, and knew that he had little girls, and we might be alone. He rushed for a doctor, and they carried the unconscious, bleeding man to the doctor's office where many stitches were taken to close the scalp. When Papa Frank wakened he begged to be taken home, knowing we were alone. Mr. White had harnessed his team in the night to bring him.

As he sat on the bench, slumped and pale from loss of blood, we sympathized and were grateful he was alive, but we were still worrying over Bounce and I asked about the medicine he had gone for. He didn't have it! What a disappointment!

He had forgotten and was so very sorry. He consoled us saying the doctor would have salve, and he'd come in a day or so. We helped him to his bunk and took off his shoes. He lay down without undressing. It would be many days before he'd be about again.

When the doctor came two days later, Papa Frank sat somewhat limply on a bench while the long bandage was unwrapped. An odd, warm, sort of sweet smell, almost sickening, came from the gauze so soaked with blood. Dubby and I stood wide-eyed and spellbound nearby, and cringed at the sight of red bumps of flesh swelled between the stitches where several inches of scalp had been closed.

As the doctor swabbed the wound with medicine, he said, "You are lucky to be alive. If this had been farther over, even one inch, it would have killed you. I don't see how you are alive as it is."

I waited impatiently for Papa Frank to ask for Bounce's medicine, whispering several times, reminding him. So, as the doctor was leaving, Papa asked him to please look at the dog's torn face. Bounce had growled savagely when he came in, and he growled again now, warning not to be touched.

Keeping a healthy distance the doctor said, "You can't do much with that. That lip will grow together all right. It's probably already binding itself." That was because Bounce had lain so still.

Cautiously, bending closer, he said, "That torn skin by his eye will draw together, too. You watch it, and if it begins to look sore and mattery, then you can do something for it. Otherwise, you just leave him alone, feed him and give him water, and he'll be all right."

Then, as if remembering, he turned to Papa Frank, "You drink lots of water, too. That's what'll put the blood back

259

into your veins."

The next time he came the wound looked better, and because it was far to come, and because his patient couldn't walk to town, he thought may be Dubby could change the bandage. But she didn't want to. It had made her sick to look at the bloody bumps. Papa Frank thought he could manage alone, but I said, "Papa, I can do it."

The doctor smiled his amusement until my fond parent said, "I think she can. I believe she will do it very well." And he told him about the good bread I had baked. He was so proud of that.

So I watched closely, just as the first time. The doctor left bandage material and medicine. It was all in my hands now.

I would have doctored it every day, had I been allowed. But every several days, standing on the bench he sat on, I unwrapped his head and bathed the stitches, telling him how it looked. He couldn't see, even with the mirror. We decided it was getting better. He helped in firmly rewrapping the bandage.

* * *

The daily struggle to keep warm turned into a battle — feeding the hungry stoves. In the fall it had seemed that enough wood was split to last forever, but now it was used up. Though larger logs were left, they needed splitting, and neither Dubby nor I could do that. Instead, we searched out fallen trees and sawed their small branches into short pieces.

Papa Frank told us to use the bucksaw and work together, using it as a crosscut. We knew how he meant, even before he insisted we bring the saw so he could show us. Aunt Carrie and Grandma Wright had pulled the long crosscut back and forth that way. How we labored, pushing and jerking the little red tool. The axe worked better for smaller sticks. Happily, the round heater could hold quite large chunks. So we managed, working almost constantly.

Bounce's lip and eye healed well, and he helped. One day he spied the end of a fallen tree peeping from the snow, and considering it the right size to take, clamped his jaws firmly and tugged. It didn't move.

He barked for help, running after Dubby and me. When we turned, he raced back and pulled again. We dropped our own loads and helped, but couldn't budge it — the heavy part was hidden. A very determined Bounce had to be coaxed to "come along," and kept struggling even after being left behind.

Papa Frank decided, "Bounce is the finest dog we could ever have found. He's worth all the extra food he eats." Bounce did more than his share of wood-carrying.

There were the traps to tend to. We had been forbidden to go alone, but when meat was needed, Papa Frank thought of what to do. Taking one of the traps kept in the bunkhouse, he showed Dubby how to open the steel wings and set it. After he had made it snap shut on a short stick, he showed her how to open it to release a rabbit, all the time warning her not to be careless and get her hands cut. We were really careful. I held Bounce back every time, while Dubby set the trap in the packed-down run.

The first time, when we paraded home with a white furry prize, the butchering was almost fun. I boldly nailed it up by its hind feet to the outside of the bunkhouse on a log at the corner, and cut the skin away at the top, pulling it down inside out until it hung over the head, as I had often seen Papa Frank do, though in much less time.

Then I slit open the naked body and pulled out the smelly

insides, letting them drop for Bounce to carry away. Now I was stumped — the head must come off! There the bunny hung, with stretched legs and raw empty body, looking half the width of its living self but three times as long, with the hanging skin touching the ground.

I skipped for my axe and chopped the body away just below the nailed feet. The messy thing fell to the ground, then I carried it at arm's length to the woodpile and dropped it over a low chopping-log — the inside-out fur dangling over the head, to be cut off at the neck — and I couldn't do it.

Dubby gained courage, grabbed the axe and boldly chopped through the crunching neck-bones as she had seen it done. I carried it into the bunkhouse in triumph. The next time the butchering was easier, but no longer enjoyed.

And so the winter weeks wandered along. Papa Frank helped to pass the hours, writing words to spell and numbers to add. Occasionally, Prodocks brought over The Argosy and The Red Book along with the groceries. We were content.

23

Where The Great Mississippi Begins

Now the sun traveled higher and days were longer. The pond was swollen with melted snows, so the muskrats again wove trails across the surface and the short cut path was gone. The old hidden road beyond the barn provided a way out. It was spring!

Budded branches waited impatiently. Papa Frank was well and strong, and he too, waited impatiently. He hadn't gone to town, and now he yearned to go fishing, and he talked of it almost daily.

Looking at his map, he said, "See here — we're close to the source of the Mississippi. Some nice day we'll start out and see if we can find it. Wouldn't it be wonderful if you could say you had seen the beginning of the great Mississippi?"

It would, indeed, be better than a lesson in school. He had heard there were streams in the area filled with fish.

Dreaming another day, he said, "I'll tell you what else we'll do when we make that trip. We'll take some bottles and gather balsam."

I looked up, "What's balsam?"

"Oh, a kind of sap that's found in little blisters on the bark of the balsam tree. It's quite valuable. It's used in medicine. And we just might be able to get enough to sell."

How exciting!

So, one nice spring morning we fed Tridget and Ruby and started off on a trail leading northwest, carrying a sack of lunch and two small bottles for balsam. Papa Frank assured us we wouldn't find more than those bottles would hold. We had wanted to take a pail. He had line and hooks in his pocket and would cut a pole on arrival.

We walked miles, following old grass-grown logging roads through timber and open brush land, with Bounce rapidly exploring ahead. At midforenoon the forest trail suddenly opened to a fairyland where tall Norways shaded smooth, needled ground. We didn't go beyond it.

This wasn't the source of the Mississippi, and the trees weren't balsam fir, but it was a place of beauty waiting to be visited. Surprisingly, off to the right stood a log cabin, quiet and shy, not even facing the road, but sleeping alone with no fence or pen for beast or fowl. Only a grindstone occupied the yard.

Straight ahead from where we were standing, the soft untraveled road beckoned down a gentle slope and continued on across a full-flowing stream, seeming to lie on the high water — for the flat, log bridge was narrow and without railings. On the far side, the road turned sharply left, curved round the foot of a hill, and wound out of sight.

Dubby and I stood fascinated by the tucked-in cabin as Papa Frank walked on. It was like finding a new home — almost. When we started toward it, he glanced back and called, "Girls, don't go over there. Someone lives there."

But strong curiosity won. The door was closed, so we looked through a window. Sure enough! Someone lived there. Pans were hanging on the wall behind a cookstove. Bounce nosed the ground, investigating.

When we caught up with Papa, I asked, "How did you know anyone was living there?"

He smiled slyly, "Because there wouldn't be a grindstone unless someone was around to use it." We hadn't thought of that. A woodsman would sharpen his axe on it.

Reaching the stream, we found it really wide and full to its banks with melted snows still running. The crude bridge stretched like a raft under our feet. We were surrounded with beauty and Papa Frank said, "I don't think we need to go any further today. This is so nice. I'll cut some poles and we can fish." He moved away to do that.

Dubby and I, preferring the bridge, plopped to our stomachs, and with heads over the edge, saw fish underneath, swimming slowly in the shadows. I called to Papa, "Come — look — the fish are all under here."

He stepped quickly and got to his knees. "For goodness sake," he laughed, "they must be having a meeting."

They all looked alike to me and I asked, "Do they all belong together? Is this their home?"

"Well, I guess it's their home while they're here," he said. "You know, home for them can be anywhere that they find food and where they feel safe with others of their kind. That should be true for people, too: Home is where your heart is — where there are people who love you."

Papa Frank left, but Dubby and I stayed on our stomachs and lifted faces to look upstream into the tumbling water rushing toward our eyes and flashing under us out of sight. Then jumping to lie at the other edge, we laughed at the sight of it racing swiftly downstream toward Papa Frank, carrying the sticks we tossed. He was catching fish, and we soon joined him with willow-poles of our own. Later on, we picnicked, with "campfire trout" on the shoreline.

When at last the time came to leave this wonderland, the cabin was still deserted. How I wished I could live there. The soft, brown yard and tall trees and quiet road all belonged to it, and the bridge and flowing water belonged to it, too. No one had passed in all those hours, but its secret visitors had spent a happy time. At day's end, a dog and three weary people with empty bottles and a string of fish, returned to the bunkhouse, completely satisfied.

Only short days later we eager explorers started out again. This time we'd find the source of the big river. It had been promised.

It was dewy-early on that clear morning, and almost from the beginning, Papa Frank used the pocket compass he always carried. Mostly, we followed logging trails and kept going west and north. Bounce wasted steps but kept close enough. The abandoned roads never ran straight. It would be easy to get lost. "If you got lost here, there wouldn't be any cows to follow either," I told Papa Frank.

He laughed at such a thought.

"Well —," I defended, "you know that's what Mrs. Steece did. She was lost and she heard cowbells, and she went over to where the cows were and began to chase them and they took her out to the road."

"Yes, Papa, that's true," Dubby said, and told it again in great detail.

"I guess that would be a pretty good idea then," he said, "if cows were around. But I think I'd rather have my compass."

When again he stopped to check direction, he held the compass flat in his lowered palm, and before letting us see, asked, "In what direction do you think we're going?" We both thought straight west. Dubby had tried to tell by the sun.

But the path had angled south. We hovered over the compass studying it, and sure enough, the arrow-end of the quivering needle was pointing opposite the direction we were going, and the arrow always pointed straight north. We were going the wrong way! But the old trail soon turned west again. All this was new to us.

About the middle of the forenoon, Papa Frank called, "Get your pins and bottles ready." He pointed to balsam trees and, stepping over, looked for blisters on the trunks, then finding some, held a bottle against the bark and pricked a blister open. A liquid, like thin glue, ran into the bottle. But there were such a few drops in most of the blisters! I could see it would take a very long time to fill a bottle. For awhile it was fun, then the whole idea became hopeless.

"We should be seeing some signs of water before long," Papa Frank encouraged as we hiked along, stopping for only the closest trees and the largest blisters, and expecting any moment to see water gushing from the ground.

He had told us that "source" meant the beginning of a river, although it did seem that the beginning should be the mouth. He explained carefully that the mouth was where it emptied into the Gulf of Mexico, over a thousand miles away. This was the source. It emptied at its mouth, though it wasn't sick.

When we came to where small streams seemed to cross, we knew it was different ground. When Papa Frank said, "Well, here we are — this is some of it anyhow," I was disappointed. There were no gushing springs, but surely they were underneath for water seemed to come from nowhere, and a wide explosion of high grasses made walking difficult. Bounce ran swishing through the tall reeds in search of things unseen.

There was solid ground, too, and trees here and there. The larger streams flowed crystal clear and full of fish. We crossed one of these, balancing on the trunk of a fallen tree. When Papa Frank put in a line farther along, we tomboys ran back to tight-walk the log and stretch bellyflat, spying on the inhabitants circling underneath.

At noon, while eating under a tree where it was dry enough to sit, Papa Frank gazed around and remarked, "This water all flows into a big lake farther over. It's the outlet of the lake that they call the beginning of the Mississippi. This is all part of it."

After seeing the river at Minneapolis, it seemed impossible that it could come from this place. But this was only an edge of miles of marsh that drained into the lake, making it overflow to start the river. Other streams joined along the way.

We couldn't linger. It had taken most of the forenoon to get there. After exploring a bit, Papa Frank looked at the compass to start home. But we didn't get far — a stream too wide for Dubby and me to cross, blocked our going. We would have to circle far back to the way we had come, or somehow get over. We followed the bank, searching for a narrow place. No stepping-logs were handy.

Finding a promising spot, Papa Frank showed us where to stand, on the very edge, then he leaped across and turned to see if he could grasp our hands. I stretched but couldn't touch him. So he gave all attention to Dubby, while assuring me he would figure out a way for me, too. After much reaching, he managed to jerk Dubby safely across and up the bank when she jumped. Then I was alone, for Bounce had simply waded a few steps and swum across. I became fearful, but Papa Frank bounded over, and after considering, squatted so I could climb on his back. I clung tightly while he made a flying leap and got safely over.

Starting ahead, I almost stepped on the flattened yellow hide of some animal that had been dead so long even its

bones lay flat. Bounce paid it no attention, although the hairy
skin formed the shape of an animal. It had been about the
size of a little puppy. Papa Frank said it was a dead coon.

It surprised me to find one dead. I had believed coons
lived almost forever. Aunt Carrie had talked about not seeing
someone "for a coon's age" when she meant a very long
time. Papa Frank agreed that maybe coons lived longer than
many other animals, but said they died of old age the same
as every living thing dies. It wasn't a pleasant thought to
carry along where spring was spilling itself.

All too soon another wonderful day ended.

* * *

With the winter-work finished, a new worry arose — Papa
might have to move to town for employment, and Bounce
couldn't be taken along. One day he heard about a new road
being staked out. It was to come through close to where he
had cut cordwood, and he was being hired to clear one mile
of it. What joyous relief.

On the morning he began work, all four of us — counting
Bounce — walked to the newly surveyed area, with sharp-
ened axes, and began searching for the surveyor's stakes that
marked the outer edges. They weren't easy to see, especially
the first time, being short and hidden in weeds. This was flat,
open country, all cut-over land, filled with much brush and
only scattered trees. Finally, after anxiously beating the
bushes, we spied a bright new-wood stake, and Papa Frank
began cutting close to one row, and worked to the center,
carrying the brush back.

That was work Dubby and I could do, and we did carry
big piles to the side. It was lovely brush with new green
leaves. And so much of it! Long branches and short ones —

just right to build teepees. While Papa Frank spent time cutting out trees, we played house in wigwams.

This was so much fun we came every day, and each morning made new teepees, leaving the wilted ones behind as Papa moved along. Soon the clearing lengthened to really look like a road. It was well our shoes were heavy calfskin and our overalls tough cloth, for the brush was sharp and snaggy.

One forenoon, when the sun had climbed high and Papa Frank perspired from swinging the axe, he joined us to sit on the ground and rest. Tossing his cap aside, he clutched both knees and looked up at the blue May sky. It was a beautiful day, though he felt most uncomfortable for his hair hung so long he looked like Moses, bald on top and ears almost covered.

Town, and saloons, had been avoided; but now, running fingers through growth curling out, he said, "I've just got to go to town. We need so many things. But I'm ashamed to even be seen on the way with this hair. I feel like a tramp."

Suddenly, he looked at Dubby. A wild idea sprung. "If we had the shears here, maybe you could trim these edges, enough anyhow, for me to get to the barber."

Dubby brightened and jumped to start for home, but we could see a house on a hillside not far away, and Papa Frank said, "Maybe we can borrow shears there, and go to Prodocks' from here, and save time. I'll hike on into town and you girls stay at Prodocks'. I can't take you in those shabby overalls."

Climbing through tangled brush to the house, we borrowed shears after much explaining and returned to the clearing in order not to be watched. Papa Frank sat down gingerly on one of the uneven stumps, and pulled off his cap.

"Now here," he said to Dubby — he was putting trust before trial — "this is what I want you to do." He drew a small comb from his pocket and, holding it against the oversized shears, explained, "I want you to lift the hair with the comb, and cut away all that comes through the teeth." He worked the blades against the comb. It looked easy. Dubby was impatient to begin. She took the tools and touched them together.

"Like this?" she asked, opening and closing the shears. "Oh, I can do that."

I stood behind the "chair" ready to advise. Papa Frank reached to fold down his ears. Bounce watched in silent wonder.

At once the tiny comb was out of sight. He did, indeed, need a haircut! Though Dubby kept a tight grip, the buried comb wouldn't connect with the shears — no matter how she twisted it. And he had said, "cut what comes through the comb." So huge chunks fell, like wool from a sheep at shearing time.

Bounce got to his feet to investigate. Papa Frank held prudently still, with head cocked at what was, he hoped, a helpful angle. As he felt the shears, he cautioned with alarm, "Don't cut too close — just trim the bottom edges. Don't take too much at a time." That, he had failed to say at the beginning; and too much at a time was difficult to judge. Dubby took what the small comb held from down deep, and was getting wells of sorts, with scalp at the bottom. Moses looked to be coming from a scalping fray.

With feet spread in solid determination and elbows fanning like wings, Dubby curved her wrist gracefully, but couldn't make it come right. "Papa, I could do so much better without this comb," she pleaded. He doubted, but felt

Dubby Gets Papa Frank Ready

of the long tufts and agreed.

"Well, go ahead and try, if you think you can do it better."

The comb went over his shoulder. Now she could really get him ready. Sadly, each snip called for another where ridges formed like siding on a house, causing endless evening-up.

I moved from side to side, pointing out places — Dubby had neglected the center-back where a tail had somehow formed. Papa Frank could only feel, and he warned again, as he anxiously tapped where she had worked, "Don't try to get all of it. I only need the lower part trimmed so it won't hang below my cap. The barber will do the rest. I'm afraid you're cutting too close." Then to me he said, "Beeny Coony, how does it look?"

I wished he hadn't asked. White bare spots, with brown tails of hair between, wasn't what he had in mind. But I knew Dubby wasn't through, and I was helping her, so I said, "It's going to be nice."

He straightened up and said, "Well, it certainly feels a lot better." Then of all things, he suddenly stood, rubbed loose hair from his shoulders, and felt his head, saying, "And that's enough now, Dubby," with a hint of alarm in his voice. "I didn't want you to cut as much as this."

Dubby was aghast and waved the shears wildly for him to sit down, pleading, "But I haven't finished! I haven't finished! I can make it better! I'm not through! I'm not through!" And, indeed, she wasn't through — but he was determined things had gone far enough. And, depending on his cap to cover it, he stepped around brushing and patting, and said, "Now listen to me. You girls take the shears back while Papa gets a little more work done, and then we'll go." We hustled away, though looking back at him in sorrow.

Soon all of us were following surveyor's stakes to Prodocks', Papa Frank striding ahead kicking a trail. Dubby whispered in disgust, "I wish he had let me finish. I don't think he's going to like it. I'm afraid he'll be mad."

I snickered cautiously, "Doesn't he look funny?"

As we watched him strutting forward to meet the public, with skin spots showing instead of familiar long hair, we doubled over laughing, and stumbled trying to keep up with his hurrying feet.

On entering Prodocks' kitchen, he jerked his cap off and stepped jauntily to the mirror hanging above the washstand, took one look and gasped, "Oh - - - - Oh, my gosh!"

Slapping both hands over the wrecked head, he whipped around to face Dubby, who explained in distress, "You wouldn't let me finish."

Turning again to the mirror, he twisted from side to side patting the downy tufts, then looked helplessly to the speech-less Prodocks' who struggled to keep sober. "I had planned to go to town. But I can't go now. I can't go at all, anywhere, looking this way. Why — why I can't be seen for at least two weeks. This will have to grow out before even a barber can do anything with it."

Taking another quick glance, he saw a clown in the mirror and burst out laughing; that's what the rest were waiting to do. But Dubby and I were truly sorry.

He found a chair and leaned back to relax and visit — no hurry now. "I had planned to take out some insurance today," he told Prodocks.

We heard him talk of leaving money if he should die, and I crossed the room to hug him, saying, "I don't want any insurance. I'd rather have you." Even after he explained, I was glad when we started home to wait for hair to grow out. He looked like a half-plucked chicken.

24

Fighting The Forest Fire

The bunkhouse stood deserted a few days later. There was a lumberjack's empty cabin closer to where Papa Frank was now cutting, and we could have it for the summer. It wasn't far from Prodocks.

"We can go back to the bunkhouse next winter," Papa promised.

The little cabin was new, with light clean boards. But, four of its kind would fit inside the bunkhouse. And it wasn't tucked in trees. Just one tree grew in this yard that faced the wide newly cut road, sweeping through the countryside. Bounce now played well with Prodocks' Shep, so we could go to the store often. That part was nice.

One morning while walking to the work area, a porcupine was sighted clinging to the underside of a low branch. Papa Frank spied it first and stopped, then pointed where to look. It was fat, more than a foot long, and covered with coarse black hairs. Bounce started over, all curious, but was called back. He would get his face full of sharp quills if he tried to grab it.

I wanted to run for my rifle. "No, we musn't kill it," Papa Frank said quickly, "because it won't hurt us. It couldn't catch us if it tried."

We walked closer. "It has probably been eating bark," he guessed, and poked it with a stick till it dropped to the ground so we might see how it could roll into a ball. "It doesn't shoot its quills, either," he said, "but you'd get them into you if you touched it. They say they are good to eat, but I've never tasted one. Anyhow, you must never kill a porcupine unless you have no other way to get food."

"I wouldn't want to eat any even if I didn't ever have anything else," Dubby said, wrinkling her nose.

"Oh, yes you would," he assured her, as we started on. "If you were lost in a woods like this, without a gun, it might be the only food you could get. That's why we leave porcupines alone. They can't run fast and are easily caught. Other people might need them."

"Well, how could anyone kill it if it kept its quills sticking out?" I wondered.

"Oh, a big club could do the business I'm sure."

We hurried along.

Although it was spring, the ground was dangerously dry. Dead leaves crackled under foot. That was why Papa Frank worried when he saw smoke about a mile away. He watched it and hoped someone was taking care of any fire. "Maybe they're burning brush, in a clearing," he said.

But next day there was even more smoke, and before starting work, we walked toward it till we could see it was really a timber fire, and spreading. Papa Frank was so mad. He kept shaking his head in disgust, saying, "Fools, fools — what fools," as we trudged back to the cutting area.

"How did it start, Papa?" Dubby asked anxiously. "Is it coming this way?"

"Someone must have been burning brush and didn't watch it. We'll have to wait and see what it does," he answered, much concerned. "Some people don't know anything. It's been too dry this spring to be careless like that. Fools — Fools!"

He stayed at his work. We watched the rising smoke, hoping it wouldn't come our way. The sky turned hazy, then cloudy, and Papa Frank said, "If we can get some good rains it might check that fire. I think it will go the other direction, anyhow. The wind is that way now. You can see the smoke is going away from us." That sounded encouraging.

By night it began to sprinkle, and the danger was forgotten. It didn't rain enough, and the next day there still was smoke and the sun was shining. "That may be only stumps smoking," Papa Frank said. The smoke didn't really seem any closer. By afternoon we could tell the fire was traveling again, though still far west of our house.

That night the wind blew strong, and although Dubby and I slept soundly, Papa Frank was up often, watching the rolling flames and smoke as the fire ate into thicker timber somewhat nearer. He still thought it might keep going and miss us. But even before daylight the wind changed, and smoke started rolling up the long hill toward the house.

He wakened us at daybreak, "We've got to get out of here, right away. Come on — help Papa pack, and we'll go to Prodocks'." I jumped to the window and was surprised to see flames that close. I pulled on stockings and overalls in record time. So did Dubby.

Papa Frank began jerking down the stovepipe, then dragged the little square stove outside and set it in the yard in a bare spot. The kitchen table was laid upside down on the stove lids, then chairs and bedding piled between the extending legs.

We tore in and out, helping, while casting anxious glances at the rolling smoke on the hill. We packed the oven, too, with food sacks. Papa Frank fastened a blanket over the heaped belongings, and hurriedly scratched all twigs and leaves from the ground around, so the fire couldn't creep close. He scraped them away from the house also, but that seemed a hopeless thing to do. Last of all, the drinking water from the pail was sprinkled over the blanket to soak it well,

especially on top. The stove had been set where we hoped
the wind might not carry sparks from the house when it
burned.

Papa Frank slammed shut the stuffed suitcase, and our
canvas telescope, then struggled with both of these, along
with other things clamped under each arm. He followed
Dubby and me, running down the path to Prodocks', wearing
our winter coats over jackets to save carrying them. I
clutched my rifle along with Tridget. Dubby hugged Ruby.
Bounce knew where to go and kept well ahead.

Now, fears centered on the heavy growth of timber
between the cabin and Prodocks'. Although flames were
coming, in back of our cabin, they just might not cross the
wide roadway-clearing in front of it. But if they did cross,
nothing could stop the fire from reaching Prodocks' building. There was not time to waste. We must help fight it or
run farther if we had to.

Papa Frank called, "I don't expect to see anything but the
stove when we come again."

"Why?" we both wailed. We thought we had prepared it
well.

"That wind will blow sparks from the house and catch that
bedding afire, regardless," he warned us.

Prodocks hadn't thought the fire was so close until we
burst in. They jumped into action even though it hadn't
crossed into their timber — the fire would come too fast then.

Mr. Prodock hitched a horse to the small plow and,
grasping the handles, started turning a strip of dark earth at
the edge of the yard on the side toward the timber. Everyone
worked. Mrs. Prodock wielded the rake and scraped leaves
and twigs away from the house. Dubby and I carried the
leaves and twigs off beyond the plowed strip toward the fire,

where she burned it. In a little while we all knew the flames had crossed the roadway, for smoke was rolling higher and thicker where the larger pines were singeing and burning.

The neighbor living south rushed over. He grabbed a spading fork to help Papa Frank, who was already digging furiously to make the strip of turned earth wider, hoping to hold the fire behind it. Every moment counted. The wind was bringing the fire fast.

As the roaring wall moved closer, the stinging rolling smoke swept down, covering everyone in that yard till our eyes stung and we choked for breath. Mrs. Prodock brought wet dishtowels for us to throw over our heads. We couldn't run away — not yet.

Papa Frank sent Dubby and me into the house to breathe better. But we came right out again. "It's worse in there than out here," I called. The door had been open, and both store and house were filled with strong fumes. Outside the swirling smoke did sometimes lift and give a moment's relief.

Papa looked inside the barn-area which had stayed closed, and saw that the air above, where the hay was, seemed clear. He called to us and waited while we scrambled up the ladder-strip on the wall. Then, boosting himself a few steps, he said sternly, "I want to see just where you'll be. Stay right here, near the ladder. Don't move. Don't try to play, but watch for any signs of fire. If you see any starting, come out."

Bounce stayed below — he couldn't climb.

We did sit exactly where he left us, being too frightened to disobey. Huddling together on the dry hay, we listened to the roaring and crackling outside. It sounded very near and very awful. Black smoke rolled against the window in waves, so it was like night outside and in.

I thought of the new cabin and wondered if it had already

burned. Smoke began seeping into the barn, and we could scarcely breathe. Papa Frank came storming in, shouting, "Girls — come out!"

We jumped to the ladder and saw his watery eyes and smokesmeared face looking up. "Come down," he gasped. "I can't stand to have you in here. This building may catch fire any minute, and I can't even see it from out there at times."

We followed him out. The plowing had stopped. Mrs. Prodock was stomping and beating all burning sparks as they fell in the yard. She, too, was black with red eyes. Her wet towel hung loosely over her head.

The rolling wall of fire was very close. Fingers of flame reached and spouted above the tall pines.

Mr. Prodock and his neighbor were on the roof leaping toward every spark that touched it. We others stomped the ground. Mrs. Prodock handed a pail of water and the dipper to Dubby, choking, "Here, you can do this." And to me, "Run, get some tin cups."

As I raced for cups, Dubby splashed water from the dipper wherever a blaze started. While Dubby and I dashed around, dousing water quickly but sparingly, Mrs. Prodock and Papa Frank carried bucketfuls.

In the heat and choking fumes everyone grabbed their wet towels often, to strain a breath of air. Only now and then did the smoke lift and allow tortured lungs to fill with fresh air. Worst of all, the smarting, stinging gasses blinded till it was difficult to see the falling sparks.

Desperately we fought, brushing burning bits from our own clothing, while almost overhead the treetops waved and curled, making a horrible roaring, snapping noise. After awhile all underbrush was gone, and everything else in that timber, except the largest pines. They were standing as before, but singed and smoking, black and burned at the bottom. Nothing was left to blow. Many of the oak trees kept on burning and falling.

The flaming wave traveled on and was lower as it ate through only weeds and brush bordering the plowed corn-field. It was over for us Greens and for Prodocks, except for smoke from smouldering stumps. And the big building had been saved!

Now, the kind helpful neighbor took off for home to save his own buildings. Papa Frank and Mr. Prodock ate a quick lunch and followed. They didn't expect to struggle there — heavy timber didn't grow close, and a plowed garden gave pro tection. Still, a close watch was kept till almost dark.

We stayed at Prodocks' that night and talked of our needs. We'd move back to the bunkhouse — the iron stove could still be used.

The next morning it was after ten when Papa Frank said, "Well girls, shall we go and look at our ruins?"

Soon we were stringing slowly along the same narrow path over which we had escaped. No reason to hurry — nothing to carry — we weren't going home.

Suddenly it all seemed strange. We were walking through growth untouched by fire! Just where had the rushing blaze turned away? We couldn't help stepping faster, looking for burned ground. Where had it divided? Perhaps pulled by the wind? Had it spared our house too?

That was impossible. It had been too close.

Then we saw the little house of new boards — standing just as we had left it! Dubby and I started to run, as if it might get away. And there stood the stove, holding the bedding, table, and everything else, still heaped high!

But in the yard, we were walking on black charred

ground! The fire had certainly been there! Around behind the house the entire smoking hillside was burned clean, presenting a most unfamiliar look. Trails of rising smoke spotted the countryside for as far as eyes could see. Stumps and fallen trees would smoulder for days.

Papa Frank seemed puzzled to see that the fire had been so close without setting the house ablaze. He walked all around the board building pointing to the ground — the flames had licked everywhere, leaving blackened earth. But the big pine in the yard wasn't touched.

When he came to the corner of the house that had faced the fire, he stopped, unbelieving. Near the ground the boards of the house were burned — charred brown — for about a foot up!

"Why girls," he called, "look here, our househas been on fire!"

He squatted to pick at the charred boards with strong fingernails. It didn't seem possible! Straightening up, he looked over the ash-covered ground, completely at a loss. "Now how could that have happened," he said. "The wind must have changed just as the fire got here. But I can't see how a blaze could have gone out after it had a start in this kind of wood." Bounce looked as bewildered as the rest of us.

I rubbed the burned boards in silent wonder. It hadn't burned all the way through, so no draft had aided it. But the house surely had been on fire.

"Papa," Dubby said, wrinkling a serious forehead, "don't you think some kind person came along and put it out?"

"No, dear — no living person was walking around here when that was catching fire."

We stood quietly beside the scorched corner, thinking

deeply for an explanation. Dubby said she still thought someone must have been there. Pretty soon Papa Frank said, "Do you know — I think Mama had something to do with this."

That seemed a startling thing to say, but he was facing us soberly, and we knew he was serious. I felt queer to think that way, and I asked, "What do you mean?"

"I think Mama, up in heaven, must have asked God not to let our house burn down."

And that really seemed to be the only answer.

We went to work happily carrying the things on the stove back into the house. Papa Frank connected the stovepipe. We were ready to live there again.

Returning to Prodocks' to bring back all we had carried, I ran half the way to tell the unbelievable news. Mrs. Prodock was cooking dinner to include us, so we waited. Prodocks wanted to go along and see for themselves how such a thing could be. They would help carry things too.

Walking on the unburned path, Prodocks looked across to their own blackened timber and felt bad. They said they wondered why theirs had to be destroyed. Papa Frank told them they should feel grateful for not losing their home. He was very thankful that our shelter and belongings had been spared.

25

A Wrong Move

The warm days came and the evenings were longer. We three cabin dwellers sat on the step before the open door and sang in the way we liked best — outside where the sound rolled away, and the woods turned dark; and the insects sang loudly in the grasses. Sometimes Papa Frank would put an arm around each of us and say, "Papa's got his girls. I hope we can stay together."

All this was soon to end. He finished the roadway and now spent too much time in town. When we had to wait alone at home, we were sometimes afraid he would bring a bottle like he had done that time at the bunkhouse. Dubby would say, "I hope he isn't getting drunk." One day he told us we were moving to Walker, but just for the summer. We were happy till learning we couldn't take Bounce. "Town is no place for a dog like that," he insisted, to our pleading. "We'll find a good home for him before we go, and we'll get him again when we come back to live in the bunkhouse," he promised.

We were heartbroken. But we did find a home for him — the farmer who lived where we had borrowed the shears said he would take him. However, he planned to give him to someone living farther away. So we didn't know where Bounce would be. And maybe we would never see him again.

On the day Papa Frank took Bounce, he made us stay home, telling us, "Anyone would have a hard time holding Bounce if he saw you girls starting home without him."

It was a sad day. We hugged Bounce's huge neck and sobbed.

Then Papa Frank started briskly away coaxing, "Come on, Bounce. Come along boy."

Bounce, all unknowing, followed a few steps, but then stopped and turned to wait for Dubby and me. He had never gone without us. After stern urging he trotted a bit farther, then whirled and raced back.

"Go in the house," Papa Frank called. "He thinks you want him to come when you stand there." And he kept pleading, "Come on boy."

We clung to Bounce, almost choking with grief; then went inside and cried bitterly.

Bounce stayed beside the closed door, torn between a master's demands and inborn loyalty.

Papa Frank came back to coax and insist till Bounce slowly followed, hesitating and looking back every few steps, watching for us to come.

Inside at the window, we could scarcely see through tears as our beloved companion slipped out of sight far down the path. Then we flung the door open, and dashed down the trail to Prodocks'.

This was Papa Frank's plan, for Mrs. Prodock was sewing the dresses she had promised in exchange for the gold rings from me, and she was ready to fit them. These were cut from her own clothes — a brown wool for Dubby and a black satin combined with pink for me, which Mrs. Prodock hoped would be especially nice, for the rings had been mine. I was delighted — the shiny pink satin was so beautiful that the black part didn't matter so much.

Mrs. Prodock told us these should be our best dresses and not worn too often, so they would still be good when fall came. There would be other new ones too: Papa Frank had bought pretty pink and green plaid gingham for summer dresses. He was relieved to have them made, for in town other little girls didn't wear overalls. He had worried about that part.

We moved a few days later to an oversized house on the shore of Leech Lake where a Mrs. Harrity lived — a close friend of Mrs. Prodock. She was the lady who came along to the bunkhouse the day Mrs. Prodock brought the cats. Now she had rented us a large room. We didn't know her very well. Our move there was to be a mistake.

So here, again on the lake shore, we could stand on the high bank and watch the white steamer, the LILAH DEE, leave the dock only a block away and churn out of the bay on its daily trip to the far shore. And just as at Snyders', there were steep steps leading down to a narrow dock where Harritys' boat was tied.

Papa Frank wished for a boat of his own. It would be so easy then to go fishing and tie the boat right there each time we got home. A few days later he told us he was planning to build one, and we would fish every day. The owner of the red-brick hotel wanted to buy all he could catch. What good fortune! To think of getting paid for such fun!

* * *

There was a large yard at the low side of Harritys' house, right where the outside door of our room opened from the lowest level. We could run out to where a creek flowed across the weedy vacant lots stretching from under the street-bridge. A creek in our own back yard! Other children played here and waded where the creek emptied into the lake, for here the bottom was sandy, and the strong flow of the stream pushed away all broken sticks and chunks of foam that floated along this walled-up section of the shoreline.

Here, too, was a boat shelter, straddling the sandy mouth of the creek. It was great fun for barefoot children to wade between the beautiful floating boats belonging to rich people at the nearby hotel and to walk the dock-boards separating the launches. And sometimes to even climb in and sit in lordly fashion and dream of going places — if the owners weren't around to protest.

It was here we met little Marie who attended Sunday School. And Agnes who held her head high. Papa Frank asked about the other children and often came to watch, trying to know who our playmates were. He decided he would build his boat, and take us fishing every day, and not be worried.

Once when he asked about other children, Dubby said, "Well — we don't like one girl very well. She walks like this —" and with shoulders pulled back and chin thrust forward, Dubby looked toward the ceiling and strutted across the room imitating Agnes, who she thought was stuck up.

"Is that the only reason you don't like her?" Papa Frank asked. "What else does she do?"

"Oh — she doesn't do anything, I guess. But she holds her nose so high. She thinks she's better than anyone else."

"Now girls," he said, getting our attention. "Listen. There is nothing wrong about holding your head high when you walk. I want you girls to walk that way, too."

"Oh, Papa," I begged. "Not like that!"

"Well, I don't know just how she looks, but I like to see anyone hold their head high. And I want you girls to know that you have as much right to put your nose up as anyone else. More right, perhaps. Your ancestry is the finest, and you can always be proud of it."

His eyes gleamed with pride as he talked of his family. I

remembered the night in the bunkhouse when he was ashamed of the way things looked. Now I understood better why he had said queer things that night.

The next day Dubby and I tried walking like Agnes, but laughed at each other's stretched neck. We decided to forget how Agnes walked.

Little Marie had asked us to go with her on Sunday to the Methodist Church, but we didn't have nice enough clothes. Papa Frank said, "I'll go to Prodocks' some day soon and bring your new dresses if they are finished. Then you can go." He was anxious that we should go to church.

On the morning he left for Prodocks', we wanted to play in the water, so he hastened off alone. It was long after dinnertime when he arrived back and we had been watching for him and wondering about him. I ran to reach for his bundle for he did have the new dresses, besides some groceries.

We were delighted with the new dresses, but laid them down forgotten when he began to explain his delay.

"Do you know what Bounce did?" he said, forcing a sad smile as he faced us. "He ran away from the man we gave him to."

"What!" we wailed,

"Prodocks told me about it." He sounded weary.

"What's happened to him, Papa? Where is he?" We piled questions.

"Just a minute now — let me tell you," Papa Frank protested, lifting his hands for silence — "When I got to the store Mrs. Prodock asked if Bounce had found us: The man we gave him to had come to the store to see if they had seen him; he had already looked at the little cabin. So they thought he had followed us."

"Where is he?" I demanded again.

"Well, that's what I wanted to know. You see, he had run away soon after I took him there, so I thought he might have gone to the bunkhouse after he didn't find us at the cabin. So I hiked to the cabin first, just to be sure, and then decided to have a look at the bunkhouse. Bounce lived there with us much longer and he would have remembered it better, and just might be there waiting for us."

We listened breathless as he told it.

"I walked in past the barn, seeing nothing, and when I hurried along the side of the bunkhouse, with no sign of Bounce, I didn't expect to see what I did see when I got to the door. There he lay in the high grass beside the step."

"Oh, Papa," we begged, "is he dead?"

Papa Frank took out his handkerchief to wipe his eyes.

"No — but he was too weak to run to meet me, or to meet anyone. He had to struggle to get up. He was thin and all caked with mud, and trembling. He had ends of rope and even twisted shoestrings dangling from his neck. Just think, he had chewed his way free even with filed-off teeth. And he must have waded swamps to get there, to be so covered with muck.

"I got down and talked to him and said, 'Shall we go to see Beeny Coony and Dubby?' I kept saying your names and he seemed to understand and moved his tail. I thought his pleading eyes brightened. Life seemed to be returning." Again, Papa wiped his eyes.

"I looked inside and our room seemed clean and waiting for us. Just as Bounce was waiting."

"Oh, Papa," I sobbed, "we shouldn't have left him."

And Dubby, crying asked again, "What did you do?"

"I took him back with me to Prodocks. He had to flop to

rest, several times, and it was a long, slow walk. We fed him and tied him, so he couldn't try to follow me. The man will get him again. I think he will stay there this time."

"Papa, do you think Bounce would have waited there for us until we came back in the fall?" Dubby asked.

His expression saddened. "He probably would have stayed there all right. He would have waited and died of loneliness I'm afraid, if I hadn't come along when I did and found him. Poor Bounce. If he wasn't so big, and so fierce, we could have him here." We were all glad we hadn't sold him and could get him back in the fall. He promised us again we would do that.

Later, when we tried on dresses and paraded around the room, he was pleased. Now we could go to church. That is the way he wanted things to be. "Mama would want you to go to Sunday School," he said. "You tell the little girl you will go with her next Sunday."

He watched with pride the morning we left with Marie. This Methodist Church was smaller than the one in Minneapolis we had attended, but classes and lessons were the same. The teacher hurried everything in order to pass out recitations for the Children's Day program only two weeks away. All who cared to speak received one. All others would sing in groups.

Dubby preferred to sing, but I wanted to speak a piece and took one with three short verses. The teacher told us we must learn our parts and come to the church Thursday to practice. She didn't say any changes might be made.

I was delighted to carry the slip of paper away, reading as I walked. Even before reaching home I had learned the words.

Papa Frank was very pleased. "It's good training for any

child to learn to speak before an audience," he said, then read it over and nodded approvingly.

"Now dear, let Papa help you with this," he suggested. "I'll read it to you several times the way it should be spoken. Then you will learn it right, with the proper tone and emphasis. You never can do as well if you learn the words first and then try to get the expression afterward." It was a bit late for that, but I listened closely and repeated the lines exactly as he had spoken them.

Later on, after he had thought about us being in the program (Dubby was to sing with a special group), he said, "I want people to know that we are intelligent and decent, even if we don't live in the right house."

He had spoken too quickly, for he couldn't explain. When Dubby said, "Why isn't this house right?" he quickly made excuse:

"The house is nice. I just wish we had more room, that's all."

But we knew he was sorry we had moved here and wished Dubby and I were nearer to Aunt Carrie. He said that children need the care of a really good woman. Much trouble was to come from living in Mrs. Harrity's house. We hadn't known that would happen. But the summer would pass with no waiting, and he said he planned to keep us with him as much as possible while fishing, in a boat of his own.

By Thursday, I was anxious to go to practice, for even Papa Frank thought I recited well.

Dubby and I, with Marie, were among the first to come into the churchyard. When the teachers who were to train the children saw us with Marie, they called her. She hurried over and answered their questions, then turned and called me to come.

I ran, ready to say, "Yes — I know my piece." But that wasn't what they wanted. They told me the program was going to be too long and that I shouldn't learn the recitation. They had made a mistake in giving it to me!

I couldn't answer. I wanted to cry instead. Then Dubby came over, and I told her what the ladies had said. Dubby protested: "But she has already learned it!" They couldn't take it away now.

The ladies said they wanted the program given by regular members only. Dubby happily explained that we had been regular members of a Methodist Sunday School in Minneapolis and had been in programs there. The teachers said that didn't count in this case, for the program would be too long.

Dubby and I were allowed to stay, and we sang with the others and waited for Marie, then started home sadly to tell Papa Frank — that I wasn't going to speak after all. But he wasn't there so we played outdoors. I forgot the disappointment till I saw him coming. Then I ran to explore the sacks in his arms and tell what had happened.

On reaching him at the doorway, all the hurt rushed back, and I buried my head against him and began in choking words, "I couldn't speak my piece." It seemed so much worse now — telling him.

"You couldn't!" he exclaimed, completely surprised, for I had spoken so well for him.

"They wouldn't let her," Dubby explained on arriving. "They said there would be too many recitations."

"You mean they didn't have time to listen to it today?" he asked, not ready to think they had refused me being in the program.

"I can't be in it at all, except to sing," I stated, wiping tears away.

He looked puzzled and patted my shoulder as he guided both of us into the house. Then he asked, "Now, just what did they say to you. And when did they say it?" He looked at Dubby.

"They called us and told us right after we got there, before the practice," Dubby said, seeming to wonder what difference that could make. "They told us we could sing, but Beeny Coony couldn't speak because the program was going to be too long."

Papa Frank got mad then, and demanded, "When do they practice again?"

"On Saturday," I remembered.

"Well," he said, as he looked down into my smeary face, "you are going to speak that piece. I'll see to that. We'll practice it together until you speak so well they'll open their eyes when they hear you."

"But, Papa," Dubby stopped him. "They said that - -"

"They who?" he blared. "Who are they?"

"Two teachers. They said that you had to be a member to be in the program. And it doesn't make any difference even if we did go to the Methodist Sunday School in Minneapolis because I told them that, too."

He said, "I know what's the trouble, and I'm going over there with you on Saturday, and Beeny Coony is going to speak that piece. They can't do such a thing." He walked to the table and angrily jerked the fruit from a sack.

I thought he might be making a mistake to go, but he was angry and I kept still.

As he stepped around preparing the evening meal, he snorted over and over, "Hypocrites! — Hypocrites!" Litle by little he spoke his thoughts. "They knew how many recitations they passed out on Sunday. And besides, some are sure to drop out — maybe get sick — or not get it learned. No — they haven't too many. That's not the reason. They just found out where you live. That's the whole thing."

He shouldn't have said it. He knew he had again spoken too quickly, for we were beginning to guess that Mrs. Harrity's bad name was the reason, and he had asked us to treat her with respect. But he seemed determined we shouldn't receive insults for something we couldn't help. He intended to go along on Saturday.

"Hypocrites" — he sputtered again — "Hypocrites!"

At the table his expression brightened. "Now, I've got something to tell you, and it's a lot better than what you told me."

We waited expectantly while he took a long drink of tea. "I found a place where I can build the boat," he said, and told of meeting a nice man who lived at the far end of town and had a big yard. "I can use the man's sawhorses and even his tools, if I need to, and build the boat there. So I won't have to litter the yard here at Mrs. Harrity's."

"I took the lumber over today," he said, "and tomorrow I'm going to begin real work on it. We'll be riding on the lake in our own boat before you know it." He smiled then, and things seemed better.

When he left the house the next morning, he carried a saw and hammer along with smaller tools. We begged to go, but he said, "No — not the first day. Maybe you can come out some of the time, but I don't want to take you the first day."

He was really planning to go along to the church on Saturday to fight for me and was expecting me to perform perfectly. So right after supper we practiced again. He instructed me to sit at the side of the room, then announced, "Now we will hear a recitation by Bernice Green." Then I rose, walked erectly to the center and turned to face him.

He showed me just how to do it so as not to look hurried or awkward. "And when you face the congregation, take time to draw a breath instead of rushing into it," he coached. He was planning definitely that I would be in the program.

"Try it over," he said again and again. I'd bow and smile and walk slowly from the "platform" to rise again and repeat it, till he was completely satisfied. I went to bed happy, though not at all sure the ladies would allow me to recite.

The next forenoon, Papa Frank worked on the boat, but came home early and went to the barbershop, and after dinner looked really nice, all shaved and in his best clothes. Dubby and I, all cleaned and braided, walked to the church with heads up, almost like Agnes. Papa Frank between us, said, "I'll show them my girls are as good as anyone else in this town."

Not many others had arrived when we reached the side of the church where one of the teachers was standing in a doorway. He asked her why they had given me a recitation to learn and then had decided not to let me speak it.

At first the lady was too surprised to answer, but then remembered — the program would be too long.

Papa Frank said, "I can't think that's true. I know enough about church programs to understand that much."

Dubby and I stood close by, a little uncertain, but proud of Papa for saying that.

The lady thought for a moment and said, "We really think the program should be given by only the regular members."

Then Papa Frank asked if the house next door was the parsonage. He intended to talk to the minister. He knew the teacher was only making shameful excuses — for he had belonged to a church — had even sung in the choir.

A wooden sidewalk ran between the church and the back door of the house. "Yes, that's the parsonage," the lady said. "But I don't think you need to talk to the minister. If you'll wait until the other teacher comes, I think we can decide something about it."

But Papa Frank's temper had risen, so he started over by himself and was soon knocking politely at the back door. We all followed him. While the minister's wife was calling her husband, Papa Frank said quietly but sternly to Dubby and me, "You girls go on away now. You stay over there with the other children."

The second teacher arrived and joined the group. Most of the time Papa Frank talked. The ladies said nothing except to answer the preacher's questions. Papa Frank said later that he told them — if they believed the Bible they would welcome everyone, especially children, and reminded them that Jesus had said, "Suffer the little children to come unto me. And forbid them not." He said Dubby and I had belonged to Sunday School, and that all his people were Methodists, but that now he was ashamed to see the way the church was treating innocent children.

The minister agreed with all he said and was smiling pleasantly. The ladies smiled too. They had made a mistake. Soon Papa Frank called us, and said, "It's all taken care of now." He explained, "The minister didn't know anything about it. And he wouldn't have wanted it to happen."

The minister shook hands with us, and told us we were to stay and practice with the others. So I was to recite after all. Everything was all right.

Then Papa Frank left. One of the ladies said to me, as we walked back to the church, "We decided there will be room on the program for you because one of the other girls may not be able to come." And I believed her.

We were happy to tell Marie, and later I spoke so well the teachers praised me. I proudly told Papa Frank on arriving home. He repeated that it wasn't the minister's fault.

The Sunday after next would be the day, and Papa Frank would be there to listen. He said, "I'm so glad you've got your new dresses to wear. All you need are new slippers and hair ribbons."

But before that day should come, we hoped to be riding on the lake in our own boat. It now had a bottom and was resting right side up with a sawhorse under each end. Papa Frank had done much marking and measuring on the bottom boards. Each required a different slant at the edges so as to fit perfectly and be strong.

Finally, he built in the seats and the oarlocks. It needed only paint. I asked, "What color is it going to be?"

He said, "Well now, I think the Greens' boat should be green, don't you?" Of course, that was a fine idea.

He took us along to help with the paint selection and to choose the oars. We picked a green brighter than the pine trees, but all the oars were alike — a natural, varnished wood. They would look nice with green.

When Children's Day came, the boat was still on the sawhorses — drying — with all cracks sealed and an under-coat of paint on. He wouldn't hurry that operation. It was so important to have it water-tight. He wanted it to be a good boat — strong — and had bolted it everywhere to make it so. It needed two more coats of paint, so there was nothing to do but wait.

Tomorrow would be the Big Day. I was prepared to recite my piece. New pink hair ribbons lay over dresses on the table, and shiny slippers rested on chairs.

Sunday dawned bright and quiet. The wait to get ready seemed like a whole day. Papa Frank took the comb and parted my hair evenly over the center, and decided Dubby had combed hers nicely. Last of all, after dresses were donned, our proud Papa, very carefully and somewhat awkwardly, tied on the new pink hair ribbons. And he did make very nice bows, twisting and fluffing until he was satisfied. Mine held looped up braids — one behind each ear. Dubby's perched atop her head and at the back of her neck.

So with matching ribbons we looked a little like sisters that morning as we climbed the inside stairs to show Mrs. Harrity how nice we looked.

I stood straight and recited for her. Just before going out our door, Papa Frank listened once more, and reminded, "Don't rush when you are on the platform. Speak up clearly, and don't be afraid, — and hold your shoulders back."

As we started for the little white church, others too, were going. Surely everyone would be there. Papa Frank walked between his slippered and bow-decked daughters, holding our hands so we would walk with a manner. For he was so proud of us.

We stepped a little timidly up the front steps and in through the open door. Then stopping in the aisle, Papa Frank stooped and whispered to me, "I'll sit back here, and you can look right at me when you speak. And don't be afraid now."

Dubby and I continued along the carpet to front seats reserved for children. I turned as soon as seated and found Papa's bald head and brown eyes. I knew now right where to look.

The room had changed. Vases of garden flowers lined the front of the platform, sending out a lovely fragrance that

To The Program With Pretty Bows

made everything gay. And, the children all looked so differ-ent. Most little girls came in white dresses, and boys wore suits, their short pants trimmed with three small buttons at the side of the knee.

When the program began, the church was completely filled. All the children marched onto the platform, sang the special first song, and marched down again. Even that seemed different from the way we had practiced.

As the preacher read the program, and began calling names, my stomach bubbled. Dubby whispered, "You know what you're going to say, don't you?" I nodded; but wished my name would be next, to be done with it. There were several group recitations — each child speaking one verse. Not many had separate recitations, like mine.

At last I heard my name and the very sound of it fright-ened me — spoken in a strange voice.

The next instant I was the only one moving, sliding out of the crowded row. The time had come. I brushed past the teacher at the end, holding white papers in her lap ready to prompt any or all who might forget.

I knew Papa Frank was watching my head and pink ribbons advancing toward the platform. What stillness! Everyone looking! I managed the three steps up, and walked slowly forward, out across the carpeted expanse, holding shoulders back as he had taught me.

But it wasn't the way we had practiced at home — turning each time to bow and speak. Now I was looking straight into a sea of faces. I stopped just back of the plants, hesitated, took a breath, and bowed slightly.

Suddenly my own voice started! It hadn't sounded that way with the seats empty and the children making noise and not listening. Too many eyes, with hats, were out there staring, and too many ears waiting. At the end of the first verse, little balls started bouncing in each heel, making both my knees wiggle, even though I stiffened as tight as I could to stop it.

Worst of all, where was Papa Frank? Everything was going wrong! Suddenly a bald head and smiling brown eyes half rose out of the mass of faces, long enough to get my attention. He reached me like a strong arm — one dear familiar face. I hoped he couldn't see my knees. He hadn't wanted me to be afraid.

The well remembered words came out by themselves. But on turning to leave, the legs that had carried me up there were wiggling sticks, hammering the carpet. Though I wished mightily to dash for my seat, it was well a slow walk had been planned — any other attempt would have spread me on the carpet.

Ashamed of my burning ears and jumping legs, I managed to reach Dubby who consoled, saying I hadn't looked scared. Desperately, I clasped both knees to quiet them.

Near the end of the program a startling thing happened. The minister announced they would be "favored with a reading" by one of their members who had arrived home from boarding school, and had been studying elocution.

A girl of about twelve rose from beside her parents in the audience. Everyone turned as a vision of heavenly blue tripped down the aisle, wearing an astonishing hat that flared up from her head like a huge lacy fan. A wide ribbon, with a bow at the cheek, held it to her head.

She gained the platform and stepped daintily forward to greet her people and give an outline of the reading. Brown curls bobbed at her shoulders, and the skirt of her silk dress fell to just below the knees in row on row of bouncing ruffles.

We program children, down at the side, craned and stretched as she spread arms wide and spoke to imaginary people, then answered for them — rushing from side to side and forward again with fingers held gracefully and high — pointing to the ceiling — then to the floor.

It was well all other recitations were over with. I was almost ashamed of mine now. But Papa Frank thought the girl had overdone all of it. He assured me he liked mine much better. We went home happy. We had learned she was the banker's daughter.

The gorgeous dress and hat weren't forgotten. As we hung our own clothes, we talked of how nice it would be to have a dress and hat so lovely. Papa Frank helped to forget, saying, "After we're through eating, we'll go and see how the boat is coming. Then, maybe later, we can use Mrs. Harrity's boat and go for a little ride."

We found the paint almost dry. After another good coat it would be ready for the water.

The days passed gaily enough. Dubby and I waded in the lake, and found it thrilling to be pulled over deep water — if a kindhearted boatman allowed us to cling to the back end of his boat.

In the evening after supper when the train came in, we were always playing on the depot platform, a block away, where a crowd gathered at that time. Often everyone watched Levi Lagoo, a laughing Indian whose scheming habit was known to all.

We were told Levi lived in an Indian camp four miles from Walker, and too conveniently close to the railroad track. He caught rides to town on the morning train more often than any other Indian, for he liked the stores at Walker. Almost every evening he was at the depot, waiting to ride home on the engine. Usually he was quite talkative at that hour.

Once in a while his squaw got to town somehow. But she stayed out of his way at the depot, and by train time she was hiding behind a barrel, where Levi wanted her to be.

One evening when the train, with one coach and baggage car, puffed in and stopped, Levi, as usual, padded his way along the platform to the engineer's cab. Faded blue overalls and shirt covered his lanky frame, and a checkered woolen cap sat over his stringy hair.

The engineer had learned that Levi had a wife, and that sometimes he made her hide till the train had left, thinking it would be easier to get a ride without her. The engineer had been told that the squaw often walked down the track afterward, reaching home long after dark. So, he decided to teach Levi a lesson.

On this evening he watched for the squaw. She was hiding well — behind a huge barrel at one corner of the depot. Levi was comfortably on the engine with his packages, waiting for the train to move. But the engineer's eyes still searched for the squaw. No doubt Levi had said she wasn't with him.

Soon the train-bell rang and the engine spit steam and started to move. Then, all at once it jerked to a stop. Everyone wondered what had happened. Heads stretched from the coach windows. The engineer had spied the squaw! She had peeked over the top of the barrel just as the train lurched forward. And now, part of her full skirt was showing, though she had ducked again instantly.

The engineer pushed Levi from the engine and climbed down behind him. Then, grabbing Levi's arm, he pulled him across the platform toward the depot while pointing to the barrel. Levi pretended not to know the reason for it all — the squaw was then really hiding. Everyone watched, amused at the performance.

It was really funny when the befuddled squaw unfolded herself and stood up — exposed to all. The engineer showed Levi how to take her by the elbow and escort her (a trembling bundle of skirts) to the waiting engine. All the while he was talking to Levi, probably telling him how a man should treat a wife.

Levi put his squaw up the steps while the engineer stood behind ready to follow her. Then when Levi started to climb on last, he was pushed back, and the train-wheels began to turn. He didn't look up at the laughing faces as the loaded coach pulled past him. Nor did he look back at those by the depot who had cheered the engineer.

He leaped to the empty track and, in long strides, took off after the train to get away as fast as he could — and maybe to get home as fast as he could, too, and settle with the squaw. Anyhow, Levi had miles to go as the back end of the coach disappeared around the bend far ahead, with his squaw riding in his place on the whistling engine. I was so glad she wasn't left behind.

26

A Black Storm Tests
The Green Boat

Papa Frank put the boat on the water when we weren't there to see it done — as he had promised we would be. When he told us it was floating, we protested until he explained, "I wanted to soak it, and test it for leaks, before you got in it. I want to be sure it's water-tight before we bring it home." Then he smiled, "I think though, that she's a dandy."

It was suppertime, and packages lay on the table. Some contained fishing tackle, and he began to spread out several reels and lines. Then he shook out hooks and sinkers — plain hooks, and some covered with red feathers that had shiny metal discs dangling.

I held up one of the fancy ones and whirled it with a finger, exclaiming, "Why — this is a hook and spinner like Grandpa Wright used."

It pleased him, "You're going to be a real fisherman, aren't you? I'll bet we'll come in with a long string of nice walleyes every evening." He beamed at the thought.

There would be no poles. The reels could lie on the bottom of the boat or be held in the hand. He told Dubby she could row, and that is what she liked best. He hoped we would want to go every day and not be home, near Mrs. Harrity. She had been calling us too often to come upstairs. Other children called her "a tough woman." She swore and smoked cigarettes and dressed in fancy clothes.

Papa Frank was worried, but couldn't explain, that unless we stayed in our own room, we would have to move. If the summer could only pass without trouble, we would get back to the bunkhouse.

The next morning we left the house in high spirits. It was the big day to try the boat. Papa Frank carried the bright new oars over his shoulder as we trudged joyfully along the dusty road to where he had built it. The familiar yard was now bare of work. We walked straight on to where the lake was showing through trees. And there — down the bank, was the green boat — floating on the water!

It was tied to a tree at the shoreline, right where he had left it. And there was much water in it! Papa Frank had put the water in, to help soak the boards thoroughly.

He pulled the boat up, tipped out the water, and floated it again. Then Dubby and I climbed in. It was a beautiful thing, with lots of room across the flat bottom. And the green paint was so shiny and pretty.

Papa Frank stepped in, put the oars in their places, and sat down. We were ready to take it home. He had built the seats so Dubby and I were in front of him as he rowed — I near the center, and Dubby at the back end. We beamed at one another as Papa Frank pulled water with the oars, and the boat moved away from the bank. It rode smoothly and quietly except for the noise of the oars in their sockets.

He said, "I'll have to get some grease for the oarlocks. But isn't she a dandy?" This was indeed a new pleasure. The wide surrounding waters sparkled a greeting.

In a little while, rounding a point, we saw Harritys' dock with the house high above it. Soon, after overshoulder glances, Papa Frank was tying-up there. Then, going in for the fishing tackle, he also fixed a lunch to take along, and filled a small pail with drinking water. Mrs. Harrity came down to see the boat and stood on the dock watching us go. She laughed, "Now don't let a big fish pull you in."

We started for the other end of the bay, with Dubby and I each holding a reel, letting the bait trail far behind, in the hope the flashing spinners would look like a meal to every fish.

"We may not get so many today," Papa Frank thought. "We'll have to find some good spots first. I've been told where to try. But we'll see."

Dubby changed to the center seat and straddled it till her overalls were stretching ready to split. Gazing across the water she said, "I like to fish this way." We all did. This was trolling — fishing and riding at the same time. Grandpa Wright had always anchored, lit his pipe, and dreamed. But Papa Frank was strong and didn't tire.

Suddenly, Dubby's reel began to spin. Papa Frank put up the oars and reached to help her, holding up the jerking line so it wouldn't run on the edge of the boat while she wound it in. In the splashing water near the boat he saw the big green pickerel and was disappointed — the hotel didn't want that kind. But Dubby was happy and pleased. He flipped it to the new clean floor.

"We won't keep very many of this kind," he said. "We'll only have to give them away, and not many people want them. But we'll cook this for our supper tonight. They're fine eating if you're careful of the bones." We knew that.

The big speckled slimy fish opened its jaws and showed white pointed teeth as Papa Frank took the hook from its mouth. It twisted into a leap that could have taken it out of the boat, had it been near the side. Papa Frank placed his foot on it. It looked like a fat green snake with an alligator's head — an ugly fish!

And so the long-planned fishing days had begun. Before long, all three of us would be as tan as the Indians skimming past in their birch-bark canoes. In less than a week, however, Dubby and I tired of it, even though we could take turns rowing.

Then Papa Frank worried again. We were running free with no one whom he could trust watching us. He tried taking us only part of the day, and that worked better. He went alone, early, while we slept, then came home to prepare a noon meal, and took us along later.

One day when one of the reels began to sing, I grabbed it from the floor, but couldn't get hold of the handle — it was spinning too fast as the fish ran with the line. It hit my fingers and hurt. I needed help and could scarcely hang on.

Papa Frank was sure it wasn't a walleye or a bass, and he didn't want it — I could let it get away. When it leaped from the water, far out, and he saw its size, he jumped to take the reel; for it was, he said, as big as a muskellunge. It was the biggest fish we had ever seen! But he hadn't come soon enough. Just as he reached for the reel, the line hung limp. The fish had cut it with its twisting and now was gone — spinner, hook, and all.

I cried, and Papa Frank wished he had helped me. As I thought about it and talked about it, I was sure we would never again see a fish that big. But not long after, as we came in from fishing, a man was on the beach with one many times larger. People were crowding around.

We ran also, to where he was lifting a monstrous fish from his rowboat. Even in that lake town it caused excitement. No one had ever seen a muskellunge of such size. The man had been answering questions, and the crowd grew.

Finally, he shouldered it and started up the hill to the meat market scales. He was a big man, and yet as he leaned forward the tail touched the ground.

The astonished group followed, and by the time he reached the market not all could get inside. Dubby and I wiggled to the front and watched it being weighed. It pushed seventy-two pounds! As it lay the length of the counter, I touched it. A most amazing sight — like the storybook picture of the whale and the giant. Everyone agreed it was the largest fish taken from Leech Lake within their memory. All evening, viewers coming to the market met others going out.

* * *

Oftentimes, late in the day when the green boat was coming home, the LILAH DEE was also splashing in to the city-dock, its paddle-wheel digging a deep furrow and causing a huge swell to come sliding over the surface, one round wave following another. We in the green boat, waited for the high rolls to rock our boat sideways and lift it up and down. This was great fun.

We had learned to ride the swell, turning the craft broadside to meet the wave. But it was dangerous to be too close, for the highest bumps could tip a boat over. Storm waves too, could be ridden this way.

One day the fishing was very poor, and Papa Frank came home early and tied the boat. Dubby and I slipped down to take a ride alone, after he had gone away. We rowed far out, facing each other grinning. The boat seemed so much bigger with one seat empty. Even the lake looked wider. We quarreled over turns for rowing and counted strokes, changing seats often.

After awhile, the long deep whistle of the steamer sounded far out in the lake. "We'll wait," said Dubby, "and ride the swell." She rowed toward where we hoped the biggest wave would roll, pulling farther and farther away from shore while watching the smoking steamer come.

Just then Papa Frank came to the bank above Harrity's dock, searching. First he saw the boat gone. Then he spotted it far out on the water with two heads in it. He bellowed and whistled, shaping his hands as a horn, "Yaho — Girls!" he called over and over at the top of his voice.

We heard him, and when we looked, were so surprised at how small he was, up there on the bank. We hadn't intended to be so far out.

Dubby fumbled with the oars and turned the boat around as fast as she could to start back. The steamer was coming with the wide roll behind it spreading like a peacock's tail. She brought the boat safely from its path while Papa Frank waited, standing now on the very end of the dock down below.

As we drew closer, he began swinging both arms high and shouting furiously — words we couldn't quite understand above the squeak of the oars. Dubby was already rowing with all her might, but the harder she pulled, the more wildly he waved, making a sort of pushing movement. We couldn't think why he was acting in such a fashion — we were coming as fast as we could.

When at last the words came through, "Stay out there!", it didn't make sense at all, and we moved still closer. He motioned frantically, yelling, "Stay away from the bank. Go back — Go back!"

I finally heard all instructions. "He wants us to go back," I repeated to Dubby, "and stay away from the bank." By this time the swell was coming, and Dubby, though puffing from her efforts, turned the boat once more and tried to get as far out as she could before the first roll arrived.

We felt a little afraid now. The fun of a rocking ride was spoiled. Papa Frank seemed mad — something was wrong. We hadn't asked to go, and had never before gone alone.

By the time the first wave reached us, the steamer was at the big dock. The green boat, bobbed up and down, riding the rolls and waiting for Papa Frank to signal us in. Along the walled-up bank, back of him, the waves were hitting high — splashing, rocking, and churning the whole area.

When we safely reached the dock, he sharply explained, "You couldn't have beat the swell, and it might have carried you on against that bank of rocks over there. If the boat had tipped or cracked apart, you could have drowned. It's much more dangerous here, while the waves are hitting, than it is out there." He scolded as he tied the boat.

We scurried ahead of him up the wooden steps and into the house. There were groceries on the table, and we began to talk about supper, hoping he would forget the boat deal.

There were the usual three cans of tomatoes. Always tomatoes, and somtimes peas, or corn. But always three — they sold three for a quarter, or ten cents for one, and Papa Frank saved the nickel. Tomatoes were good on hot days, eaten cold from a dish.

"Are we going to have tomatoes again, Papa?" I asked.

"I suppose you want corn," he said and smiled as he turned to see if some were on the shelf. Dubby and I stole glances and I thought, now he's forgetting about the boat deal.

But sitting at the table later, eating corn, he preached seriously about danger. "Don't ever be afraid, no matter what happens. Even if you are in very real danger, you won't help yourself by being afraid. Many people drown who might be saved if they didn't become frantic and lose their senses."

Bo-Shoo — Bo-Shoo
(bonjour)

We hadn't been much afraid that afternoon, but he had been terrified. I couldn't quite believe him, and said, "But Papa, if you really were drowning, you'd need to be afraid."

He shook his head quickly, "No — you wouldn't need to be at all. Listen — what good would it do you to be afraid? When you're afraid you can't think, and then you can't help yourself, and no one else can help you either. No matter what the danger is or where you are you will have more chance of saving yourself if you aren't afraid." We argued a little and asked questions, but learned much.

Little more than a week passed before that advice was put to a test. It was Sunday, and stifling, even in the forenoon. Papa Frank decided to row across the bay and cool off. Taking a picnic lunch, the Sunday paper, and a book, we left. No breeze lifted the heat, and as the oars cranked the boat over the water, the liquid mirror, surrounding us, threw fire in our faces.

We passed the city-dock where its fat legs waded out to look at us, and slipped on toward the far end of the bay where canoes crossed, as if on a watery road, to the Indian Reservation.

A canoe was seen coming from behind, with an Indian kneeling in the center, picking deftly with his paddle and making hardly a ripple, yet cutting his craft through the shining surface with the speed of a sailboat. He would soon pass us, and Papa Frank said, "Do you want to say 'hello' to him?" We weren't sure, but he urged, "When he passes us, you say, 'Bo - shoo' (bon jour)."

We both repeated, "Bo - shoo," and it wasn't hard to say. Bon jour, the French word for hello, was used by these Indians.

As the canoe passed, Papa Frank nodded, and the Indian

did the same. Then Dubby gathered courage and called, "Bo - shoo," after he had passed. The tan Indian looked back quickly and answered, "Bonjour, bonjour," grinning happily and nodding vigorously, twice, to make it genuine. It had pleased him, and he glanced back several times smiling. Soon only his blueshirted back showed, far beyond.

We continued across the bay and landed where trees were close and the shoreline low and sandy. Papa Frank settled to read in a shady spot, but we went exploring. Surely no one had ever walked in this place, we thought. Not another person was in sight now, nor were there any landing docks near. We were alone and free. Farther back were trees that could be climbed, almost like at the bunkhouse.

Scrambling up, "Charlie" and "Fred" were soon sitting on high branches singing the sawmill song, but properly — Papa Frank might hear. With so much freedom we soon turned to breaking branches and building walls and hadn't thought of eating till Papa came. Seeing our sweaty faces, he said, "Why don't you girls stay out by the water and not play so hard in the hot woods." But we were in water every day. Playing lumberjack was better.

It grew cloudy. Papa wanted to start home, but we weren't ready to break camp. Finally, much later, he called sharply and came running, "Girls — come on! We'd better go." A storm was coming and the sky was darkening. His voice was urgent.

We hurried to the shore and could see black clouds rising fast. He watched the sky anxiously. "I don't know whether to try it or not. I think, though, we'd better make a start. If we don't go now, we'll have to stay all night. The lake will be rough for hours." Little ruffles were already skipping across the water with the advancing wind.

He looked at us, and said, "It may turn cold and rain all night, and there's no place where we can go to get dry. You'd catch your death of cold." We had no wraps.

That decided him — we ran to the boat, pushed it from the sand, and jumped in. In just moments he had it swung around, and the shore receded rapidly.

From then on it seemed we barely moved, though he was pulling furiously. He looked up over his shoulder, at the advancing storm. "We should have started sooner," he said. Scudding wavelets were already slapping against the sides. He considered turning back, but decided, "If we can just reach land on the other side we'd be nearer home and can walk the bank." Soon he wished we hadn't left the other shore — "We could have turned the boat over on ourselves for protection." He thought of that now.

The clouds looked blacker every second. All of a sudden, heavy drops of rain fell into the boat and peppered the surrounding water. Papa Frank joked, "We'll get cooled off now." A whistling, cutting wind swept past, whipping the water and shooting gray scuds across the surface. In no time at all, the fury of it sucked up waves. Lightning streaked through the clouds, and suddenly the whole sky crashed open!

The rain plastered our hair and faces, and soon water was washing the bottom of the boat. He told Dubby to get the small pail from behind her and dip out water. "Whatever you do, don't let go of that pail. We will need it," he cautioned. She changed to the center to begin bailing out water.

Like a black curtain drawn across the sky, the rolling storm clouds covered all of the blue. It seemed as if the end of the day had come. The water turned green, and every wave carried a ridge of white foam. Each thundering wave loomed higher, and heaved itself against the small craft like a mad bull boosting its enemy from the earth, tossing us up and dropping us, amid towering foaming ridges.

Papa Frank was thankful now for every extra bolt he had used. With straining muscles, hardened from swinging the axe, he gripped the oars and struggled to stay right-side-up. Fright filled his eyes as he begged us to hold tightly to the seats. Each time a high wave moved against the boat, it seemed that surely we could never overcome it, but that it would roll over us instead.

It was then we learned to ride waves many times higher than the swell from the steamer. Papa Frank spoke up as calmly as he could, "Girls — lean this way — watch me — do just as I do."

He leaned sideways, away from the oncoming wave, to avoid cutting into it. Then when we sat high for an instant, as though riding on air, and before being dropped into the trough again, he straightened up and centered himself on the seat. On the downside dive he leaned the opposite way to level the boat so it wouldn't dip water. We watched his movements and shifted our weight exactly as we saw him doing.

Most of the time Dubby was on her knees in the bottom. She kept doing everything — crawling from side to side balancing the boat, and trying to bail water, too. As each wave was mounted, she clung to the high edge of the boat with one hand, while clutching the pail, ready to dip with the other. But when the boat was so tipped, the water ran to the low side and she couldn't reach it. Only when the boat leveled in the trough could she dip it out. Then she did it fast. She was saving us all, doing that.

Papa Frank continually warned her that keeping her

weight on the top edge and hanging on was more important than bailing, for we would tip over if she stayed where the water was.

Riding the rolls was almost fun, I thought, except that Papa Frank's brown eyes looked so wild. He urged Dubby to dip faster, for the rain and the top ruffles of waves, spilling over, had deeply covered the bottom. I looked at him and called, "Papa — are you afraid?"

He answered quickly, "No, I'm not afraid. You aren't, are you?"

I might have said yes, but knowing what he expected, I shook my head no. It was a blessing that we were trained to never be afraid of storms. The lightning had pierced constantly, and the thunder cracked and boomed.

We were drenched, water over our feet, and rain washing our heads. After awhile Dubby's arms tired, and she couldn't dip as fast. "Are you tired, Sister?" Papa asked. She dropped her shoulders in answer. I had begged to help bail, and now began to move from my seat to change places.

Papa Frank seemed terrified. "NO — YOU SIT STILL! And HANG ON," he ordered. I think he was afraid I surely would lose my balance or be washed out. "We need Dubby right there." There was nothing for each to do but stay where we were and do what we were doing.

Before long, water in the boat was splashing like a lake all by itself. Papa Frank knew that if much more fell in, we would be washed out as it capsized. He really thought it would happen soon, for he spoke out with all the brightness he could show, "Girls — if the boat tips over, hang tight to it, for it'll float upside down. But if you do get washed away and go down, don't be afraid, because you know Mama will be right there with you and take you in her arms."

Sighting Home From A Sinking Boat

"What!" Dubby shrieked. She hadn't thought about drowning. She thought the only danger was from tipping, and we had learned how to keep the boat right-side-up. "Why will we go down?"

"The boat can't hold much more water without the sides dipping," he told her, as we all leaned again.

"But, Papa," I called, "Mama is in heaven. She can't be down here to save us."

His face was strained with effort, and he couldn't find words to answer, so he only nodded — yes. Then he said, "She will be there waiting for you, and keep you with her."

It was too difficult for me to think she would be waiting below, in that dark water, and not come to the boat. All at once, both of us knew what he meant. Our Mama had died, and if we were with her, then we would be dead, too.

"You mean we'd be dead?" I called as I clung to the seat and the water swished my legs. I was frightened.

Slowly he shook his head no, saying, "You would be in heaven, with Mama." I tried to think about that, but couldn't. I didn't want to sink, or even go to heaven, so I bowed my head and prayed, the way it had always been easiest to pray: I asked Mama to help, because she was right there with God and could ask him much easier.

Dubby, all of a sudden, began splashing water out with all her might, no longer tired. In only a few minutes she had bailed out more water than was coming in. In spite of the rain there was less water in the boat. She changed hands to keep swinging it out, stopping only to cling as we rode over a crest.

Before long, Papa Frank became hopeful and began trying to make headway between waves, although he wasn't sure of the exact direction to go. It hadn't mattered before. All he had tried to do was stay right-side-up. He asked me, sitting in the back end, to look for the town while on top of a wave.

It was so dark that all of the distant shoreline looked only black to me, except a spot far ahead to the left where a few lights were showing. From this top view, the whole lake looked foamy white. I pointed quickly with one hand while clutching the seat with the other. Then, whenever he asked, I directed. The rest of the time I prayed.

At last the rain stopped, all but a sprinkle, and the wild wind lessened, but the waves didn't go down. Although the big ones adopted the smaller ones, and became farther apart, they were still as high. Now Dubby had more time between waves.

It had turned very chilly, and we looked toward the lights of town with thankfulness for we were gaining.

But at the last, Papa Frank had to struggle with all his might to get to shore, for the waves seemed determined to carry us past. Surprisingly, the sky was light again, but not bright. He couldn't risk tying at Harritys' dock, so he brought the boat to the sandy shoreline below the hotel — the wading place. Boats of all kinds were here, hugging the shore.

During the storm no one had been near the lake, but now people from the hotel were waiting. They had watched Papa Frank trying to come in. It was unbelievable that a boat had stayed rightside-up on such waves. Mrs. Harrity, waiting with the others, said she never supposed we were in that awful storm.

Papa Frank patted Dubby's shoulder and said, "Here's the little girl who saved us." Dubby was a very tired little girl right then.

So the day that began burning hot, ended gray and cold.

We three wet survivors walked shivering up the path, and as we opened our door, the heat of the shut-up room felt good.

Later, at the table, Papa Frank said, "I feel as though we've had our lives given back to us. We should feel very grateful to God. He helped us through."

Dubby, sitting in her nightgown, drinking milk, looked at him and said, "Papa — God did make it stop raining, didn't he?"

"You thought we were going to sink, didn't you Papa?" I said. He nodded a reluctant yes. But in my own mind I was sure my prayers and Mama had helped most.

27

Wrong Things Happen

Days turned to weeks. When we weren't fishing, Dubby and I waded and played. Papa Frank advised us more and more to stay in our own room and not see Mrs. Harrity.

Once, when we started to sing a song she and her daughter had taught us, he stopped us, saying, "I don't want you ever to sing any song you hear around them. And I want you to stay away from them entirely."

Trouble might not have come if we had minded, but Mrs. Harrity called often and had cookies, so we didn't refuse to visit her. She was always nice to us.

One day, when she was rocking and singing in her parlor, and expecting us to follow along, Dubby carefully explained that Papa Frank wouldn't allow us to sing songs that she or Louise sang. Telling that was a mistake. Mrs. Harrity stopped singing, and for several minutes rocked faster and looked out the window. Then she said, "So that's it — your father thinks he's too good for us, does he. Well!"

Dubby knew she shouldn't have told her. So she said to me after we left the room, "Don't tell Papa I told her what he said."

Each day brought change, because Papa Frank changed. He began talking longer with men on the street. On days when we fished together, he took the catch to the hotel as he had always done. But instead of coming home with food, he stopped at the saloon and stayed too long, drinking all the while, and he wasn't hungry.

Then we often looked into Mrs. Harrity's kitchen to watch her fry beefsteak without a pan. She plopped the raw meat onto the dry hot lids of the stove. It spluttered and smoked as she lifted and turned it constantly. The greasy smoke floated out the open door. She said it was the only way to cook a steak properly. I didn't want any, for it looked half raw when she cut it on her plate. In our own room we ate bread and butter with sugar or jelly.

One evening, when Papa Frank was late getting home, and found us hungry and waiting, he felt very bad. That night he told us, "Papa is going to stop staying at the saloon. I'll bring beer home instead." He promised us earnestly.

He kept his promise for awhile. He carried the beer in a syrup pail and sat at the table at home pouring it into his glass. Then, after only a few days, he again stayed in the saloon too long. He didn't at all want to do it, and he said to us one night, "I think we never should have moved to town. We should have stayed out in the timber all summer." In a desperate effort to stay away from the saloons, he worked out a plan with the bartender to have Dubby and me go to the back door and then in, just far enough, to peek under the cut-away door so he could see us and get our pail and fill it. That failed too.

Mrs. Harrity began to tell Dubby our Papa was bad and talked of many things that weren't true. Dubby was afraid to tell him any of it.

One day when we came from playing, Papa Frank and Mrs. Harrity were talking angrily in our doorway. He sent us away, for she was spitting vile words. He sounded cross when he called us, and he was cross all evening.

I think if Papa could have stayed out of the saloons, all the horrible happenings might never have come about. More and more he remained away and always avoided Mrs. Harrity. Sometimes he talked about the bunkhouse, of moving back and bringing Bounce home. That is what Dubby and I wanted most.

Days dragged on, and sometimes we would find him on the street talking to other men about the tariff, and the new President, Teddy Roosevelt, and calling himself a stand-pat Republican. But most of the time he was in one of the many saloons.

I often watched his face when his eyes were red, and tried to understand, but I couldn't. He had told us that he didn't want to drink and get drunk, and it seemed that if he didn't want to do it, he didn't have to.

All the while, Mrs. Harrity was scheming to hurt him. She knew he loved us, for he had struggled to keep us with him. So she decided to try to have us taken from him.

One afternoon when he was gone, she called us to come upstairs. In the parlor her daughter Louise was playing the piano, and we had often sung with her and had fun. This day she told Louise to keep us there because she was "going over to see the authorities," about having us taken away from Papa.

Dubby had known a little about it. She knew Mrs. Harrity was planning that we were to live with her, and Dubby knew Papa Frank wouldn't want that. I felt caught — everything was wrong. I couldn't sing. I looked out the window and wished so much he would come, and that he wouldn't be drunk.

Later, when Mrs. Harrity was home again, we watched for him through the lace curtains. She had told us we were to stay with her for supper. Even before suppertime, we saw him coming with paper sacks. I wanted to run out and meet him, for everything was all right — he was bringing food. But they held me back, and Mrs. Harrity warned us to be quiet.

We heard him go inside, and for awhile he walked around in the room below, preparing supper. Once he went outside and looked for us and called. In a few minutes he went out again and called. I choked back tears as I stood shaking and wanting to answer and go home. It seemed terrible not to answer.

In a little while he came up the inside stairs to Mrs. Harrity's door and knocked. She motioned for Louise, Dubby and me to get back out of sight, then reached for the doorknob. Her silk dress, which she had worn to town, looked elegant, touching the floor, although she had tied on an apron because she was starting supper.

We heard Papa Frank's voice, so dear and familiar, as he asked politely, "Mrs. Harrity, are the girls here?"

I couldn't believe we were not to answer him and go. I wanted to run and tell everything, but Louise held me.

Mrs. Harrity stiffened and glared at him, saying, "Yes, the girls are here — and they're going to stay here!"

I edged over far enough to see. Papa Frank's brown eyes, a little red, were questioning her, unable to understand what she meant. Seeing her angry manner, he demanded, "Why — what do you mean? I have supper ready for them. And I want them to come."

She blared, "They're not coming. They're staying right here with me." When he took another step up to look around the room, as though to come after us, she braced her arm in front of him across the doorway. He became very angry, but said patiently, "Mrs. Harrity — you can't do a thing like this. They are my girls. They belong to me, and I want them to come home."

Dubby seemed to be sorry she had been so friendly with our landlady, because now when Papa Frank stood there asking for us, she too, wanted to go and started toward him. Then he looked straight at her and said, "Come girls."

Dubby turned to me and I moved to go with her. But before we could reach him or say anything at all, Mrs. Harrity spoke words to Papa Frank that changed our lives forever. Looking like an angry cat she snarled, "Oh yes I can keep them here. And that's what I'm going to do. Those girls are never going to live with you again. I saw the authorities this afternoon."

Papa Frank couldn't answer. He took a step backward on the landing and hesitated, as if he'd been struck. His eyes flashed, and instantly he seemed to have made up his mind. He started down the steps, snapping back at her, "I'd sooner see them dead than with you!"

Only seconds later, she gasped, slammed the stair-door shut, and turned the key while screaming to Louise, "Run— take the girls and run. He's coming with the gun."

Louise grabbed my hand, and Mrs. Harrity gave Dubby a push toward the front hall. We tore off across the street, running wildly, to find a hiding place. Louise thought it safer to get as far away as possible, so we sneaked around houses and barns and kept running, keeping out of sight, stopping only to see if he was following.

Finally, several blocks away, we paused for breath and watched from behind a shed, wondering what to do. The excitement of running had held back all thought of the outcome until now.

"Where will we go?" Dubby asked Louise, who was anxiously peering around the corner of the building and breathing deeply. Running was harder for her with her long skirts. She said she thought that after awhile we could sneak back to her mother, for surely someone would take the gun away from Papa Frank.

But that idea was forgotten the next time we dashed across a street, for we saw him! He was about three blocks away, on the high bank of the railroad track, standing, looking in all directions. He still had my rifle in his arm! The long barrel showed plainly as it extended from the crook of his elbow, for the sky was light behind him.

I hadn't believed he wanted to harm us. I had thought this was the way other children sometimes ran from whippings, though never Dubby or I. I had thought we would soon go home and eat supper and go to bed—refusing to think he would hurt us. And I had been trying to tell Louise and Dubby that, all the while.

But now, I stood in the street watching in disbelief instead of jumping out of sight as Dubby and Louise had done. They were calling wildly, "Come on! Come on! He'll see you!" Suddenly, I turned and raced to catch up, sobbing and trembling. He hadn't seen me. We were sure of that, for he had kept turning and looking, waiting for us to come into view.

The whole world had changed in those few seconds. We were afraid to go home now and didn't know where to go. Then Dubby, too, began crying, and that made everything worse. We ran now without stopping, only watching to make sure we were out of his sight. We wondered if he had harmed Louise's mother to get her to release us.

Seeing a lady in her front yard, we went to her and asked for protection. She hurried us inside. We ate supper there and afterward Louise sneaked back home. We didn't see her again for many days. After dark the lady took Dubby and me to the home of one of her friends where she said she thought we would be safer.

We remained there hidden for two days, which to us seemed like months and years. Dubby wished so much to tell Papa Frank the things Mrs. Harrity had said, but now she was too uncertain. On the third day a strange man came, but he didn't take us home — we never again went home. He took us to the hotel — the one beside the lake and Harritys' yard, where we had always played. But we were not allowed to go to Harritys', or to play outside. We could only watch our playmates from the windows. That didn't matter so much because we were still afraid of Papa Frank, although he was no longer at Harrity's house.

Being at the hotel was, for us, almost fun at first. There was a piano in the parlor that joined the dining room where we might sing or practice. Quite often someone was playing. And it was fun to eat at the dining room tables, and watch a waitress carry the trays in and out to the kitchen, and to listen to her call an order to the cook through the round hole in the swinging door.

We soon became friends of the cook and others in the kitchen. Here we were amazed to see the dishes sliding around in the huge sink without breaking. The women tossed, dried and stacked them fast. I thought they weren't even trying to be careful, but the thick rounded edges slipped safely together.

Sometimes we helped and got extra treats. I asked the women why they didn't do as the camp cooks did, and pour hot water over the dishes instead of wiping each one with a towel. They only laughed and said, "The missus wouldn't stand for that. Those were tin dishes, and streaks don't matter anyhow in camp."

One day the hotel-keeper's wife, who was 'the missus,' told Dubby that we would be at the hotel only until arrangements were complete for us to be taken to the State School at Owatonna. We were to be placed in a home for children. Dubby came running, and broke into choking sobs, "They're going to — put us — in a reform school!"

We thought of the school at Eldora and were shocked. We didn't want to be put in a place like that. A State School! I couldn't think why we would be sent away. We hadn't been naughty or done anything wrong. I, too, began sobbing, remembering the school at Eldora where we had watched boys being marched along the sidewalks and across the lawn. We had felt so sorry for those boys.

Now we would be marched and made to sit in groups, instead of running wherever we wished. And maybe people would look at us and feel sorry, or think we had been bad girls. It was all too awful. We cried bitterly.

Dubby decided to do something to keep it from happening. She managed to sneak over to Mrs. Harrity for help. She even hoped to see Papa Frank and tell him about it. Anything would be better than being in a reform school. But Dubby came back to tell me she had failed: Mrs. Harrity didn't know how to help, and she didn't know where Papa Frank was either. She had seen him only once since the night we ran from him. The police had arrested him that night, she said, and he had come for his clothes a few days later. She told Dubby not to try to see him because he still might harm her. She knew he was trying to find us, and she hoped he never would.

She was angry, too, with the police for taking us to the hotel. She said to Dubby, "They could just as well have let me earn that board money. Old bigshot (the hotel-keeper) will put in a big bill for it, and get it in his own pocket."

We both wished so much to see Papa Frank, even though

we were still a little afraid. I couldn't think my papa didn't love me. If only he wouldn't be drunk he could help us, I was sure, just as he did that time at the church. But he was drunk too much, now. I remembered he had promised us a home. But Mrs. Harrity's room wasn't home. And even the bunkhouse wasn't a real home. Oh, where is home, Papa?

One day we were told that court proceedings would be held at the court house the next morning, and we must be present. A judge would be there, and Papa Frank, too! After that we would be sent to the school. It must all be made legal. But we must first be taken away from Papa, and he would no longer have anything to say about us.

That night we went to bed with terrifying thoughts about court proceedings. One thing gave hope — Papa Frank would be there. And we knew he wouldn't let us go. He would do something. We talked for a long time — our heads spinning with ideas. Maybe we could go back to the bunk-house and get Bounce. We were so lonesome for Bounce. Or maybe we could even go to Aunt Carrie. Or to Aunt Nellie in Minneapolis.

The next forenoon the hotel-keeper's wife helped us get ready, and tried to comfort us, saying she would go along and stay close the whole time. We walked the several blocks to the courthouse. It stood away from the street and alone. A long walk led to the brick structure that looked like a prison to us. With legs that trembled we climbed the stone steps — six of them.

From the wide hall we entered a large barelooking room to wait for whatever might happen. Papa Frank wasn't there, nor anyone else. Dubby and I began watching the door, but it was still early. He would come any minute, we were sure of that. We would tell him everything, and he would make things right.

The high-ceilinged room looked much like a school with rows of empty seats. There was a flag up front and pictures of Washington and Lincoln on the wall. There was one thing different — extra seats were near the large desk at the front. No teacher ever had special seats for a class. There was also a huge armchair very close to the desk. It had a high back and wide arms and looked most important standing alone on a small platform.

We waited and wondered and finally sat down. Then three men came in and stood talking near the door. A little later Mrs. Harrity and Louise arrived.

Dubby turned to the hotel-lady and said, "There's Mrs. Harrity," but she was quickly told, "You stay here with me." Louise and her mother sat down together, farther back.

Precious minutes were passing. Oh, where was Papa Frank? I watched, never taking my eyes from the doorway. Surely he would step in the next moment. Instead, another strange man strode in. Everyone seemed to have been waiting for him. He walked to the desk. The hotel-lady told Dubby he was the judge.

I whispered to Dubby, "Why doesn't Papa come?"

Dubby was watching the door too, and her forehead wrinkled anxiously, "I don't know."

It was now too late to talk to him beforehand, but he was still our only hope. He could save us if he would only get there.

The three men then took seats, facing the big chair which was the witness chair. After the judge at the high desk had said some funny words and rapped for order, one of the men rose and began to talk. He was a lawyer. He asked Mrs. Harrity to come to the high-backed chair. She raised her hand, promising to tell the truth, and then sat down and said mean things about Papa Frank before going back to her seat. I watched the door. It seemed all wrong to have this going on before he got there.

Then Louise was called. She raised her hand and got into the chair and told about running with Dubby and me while our father was looking for us with a gun. One of the three strange men told about going to our room at Harritys' and finding very little food there.

Then Dubby had to raise her hand and get into the huge chair. She tried to tell them why there hadn't been much food in the room. She told them Papa Frank always brought whatever we needed each day. She told them the room at Harritys' wasn't our real home — it was in the woods, and we were going back there. She said Papa Frank was good to her and that she loved him.

But when they asked if she had ever seen him drunk, she had to say, "Yes." And when they asked if she had gone to school the past year, she had to say, "No." She had promised to tell the truth.

I stood beside her and could see into the hall while listening to the talk. I couldn't understand why they weren't waiting for Papa Frank. Then they told me to sit in the chair. I began to cry and said, "I want to wait for my papa." But Dubby got out of it and I had to climb in. I held my hand up the way others had done, and promised to tell the truth. The side arms were almost as high as my shoulders; two more children could have sat with me. Dubby stood close, for I was trembling.

They asked me if I was Bernice Green, and I wondered why they asked that; didn't they know it? And then the question, "Is Frank Green your father?" Just as though they didn't know that either. A lawyer began asking the same questions they had asked Dubby. I told them my papa could explain, and that I wanted to wait for him.

As I sobbed, the lawyer began talking very earnestly to make me understand that I must not wish to live with Papa. "Why," he said, throwing his arms out in a hopeless way, "your father doesn't care anything about you, or he'd be here now. He's probably drunk this very minute."

I couldn't think of anything to say. Papa Frank hadn't come, and I didn't know where he was. But never, never had I thought that he didn't "care anything" for me, as the man said. Dubby slipped into the seat and put her arms around me, then tried to wipe my eyes while we cried together. I rubbed my face on Dubby's sleeve, but there was no use trying to wipe tears away; they came too fast. We needed handkerchiefs.

The lawyer talked on, "He didn't provide a proper place for you to live. He didn't have you in school."

Then I looked up and said in a choking voice, "He taught us lessons at home though."

The lawyer only shrugged, as much as to say - that doesn't amount to anything. I knew he didn't believe me, because he didn't know Papa Frank was an educated man.

I thought, if only someone would come and say something good about Papa. If only someone would help us. I knew that maybe he was drunk right then, as the lawyer had said, but to think he didn't love me, or Dubby, was too terrible. I wouldn't believe that was true, even remembering the gun in his arm.

"You will be much better off away from him," the man was saying. But I remembered, too, that he always wanted us to learn about everything. And he was very good to me and to Dubby, except sometimes — sometimes when he was drunk; but he couldn't help that either. He didn't want to be drunk. He had tried to stay out of the saloons. I remembered that, too.

While we clung together in that huge chair, the judge decided. We listened to the talk. Nothing was going to keep the world from ending. Tears and pleadings didn't count. Dubby begged them, saying, "We don't want to go to a reform school. We could go to our Aunt Carrie again."

The lawyer then tried to tell us about this school at Owatonna. It wasn't a reform school he said. It was a State School where children were taken who had no parents. He said, "You girls will like it there. You will be taken care of and receive an education."

So the papers were signed. It was over. And Papa Frank hadn't come! We were to be taken away. Soon everyone stood up and left. Nothing had stopped the awful thing from happening.

Outside, Dubby and I, brokenhearted, went down the front steps with the hotel-lady and followed the long walk to the street. We felt forsaken. We had been told that legally Papa Frank was no longer our father and could have nothing to say now, and that we belonged to The State. It seemed there was no one who cared about us.

Mrs. Harrity and Louise had waited in the street to tell us they were so sorry, but the hotel-lady reminded Dubby, after Harritys' walked on, that Mrs. Harrity had started most of the trouble. "I think much of the blame placed on your father came because he had you living at her house," she told us.

We walked very slowly along the wooden sidewalk in the high sunshine, all hope gone. We were going to prison. To us a reform school and a state school were the same — a prison.

We watched the stores and saloons as we passed, hoping to see Papa Frank and tell him what had happened.

"I don't see why he couldn't have found a better place for you to live," the hotel-lady said, still thinking of why this had all come about.

"We went there because Mrs. Prodock knew her," Dubby explained briefly.

"Who is Mrs. Prodock?"

"She was our neighbor out in the woods."

"Oh, I see." The hotel-lady began to understand how it had all begun. "It's too bad you ever moved into town," she said with sympathy, "but you should have been in school, too."

Horrible days followed. We were kept inside for fear Papa Frank would steal or harm us. Little Marie and all the others played just below the hotel at the lakeshore — where the creek flowed in from Harritys' yard — where the launches were safely floating in their shed — where the water was clean and the bottom sandy. We watched from the window and wished we could be out there.

Word came from the school that it might be another week before anyone could come for us. Four days had gone by since the forenoon at the courthouse, and Papa Frank now knew where we were and he had asked to see us, and had been refused.

Because he wanted so much to just look at us, he watched the hotel most of the day. Often, when I saw him from a window, looking so dear and familiar, walking straight and squareshouldered and not at all drunk, I wanted to run out to him. But that wasn't allowed. And, too, I was still a little doubtful. A queer lost feeling came over me when I remembered he was no longer my lawful papa. I wondered if he knew we were to be sent away.

The hotel-keeper decided it was wrong to keep us shut in while our father watched outside. He arranged to have him ordered out of the county, "So everyone can rest easier," he said, "and the girls can play outside with other children."

The hotel-lady found Dubby and me in the kitchen and told us: "After tomorrow we won't need to worry about your father. He's been ordered to be out of the county by six o'clock tomorrow night. He's been told that he can come and see you girls before he leaves; but just once, to say good-by. So I suppose he'll come tomorrow sometime."

Our hopes soared. We could hardly sleep that night for planning all we might say to him. But we wondered if he still cared to help — he hadn't come to the courthouse to keep it from happening.

It was late afternoon when he came. We had expected him long before that and had begun to think he might not come at all. When the hotelkeeper called us to the front office I was almost afraid to go. But when I saw him sitting in a round armchair pulled to the center of the room, he was the same dear papa, with smiling brown eyes and bald head. He spread his arms wide and leaned forward when he saw us coming slowly through the doorway. We rushed to him, and he folded us in tightly as he murmured with shaking voice, "Papa's girls."

He kissed us hungrily, first one and then the other, again and again, as though not able to say words. All at once I knew that what the lawyer had said wasn't true, and he did love us. A right-feeling came back. I wanted to ask him everything, just as I had wanted to go to him the night at Harritys' and tell him what was wrong, and they had held me back.

So now I said, "Papa — you didn't want to kill us, did you?"

He pulled my head against him and answered in a low tone, "Darling." And then very deeply, "No." He held me close for a moment and added, "Papa doesn't want to talk about that."

Dubby, too, wanted to tell everything, and she burst out, "Papa, they're going to put us in a reform school!"

He reached in his pocket for a handkerchief to catch tears as he answered, "I know it, dear, but it's not a reform school, and Papa won't let you stay there. I'll get a good home ready for you and sister and then we'll be together again. This has all been a bad mistake. If I could only tell you so you would understand. If you were older I could tell you everything, and you would know it wasn't all your papa's fault."

He said to me as he took his arm away, "Papa wants to talk to sister for a few minutes alone."

Before I stepped away, I asked the question that had been in my thoughts all the days, "Why didn't you come to the courthouse?" He seemed not to know how to answer, and I wondered a little if he had been drunk, the way the man at the courthouse had said.

After a moment he told us quietly, "I didn't know it was the day." But that didn't explain it well enough.

The hotel-keeper stood close to the locked outside door. No one else was in the room. Papa Frank wanted so much to talk to Dubby alone that he said to him, "I'd like to be alone with the girls for a few minutes. I have some things to talk about I'd rather say to them alone."

The man said rather bluntly, "Go ahead and say anything you have to say." And he stayed at the door. He was there to keep Papa Frank from taking us out and to keep others from coming in.

I stepped back to where we had entered, but I could still hear most of it, as Papa Frank drew Dubby close and began to talk very earnestly. He told her that although she wouldn't understand now, he hoped she would remember all he was saying, then when she was older she would realize, and could explain everything to me. He told her that jealousy was the cause of all the trouble — the hate that goes with jealousy. Certain women had wanted to do the meanest things they could to him and had schemed to take his girls away. He had known all that.

Dubby then told him Mrs. Harrity had said he didn't care for us, because he was spending his time with a woman friend, and we were only in his way. And maybe we might get a stepmother who would be mean.

Papa Frank hadn't known we thought he didn't love us. "Oh darling," he said, as he hugged Dubby, "and you believed her? You let her tell you that I didn't love you? Remember this," he begged, "the time will never come when your papa doesn't love you. No matter what happens, always remember that, won't you?" He talked on — wiping tears from her face, and from his own, and making her know that he loved her.

Then I took her place and felt the comfort of his strong arms. "It makes Papa feel so bad to have you think he doesn't love you. And to think you have been afraid of him!" His tears ran on my cheeks while I gripped him tightly to show I did love him a lot. I hadn't believed what they had told me — except for a short time — when he had the gun.

He said, "Some day you will understand. Dubby will explain." There was nothing left now for him, except to try and make our going easier. "Be a good girl and Papa will come for you. We will get everything straightened out somehow," he encouraged. "Always remember — Mama is watching over you."

"But I don't want to go, Papa! Why do we have to go? Why can't we go to Aunt Carrie?" I pleaded. I had thought all along that he would save us. Now he was here, and he too was talking about us going—just as though he was helpless to stop it. "Can't you do something, Papa?" I begged.

He could do nothing and knew it. Although I felt sure he wanted to comfort me, he could only choke back grief and wipe his eyes. "Papa will do all he can dear," he managed to say. "You can be sure that some day there will be someone there to get you. Try and be good girls, and do everything they tell you to do, and you will get along all right."

All hope was fading. Even Papa Frank could do nothing. Dubby was standing close with new ideas for help. He again shifted girls and took Dubby. But all was lost — we couldn't go back to the bunkhouse, or get Bounce, or remain free. As we began to realize this, we cried even harder. And I know Papa wished we wouldn't beg so hard. It only made the parting more unbearable.

He told Dubby one more thing to think about as she grew older: "Always remember this, dear — don't let outside people influence you." She knew he was saying it because that was exactly what she had done, and it had caused so very much trouble.

Just out of sight, inside the half-open door of the dining room, a group stood listening and wiping their eyes: the hotel-lady, those from the kitchen, and two women boarders — I had seen them when Papa asked me to step away.

The hotel-keeper, still by the door, spoke up and said, "Come, come now — this has gone on long enough." He, too, was crying, and it must have provoked him a little.

Papa Frank paid no attention, but kept talking to Dubby and kissing her, as he held her close. Soon the man spoke sharply, "Come on now, you'll have to go," and he pointed to the big clock on the wall. "You have only a half hour to get out of the county."

Papa Frank reached for me to come back, and he said, "Just once more," as he took me on his lap. He reached arms around both of us, and told us how proud he was, and reminded us, "Never think that other children are better than you are. You are fine girls. Just as your Mama wanted you to be. And please, darlings, be obedient when you get to the school, and do everything they tell you, for her sake."

The clock kept ticking till only fifteen minutes were left. The hotel-keeper was pacing in a circle. People were waiting outside, and again he stepped out to explain. Now, he kept pointing to the clock.

Finally, Papa Frank flared at him, "You needn't worry about me. I guarantee I'll be out of this county by six o'clock."

"Are you crazy, man? You haven't enough time left, even now, to do that."

"You leave that to me," Papa Frank told him. "I've got it timed, and I'm not leaving here one second before I have to." He clasped us closer and said, "Beeny Coony-Snakey Biddle-Bum Bum Bum," and I think he was recalling the day I stomped my foot and called myself that. And then, he groaned softly, "Oh — how I have failed your mama."

He, too, kept eyes on the clock now, as he clung to us to use every precious second. Then, looking quickly at Dubby, he said, "Good-by dear — you take good care of sister." And to me, "Good-by dear — remember, Papa loves you."

Releasing us he rose, choking, and walked swiftly out the door as it was held open, speaking to no one.

We followed and called, "Good-by." He glanced back quickly to answer, while rounding the corner of the hotel.

Those who had listened from the dining room, now came tearing out and joined the group waiting outside. All watched from the side of the building, in view of the lake. They were probably curious to know how he could get out of the county in ten minutes.

He was departing swiftly, down the wide gravel path, in long leaping strides, and really running when he reached the shoreline at the foot of the hill. And there was the green boat! Loaded with his possessions. Without looking up he pushed it from the sand and jumped in — reaching for the oars.

With tremendous strokes he pulled straight out, and before long, began glancing sideways to the west shoreline as though measuring with his eye. Suddenly, he turned the boat at a sharp angle, and rowed toward that shore — which was close to another county. Now, from the side view, the rounded hump of total belongings, piled and covered at the back end, could more plainly be seen.

"So that was his plan," the hotel-keeper remarked. "Quite smart at that, I guess. The county line is over there."

One of the women said, "Oh — do you suppose he's going to jump in and drown himself right out there where we can all see it?"

"Sh," the hotel-lady warned, and touched the woman's arm. Dubby and I were standing close, crying bitterly — our eyes stinging. She put her arms around us. Others left, but Dubby and I stayed till the boat grew small. We waved, but couldn't see him answer.

* * *

Brighter days followed. The hotel-lady provided strong pillowcases for floaters, and we waded and floated in the lake for hours each day with playmates, but such freedom was not to last. The matron from the school would come. We must be ready.

28

Within The Walls Of Cottage Five

It was decided that I needed shoes worse than a rifle. A gun wouldn't be allowed at the school anyhow, so the hotel-lady inquired at the tiny trading post by the depot, and found that a trade could be made.

On the day we purchased the shoes, I was allowed to carry my precious Winchester the short distance. I held it lovingly in my arms while trying on the shoes. My most prized possession was being taken, just for something ordinary, and a few dollars in cash.

They put on a horrid pair — too big — and needing cotton in the toes. The ugly bright tan, almost an orange color, was what Indians wore when they didn't wear moccasins, and that was the kind kept here to please those who brought articles to trade. I felt very foolish trying them on — knowing it was an Indian store.

I gazed around. It had always been fun to come here, and buy long black licorice sticks, and yellow marshmallow bananas. And to look at the woven beads and doll-sized canoes of birchbark. But now the room had changed. The whole world was wrong.

Time went too fast for me. I worked the bolt of my rifle back and forth a few times more, and then had to hand it to the storekeeper. He gave the hotel-lady three dollars and fifty cents, besides the shoes. The lady said it was a fair trade, though it wasn't.

We walked outside; I was wearing the shoes, all buttoned up over my ankles. After taking a few steps, I heard them! They squeaked — the way Indians wanted shoes to squeak. I looked down and hated them. Now I would be heard as well as seen coming. Dubby was glad to keep her own black ones.

The day came to leave. All along we had secretly hoped to escape, and reach Aunt Carrie, but we had no money for a train ride. A plan had come about — the hotel-lady was taking us half way, to meet the matron where we would change trains. She was happy to do this, and visit a friend in that town, and we were glad she was going.

When the train came in, all our playmates were on the depot platform. We tried not to cry, for our eyes smarted from crying all morning. Sitting by the open window in the coach, looking down at everyone, even the thought of a train ride couldn't stop tears. Soon the train began to move and we were on our way.

The ride was long, and it was dusk when we stepped from the coach at St. Cloud. The matron was there to take charge. After eating at a cafe, we returned to the depot to wait for the other train. Dubby and I walked outside on the platform, planning to get away.

It was now entirely dark, and although we had waited for darkness, the black shadows threatened from under the plank ends of the raised platform. Something might be hiding. So we hesitated. Few people were in the depot, and no one stayed outside. The matron looked now and then.

Somehow the nearby buildings took on strange shapes. Their lighted windows stared like watching eyes. So we stayed with the matron, and when the train came snorting and clanging in, climbed up with her and settled into the plush seats and went to sleep.

Hours later we were wakened and told: "This is Owatonna." The word sounded terrifying. The matron guided us down the aisle, and at the lower step a man took our luggage. He spoke to the matron and walked with us toward a hack that was backed and waiting. The matron explained he was from the school and had come to meet the train.

The hulking vehicle was lighted inside, and two heavy horses stood at the front. He helped each of us up onto the steps, bracketed below the door at the back end, and we climbed into the hack. He slid the luggage in behind us and closed the door. In moments he was on his high seat on the outside front, and the horses started to walk.

The rig rolled forward slowly. Only the scrunching of steel-rimmed wheels on the sand told we were moving. A benchlike seat ran along either side, where ten or twelve children could sit and face those across. The stiff window shades, behind, were pulled down, and an odd-shaped lamp provided the light from high in front.

When I twisted to peek out from the edge of the curtains, all looked black, and very still, and strange. I could hear the driver speak to the horses now and then, and the hack jiggled a bit as it bumped over rough places. But it moved steadily and we with it — thinking wildly of escaping while there was still time, but the matron was sitting too close to the door. The horses walked the entire distance — slow and heavy — the way horses haul a hearse.

At last the driver "whoad" his team, and when we jumped from the hack, a three-story brick building loomed before us in the darkness. Not far away was another one. Had it been day we would have seen still others, even larger, and all red brick. The driver brought our luggage while the matron opened a door at the very corner of the building and entered a dimly-lit hall. We followed.

At once she pressed a button, signaling to somewhere that

we had arrived. As we waited, I looked through a wide doorway across the hall where three broad steps led down to a large darkened room. It was filled with many rows of small chairs, each chair holding the clothes of some undressed little girl who had folded everything neatly over the back. A pair of shoes, placed properly together, waited under every chair.

In only minutes two matrons came down the long stairway that led up from the hall. They wore dressing gowns over nightclothes, and looked sleepy, but both spoke kindly as they took over from the traveling matron who then left.

We weren't taken to the darkened room to undress, but were ushered up the stairway to a room with a bathtub! We were amazed when one of the matrons began running water into the tub, for the clock in the hall had said 2. Dubby was quick to tell them, "We had our baths at the hotel just before we started." But without even listening they helped us undress, to hurry things. We felt awkward, being helped. The tub was so large we sat facing each other while each matron sudsed and scrubbed one of us. Afterward there was more.

Along the wall, several gray marble washbasins stood sturdily in a row, and the matrons began unbraiding our long hair to wash it. Dubby protested again, "Oh, it always takes so long for our hair to dry." She said we would catch cold from wet heads at that hour — an unheard-of thing!

The matrons went right ahead — placing stools for us to stand on, and bending us over, to wet and soap our heads. I had never felt such rubbing and squeezing. I looked across to Dubby at another basin and saw her being jerked in the same manner. Running away might have been better than this, I thought. The matrons were hurrying to get back to bed.

Finally, the one handling me reached for a pitcher, and

without warning, splashed water all over my head, and the back of my neck as well. I cried out, "Oh—that's cold water!" thinking surely it was a mistake. Dubby, too, was yelping. We had never known such fast treatment. But it had been done knowingly. "The water will keep you from catching cold," the matron said.

In a short time — scrubbed from top to toenail — we were taken through the hall again, and up another wide stairway. Had it been a happier time we might have laughed at each other for looking like the Turks in our story-book, with the heavy white towels wrapped over wet rolled-up hair, and white nightgowns hanging to our ankles. But now we could but frown in disbelief.

Through a wide doorway, we entered an immense room where a sea of white iron beds were waiting - row after row — close together. The dim light from the hall shadowed softly over a sleeping child in each one. All was quiet.

There were no empty beds, so I was placed with a little white-haired girl, and room was found for Dubby several rows away. I felt most queer going to bed at such an hour, in such a place, with my head wrapped so tightly it felt like a keg on my shoulders.

Two or three heads bobbed up and looked in my direction. In a few minutes, somehow it didn't seem so awful, with others sleeping so near, and the soft light outlining so many beds. I soon slumbered.

At six o'clock a bell woke everyone. Some began sitting up. The little girl with me was surprised to find me there, and asked, "Who are you?" Other girls in nearby beds asked questions too, and all were ready to tell me what to do.

In a short time, a parade of yawning, stretching, nightgowned girls passed into the hall. I could see Dubby in line ahead. She had taken off the towel and was shaking her hair to finish drying it, so I did the same.

The long double line ribboned softly down the stairway, and on around, unending to another flight, bare feet sliding quietly on the polished wood. In the lowest hall the leaders guided the flowing line into the large room I had seen the night before, where everything was folded neatly — nothing heaped, or hanging, or dropped.

Each girl reached her own small chair and sat down to pull on long black stockings and dress herself. Dubby and I were assigned to places and given clothes exactly like those the others were putting on. Every piece was marked: Inside the neckband of the gray and white checked dresses, and on the white muslin underwear, "ctg 5" told us we belonged to The State. This was Cottage Five.

Everything was new except — except — my shoes! They brought me the hated orangey-yellow Indian shoes that squeaked, and told me, "These are too new to throw away." Everyone else had black shoes — nice shiny ones. Even Dubby got new ones.

While I was busily dressing, I was told that I had slept with "Annie the Po-lock." Although I didn't know why that wasn't all right, I soon realized there was something very wrong about it. Whenever one girl passed the word on, "She slept with Annie the Po-lock," there were grins and snickers.

Annie, I found out, couldn't always understand what the others were talking about, and so they laughed at her. I began to feel ashamed because the matron had put me with Annie. Did the matron think I was dumb, too? And Annie was a homely child. Her hair looked dirty-white in the daylight and hung like cotton string. Poor little half-wit Annie.

Each girl, without crowding, took her turn at the row of marble lavatories up front, where all toilet needs were together. I rather liked to stand behind the row of basins where some were still washing their faces. I could look past them into the mirrors lining the wall and see reflections of others combing and braiding their hair, or having it done by the matrons. I was proud not to need help.

As each child finished, she tripped to her own chair to wait. I could see Dubby across the room, with girls her own age. Talking was allowed — quiet talking. Everything was done by the clock. A lot of time was used dressing — those who finished first couldn't play anyhow. I didn't like that part! But when the morning singing fanned the ceiling while waiting for the breakfast gong to ring — that was fun. We would go to another building to eat.

When the bell sounded, we all moved into a double line, up the three steps and across the hall to the corner door — the one Dubby and I had come through only five hours before. Once outside, our line waited on the narrow walk.

Here, in the daylight, I was surprised to see so many red brick buildings. Sidewalks from other cottages wound out to join a longer one leading to a very large structure in the center of the grounds. That massive imposing structure, which looked like several buildings fastened together, held the Superintendent's office and home, the big dining hall and kitchen, and the chapel and schoolrooms, we found out. So it had to be big.

As the cottage 5 girls stood ready to march, the matrons urged all to "keep the line straight," and although we were ready and waiting, it didn't mean we could march. Other lines, on other walks, waited their turn. But the fresh air of the summer morning was pleasant.

No child could call out to another, or take a step that might make the line crooked. I felt like the coyote, chained on the roof at Brainerd, whose owner thought he had it tamed, but whose endless pulling at the chain showed discontent. My spirit tugged.

As the line of cottage 5 began to move, Dubby could tell just where I was walking, for the yellow shoes squeaked sharply on the bricks. Lines of boys could be seen far over! It was surprising to learn that boys were at this school.

To reach the dining hall our procession passed along the rear of the central building where a wide doorway, several feet off the ground and used for unloading, allowed us to look into the bakery and kitchen. Boys, wrapped in square white aprons, were busy, and several stood in the opening watching all the girls and smiling as we passed — their work done for the moment.

This part was rather fun, I thought, to pass where someone could see that the line was even, and that you were walking straight. The day was soon to come when I would wish I could hide instead of pass that door.

The marchers broke into single file to enter the dining hall. Moving along past the breadslicing table and serving area, we walked to our certain tables and stood behind our own chairs. The tables were not endless-long affairs with benches, like a lumber camp, but nice cloth-covered smaller ones, surrounded with twelve chairs.

The boys entered a different door on the far side, in an orderly manner. When everyone had reached his own place, a bell sounded and the vast noise of sliding chair-legs rose, then subsided at once. It grew very quiet as all heads were bowed. Low-spoken words rumbled like distant trailing thunder.

Heads bobbed up to smile, and at once a parade emerged from the kitchen. Boys carrying large bowls of steaming cereal stepped swiftly to each table and placed one before the host or hostess at the end, who dished each one's bowl as it was passed around — taking note that every child was served, and that they ate all of it. The kitchen boys then kept carrying kettles of it around, and ladled into the host or hostess' large bowl whatever amount they asked for — according to how many wanted more. None was wasted.

There was much movement throughout the room, from children going to, and coming from, the bread-slicer. The bread-plate on each table was emptied often, just so turns could be taken carrying it to get more. Long loaves lay on the breadbench, and an older person stood there constantly, cutting it as it was needed. So mealtime was not unpleasant.

It was vacation time here, the same as at any school. It was August, and to Dubby the hours were too long. But there was a tree-shaded, grassy play area for cottage 5 where various games were often played at the same time: pump-pumppull-away, last couple out, or drop the handkerchief. The favorite of all was Statue, and I chose that most often. As the leader whirled each one by the hand and let go, they stiffened at the exact position she put them. After several were quickly swung and left holding their statue-like pose, the leader chose the one she thought nicest.

The "statues" looked ridiculous with mouths open and arms reaching toward the sky, or sometimes half falling, with one knee on the ground. I tried many times before being chosen, thus getting a turn as leader.

There was excitement and planning among twenty of the girls in cottage 5. It was their turn to attend church in town on Sunday morning. That sounded almost funny to me. I had never thought going to church was a special privilege, but I was told that it was: They would get to ride in the hack, and to wear their hats and Sunday dresses! But all other Sundays they had to stay on the school grounds and go to the chapel there.

A happy dressed-up group waited outside on that bright Sunday forenoon, wearing white stiffstraw sailor hats and gray and white striped seer sucker dresses with a clean handkerchief tucked into each pocket. Dubby and I had been included and felt so very dressed up as we climbed into the hack with the others. It didn't seem so much like a hearse now, seeing how well the others liked it. We smiled as we faced one another from the two long seats. It was a gay short trip.

The driver didn't go close to the church and dump his load. He stopped, over a block away, so we could walk there, just like everyone else. We were all proud to sit very quietly in the pews, wishing we could come often.

At cottage 5 there was a very large empty room on the second floor. I was most curious about it. From the hall, its polished floorboards looked like glass. It happened that a few days later it was too wet for outside playing, and we learned this was a place for exercising — arms up and down and out and back. We stood in rows and worked in unison as a matron called instructions — twisting, squatting, bending and resting.

After that we all filed into a long closet and each girl grabbed a pad from hooks along the wall — pads of old stockings. One little girl told me it was now time to polish the floor. She handed a pad to me quickly, so we wouldn't lose our place in line. I was most surprised that the shimmering floor was to be polished!

We rag-toting workers formed two rows across the room, facing floorboards the long way, and then dropped to our knees, side by side, clutching pads in front of us — pressed firmly to the floor — waiting. One of the group, a girl of maybe twelve, stood ready to call. She began suddenly, snapping the words sharply and evenly: "Rub --- two --- three --- four. One --- two --- three --- four."

The rows of kneeling girls pushed out, and back, and out, and back, looking like washer women over flat washboards — our rounded backs bobbing down and up in rhythmic movement. Suddenly, at the call of "Move," boths rows scooted forward about two feet and we started again, "Rub --- two --- three --- four --" steadily and heavily, continuing across the wide shining floor. Then reversing, and shifting sidewards, and turning pads over, we started back: "-- two --- three --- four."

I could see no sense in working so hard to polish wood already as shiny as glass. To me it was real punishment, and I hated it. The girl calling seemed delighted to see us press down as she ordered, "Rub ---," and I longed to be in her place.

When a young friend came to see the girl, she talked and laughed, and only now and then turned to look at the bobbing rows and say, "Move" and "Rub," to keep us going. One little girl next to me explained, "She lives here at the school, but her relatives send money for her board. That's why she can be the caller." I wished someone would send money for me.

So life at the State School had begun. Although Dubby and I were under the same roof and could talk together at times, we slept and ate and marched with girls our own age. I didn't sleep with Annie the Po-lock after that first strange night. I got my own bed — like the others. I was learning, too, how everything was done, and at what time on the clock.

After supper, the evening hours were nice, when everyone could stay outside on the thick green lawn. It wasn't the play area, but Tag was allowed. It was a cherished privilege to be in the twilight as the sky was softly drawing its curtain on the night. Many sat in groups, singing, not ordinary songs, but the kind that made a game of singing. There needed to be three groups close together, one group to begin, and the next to join at a certain word, and when the third group came in, it all fit together harmoniously. Strains of the favorite round came from all corners of the yard: "Row-row-row-your boat, gently down the stream. Merrily-merrily-merrily-merrily, life is but a dream."

I began to look forward to the evening time. I could go to Dubby and sit with her and talk, but most of the time I stayed with my own group. Then one evening Dubby came close, and slid down beside me and whispered, "I don't believe anyone is coming to get us out of here. And I just hate everything. I'm making plans to run away and get back to Papa."

I turned to her — startled at the thought.

Dubby kept whispering, "There's another girl here who doesn't like it any better then we do, and she wants to go with us."

I looked around cautiously. It seemed that the nearby children in gray checked dresses, and the matrons too, must surely know what Dubby was whispering. "Oh, we don't dare do that. We might get caught," I breathed.

But Dubby said she was sure she was planning everything perfectly. After thinking a few minutes, I was tempted. For it really would be wonderful to get back to Papa Frank — if only it could be done. But I was too timid.

Dubby saw me avering, and warned, "Don't you say a word to anyone or we'll go without you. I'll talk to you again tomorrow night. My mind is made up, and we're going whether you do or not."

The rest of that evening I felt separated from all around me. At bedtime, even my own bed seemed to be knowing the secret. I was quite sure I didn't want to run away. It was too far to go - without money. And Papa Frank had left Walker. We would have to look for him. I planned to make Dubby change her mind and wait to get out some other way.

The next day was Tuesday, and we had been there eleven days. It had seemed months. The evening was warm when we gathered again on the lawn. I was playing a tag game when I saw Dubby waiting and walked toward her. We sat down together. Dubby seemed very excited, but tried not to act that way. Ellen, the girl who wanted to go along, was standing near. She looked scared.

I didn't have a chance to beg Dubby not to try it. The first thing she said was, "We've decided to go right now. We've been talking it over, and we don't want to stay another day. We're going to walk around a little and get back of the building when no one is looking. And you come around from the other side and meet us."

Dubby got up and started away. I was afraid to try to stop her, for the matron, standing not far away, might notice something wrong. As Dubby and Ellen strolled off, terror struck me, and for a wild moment I didn't know whether to run to the matron and tell, or to run after Dubby and beg her not to go. I ran after Dubby and Ellen who were walking slowly, trying to look aimless and innocent, and I pleaded, "I'm afraid to do it. Let's don't do it. Let's wait. Please, Dubby."

Dubby looked at me, as though wondering for a moment just what to do about me. Then she said, "You can stay here if you want to. We're going. And if you don't want to come along, we'll go without you. We'll have to hurry too, and get a good start before they miss us." I watched them walk toward a corner of the building without me.

The moment they were out of sight I was terrified — afraid of being punished for what they were doing. I followed. They were standing on the narrow strip of lawn behind the building, waiting to be certain no one was following. Again I begged, "Please, Dubby." But Dubby said she was afraid to wait and get caught now.

Just then Ellen made a dash down the edge of the terrace, into the cornfield, and Dubby, at her heels, urged me to "Come On."

Frantic, I again thought of running to the matron. I stood alone now, the huge building at my back and the rows of high green corn in front, where Dubby and Ellen were waiting, almost out of sight. They had turned to look back and were now motioning desperately for me to come.

I had to decide, though shaking even worse than on the platform at church. Suddenly the thought that Dubby was going to Papa Frank brought action. With a pounding heart, I dashed wildly into the rows of corn and was soon beside them. We three girls in gray checked dresses had but one thought now — to get away as far, and as fast, as possible.

The cornfield was broad, even though it was so near the city, but we soon reached the other end of it, hurrying so much. Here was a road. Now there was real danger. We saw houses farther along that would have to be passed. We were sure this road led out of town.

Pausing to consider, Dubby decided it would be better to risk passing the houses and get far ther away, than to wait for darkness and be missed at the school when playtime was over. Then we would surely be caught.

No one was in sight as we stepped from the green rows and quickly crossed the road to a cinder sidewalk that would take us past the houses. Now great care was needed. Dubby instructed, "Walk slow. Don't act in a hurry." It was hard for me to hold legs to a walk when I wanted so desperately to run.

Coming closer to the first house, where a man and his wife were sitting on the porch, it was difficult to keep going. Dubby again warned, "Walk slow. And keep talking together as though we're just out for a walk."

Ellen said, "Won't they guess we're from the school with these dresses on?"

"Yes, but maybe they'll think we're just taking a walk if we don't hurry," she explained. It seemed to me that my yellow shoes had never squeaked so loudly.

We felt silly, strolling that way, and began to giggle when we looked at one another pretending to be visiting, and could think of nothing to say. As we passed the house, Dubby glanced up and smiled in a very friendly manner and said, "Good evening." The lady looked at us steadily, and then called, "Where are you going?"

"Oh — just for a walk," Dubby answered sweetly, trying to sound natural.

"Do they let you go for walks?" the lady asked.

"Oh yes. We're only going to the next road and then around," Dubby told her, pointing ahead and swinging her arm back toward the school.

Because this was not a reform school they seemed to

believe her, and no one followed. Dubby looked older than she really was and Ellen was tall for eleven.

Continuing the evening stroll we passed all houses, and far down the road turned toward the school as Dubby had said. But once out of sight, our anxious legs dashed across into another cornfield and rushed stumbling through the rows, cutting back at the far end to the country trail we had started out on.

There, breathless, we paused to rest and wait for darkness before venturing out. Being so anxious, we didn't wait long. It was still light as we trudged in the sandy trail, watching ahead, and taking turns walking backward to check the rear for any rigs that might creep into sight — and teams did come from behind. Twice, we crept down into high weeds and brush, and waited the long time it took for a horse and buggy to get to us, and pass out of sight again. And mosquitos were in the weeds!

As the night came down very black, trouble arose that Dubby hadn't planned for: Ellen was afraid of the dark! Dubby and I laughed at her complaints. We were glad to walk along in the blackness.

Dubby talked of her plans. She said, "We will keep going till we're so far away they won't guess we're from the State School. If we come to a town, we'll go to the depot and tell them our father has worked for a railroad, and they'll let us ride, I'm sure. Maybe they'll even help us find him."

But now, in the blackest darkness, an approaching rig could no longer be seen, and suddenly our first warning was the startling noise of a horse snorting away gnats from its nostrils. We ducked into weeds as the soft-grinding wheels passed in front of us. From here on, walking close together, Ellen stayed in the middle — clutching her protectors' hands. She needed support.

Even in darkness it was easy to see the light sandy road close around our feet. As it grew late the air chilled, and our bodies shivered — without jackets. A fog gathered, like white steam, close to the ground, and floated in waves. Ellen quivered — more from fright than cold. She was sure the white misty forms were ghosts, and she wanted to turn back, but was afraid to, alone.

We had passed several farmhouses where lamplight glowed from the windows. Ellen begged to stop at whatever house we might come to. But Dubby said she thought it too soon. Then no more lights were seen. Farmers were in bed, and fog and blackness hid everything. Dubby's determination seemed to sag, along with her feet. The only time for rest had been while hiding.

We plodded ahead without talking. Only the squit - squit - squit - squit of my shoes told that anyone was walking in the blackness. It was quiet, far out and around. Everything slept — except the merry singing crickets along the grassy roadside, and the dogs that now and then barked alarmingly from a distant farmyard. Always, when passing a yard that was near the road, a watchdog barked violently till we were well beyond. Once, after planning to stop, angry bellowing held us off. If Bounce could have been there he'd have protected us.

In such deserted stillness and lateness, it was terrifying to hear scratching wheels coming up close behind. This was our last and most trying experience. I knew Ellen didn't want to hide! I knew she probably wanted to call out and be rescued from the circling ghosts.

Dubby and I dragged her backward and covered her mouth, though trying to comfort. She refused to enter threatening tangles that loomed behind, and it seemed that anyone riding in that passing rig could hear her teeth chattering. Or any horse might shy. The buggy showed through the fog, but no talking came from it. Someone was riding home alone.

We had been lucky: Dogs had stayed home, or were riding in the rigs with their owners. Each time, that had been a worry.

Finally, Dubby was sure we had walked to where people wouldn't know about the State School, and it seemed that morning would come soon. So, following wheel tracks that turned off to the right, we entered a farmyard where a barking dog came rushing out. Dubby saw it was a Shepherd, and she spoke softly and petted it. It acted friendly.

No light showed in the house, and the path to the back door could only be guessed at. Dubby had thought of a lot of things to say — expecting many questions to be asked. She knocked, and as we shivered and waited, she whispered, "Now remember, we'll tell them we were on our way to our aunt's house and got lost. And we want to rest until daylight, to find our way." To Ellen she said, "Remember, you're our sister, and that's why we're dressed alike." It all sounded good. Dubby had everything fixed.

We all knocked several times . finally, inside the window, a light spread from a back room, and the moving shadows and light flickered brighter as a lamp was carried to the kitchen. Then a man opened the door — lamp in hand. Dubby spoke first — the man seemed too surprised to say anything. "We wondered if we could come in and stay all night," she asked, in her best grown-up manner, shivering in spite of great effort to hold her arms tight.

He looked at the three eager faces, and he saw the three

checked gingham dresses. Then he answered, "Well — I guess so."

We entered the warm kitchen gratefully as he held the door. He left us on kitchen chairs and returned to the back room to tell his wife. A pleasant lady came almost at once and smilingly greeted her visitors, seeming not at all surprised or even curious. Dubby fidgeted, then began to explain things. The lady listened to her tell about being on our way to our aunt's home. She seemed to believe all of it.

The wooden clock on the shelf talked steadily with its hands showing half-past-one. We wanted so much to know how far we had walked, but didn't dare ask the distance to Owatonna — those people just might know that a school was there. The lady brought cookies from the pantry while her husband carried milk from the cellar and filled our glasses. But he had little to say. The food tasted wonderful to us chilled travelers. When the wife slipped upstairs to prepare beds, the farmer passed more cookies and managed to talk of the weather — the fog.

Soon our three wilted bodies, needing sleep, were guided up a narrow inside stairway and into a room where bouquets of blue flowers smiled from the papered walls. Even on the ceiling tiny ones paraded crosswise. The soft bed that I climbed into was the whitest, nicest bed I had ever touched. The lady called it a featherbed. Even the pillows seemed softer — all ruffled. This was the company room. Dubby and Ellen were together in a larger bed in the next room.

After the lady slipped back downstairs, Dubby tiptoed to my room, and coming close to the bed, whispered, "They didn't ask us about our folks, or where we lived, or anything. I wonder if they know. We must get up early and get away before they find out." Dubby had told the lady we wanted to get started early, for our aunt would be waiting. She had promised to call us, asking nothing about our aunt who had allowed us to start across country alone.

Dubby started to leave, then turned back. "I think we'd better say our prayers tonight," she whispered, and knelt at the bedside. We moved heads closer and breathed our own prayers softly — Dubby's being different from my: "Now I lay me —." We wouldn't know until the next forenoon all that the kind farmer and his wife were planning downstairs — there was no telephone in the house, but a neighbor living a mile away had one. The farmer intended to quietly mount a horse at daybreak and use that phone. He would tell the school they'd hold the runaways until some-one could come.

The sun was high and bright when we awoke. Dubby was concerned — we had overslept. We began to dress hurriedly. The gentle lady came upstairs when she heard movement and wasn't at all anxious to help us hurry. She sat on the edge of the bed and smiled sympathetically. She had been very quiet downstairs, hoping we would sleep late. She said she knew we needed sleep.

"I've been thinking," she said, "that if you girls still have a long way to go, I'd better fix a lunch for you to take along. Maybe after breakfast you can help me. We can bake a batch of those cookies you liked so well last night. Your aunt might like them, too. You can carry some along to her."

"Oh," Dubby protested, "we can't take time to do that. She'll be worried because she is looking for us. We'll have to start right away." The bright daylight lent urgency to our dressing.

The lady said, "But you want some breakfast, don't you?" We all did want breakfast.

The kind young wife seemed to use much time preparing the meal. She now asked the questions that Dubby had expected, and we were glad that she seemed to believe all of it. We lingered over breakfast — enjoying extra helpings.

As each minute passed, Dubby became more confident, for the lady and her husband seemed so willing to help us. Dubby whispered and reminded me we had no money and would have to stop again for food, so she decided to help cut the cookies as she had been asked to do. Then we could carry along a lunch.

Ellen and I explored behind the house and found a pile of old bricks beside a mounded cave. Soon the outline of a playhouse took shape. "I wish we could stay at this place," I said, and I knew Ellen would gladly stay anywhere rather than walk with ghosts.

Ellen agreed, "I do, too. But we can't stay very long. The school will be hunting for us."

The sun climbed higher, and after awhile Dubby came outside. She didn't seem in such a hurry now. I told her I wished we could stay at this nice place — remembering the soft white bed I had slept in.

Then Dubby surprised us saying, "They want us to stay again tonight because we walked so late last night. They think we will be too tired to go all the rest of the way today. They want us to wait and get an early start tomorrow." She stepped closer and whispered, "I don't believe they know about us at all. They don't have a telephone. She said we could call our aunt from here if they only had a phone." Dubby grinned, "I'm glad they don't have one." We all smiled at that lucky situation. Who would we call?

After thinking a moment, Dubby looked determined again, saying, "But I think we'd better go on. I'll tell them we want to get started as soon as we can. The cookies are all ready to bake when the oven gets good and hot."

She hurried around the corner to the kitchen.

It was about a half hour later that the Shepherd dog ran from the back step barking, as a team turned into the wide yard. For a moment Ellen and I looked at each other. Could it be someone coming for us? We peeked around the house and saw a nice surrey with its top edge waving with fringe, and a man and lady sitting in the front seat.

"Oh, they're getting company," Ellen said with relief. "Don't let them see us." And we dashed back to play again.

"What about Dubby?" I wondered, but worried only a moment, being quite sure Dubby would know what to say.

Only minutes later we heard her, calling in an unnatural high voice — a squeal, that somehow formed, "S-i-i-s—ter." Then she appeared at the corner, stumbling toward us with eyes shut tight and mouth stretched wide for breath. "They've found us!" she sobbed between gasps.

Ellen's and my first impulse was to run, but just then the farm lady and her husband, with the man and woman visitors, came following. The farm lady put her arms around Dubby and tried to comfort. Ellen and I, sobbing and shaking, stepped slowly closer. "They knew all the time," Dubby squeaked.

We had been trapped, and now we looked accusingly at the lady who had been so kind. But she, too, was crying — into her apron.

We soon found out the "company" was the school superintendent and his wife, who had been driving steadily since the call at daybreak. The surrey was the superintendent's private carriage, and we had never seen it at the school. We were surprised that anyone, other than the hack-driver and a matron, would be there.

The wide world had crashed, but soon our bitter disappointment changed to a quaking fear of punishment. What would happen now? Dubby hadn't planned for that.

Mr. Lewis, the superintendent, didn't look angry, and didn't at first say anything to us. We were crying too hard to listen anyhow. The farm lady tried to talk to Dubby who had trusted her and whom she had tricked. After a bit, Mr. Lewis said, "You musn't blame these people. They did the right thing in letting us know, and we're very thankful to them."

We all walked slowly back to the kitchen door, to the smell of cookies in the oven. Later, the farm lady passed a plateful and filled a paper sack to be taken along.

Slowly, we all moved toward the waiting team and surrey, then stood talking. The nice lady said to her gingham-clad visitors, huddled together, wiping eyes, "I hope you girls don't hate me too much. We didn't do it to be mean to you. We did it for your own good. I just couldn't let you go out into this wicked world with no one to look after you."

Then she smiled brightly and said, "I wish you girls could come and make us a real visit sometime. Maybe we can arrange something like that some day soon. Would you like that?" We looked up, nodding "Yes," but couldn't quite manage smiles.

Mr. Lewis agreed. It would be nice for us to visit later on. And they talked about it. "I mean I'd like to have them come and stay several days, or a week," the lady said, as she put an arm around each of us in turn and bid us good-by.

Then, at once, we climbed into the surrey, and the quickstepping team trotted from the yard into the outer road leading back to the school. Dubby and Ellen slumped in the back seat, with Mrs. Lewis between. I sat in front, close to the patentleather dashboard. Here, I watched Mr. Lewis slap the long leather reins to make the horses trot.

After a while the sobbing in the rear changed to soft crying. I looked back at Dubby and saw very sad red eyes that also held a look of fear. Then Dubby could wait no longer. She whimpered, "What are you going to do to us?"

Mr. Lewis hesitated for a moment and asked, "You mean, are we going to punish you?"

"Yes," Dubby sounded pitiful. "Are you going to whip us?"

"No, I don't think so," he answered, his tone calm and serious. "I'm not thinking about what to do to punish you. You aren't bad girls. What I'm thinking is — why did you do it? I feel that I'm the one at fault. I feel that I have failed somewhere. What is so wrong at the school that made you so unhappy? Why did you run away?"

We were too surprised to answer. Dubby and I had never seen the superintendent, or Mrs. Lewis — having been at the school such a short time. This man and woman acted like a father and mother. I was amazed to hear Mrs. Lewis say, "You had us worried to death. We looked for you all night long."

"Yes," the superintendent said, "Mrs. Lewis and I haven't had any sleep. We've been looking for you ever since you were missed last night. We've been up all night."

This was unbelievable! I didn't know that anyone would care enough to stay up all night and search.

Finally, Dubby's curiousity couldn't wait. "When did you miss us?" she asked. We had wondered so much about that.

"They didn't miss you until bedtime, when you weren't at your own chairs to undress. The other children missed you. Just where were you trying to go?" He had many questions.

"We wanted to find our father," Dubby sounded so

disappointed.

The farm lady had told him Dubby's story about going to see an aunt. "Then you weren't going to see your aunt?" He looked halfway around, and I saw a sly smile on his face.

"No," Dubby answered.

"Well, how did you ever think it would be possible to find your father?" The superintendent pushed his questions. "No one knows where he is now."

"Well," Dubby explained, "we were going to see if the railroad would give us a ride back to Walker, and we could hunt him from there."

Mr. Lewis shook his head hopelessly. "What makes you think he would make a home for you now, when he didn't do it before?" A wise question.

"We did have a home with him in the woods," I defended, "and he wants us back. He told us he would get a home ready for us and get us back."

"But you need to go to school, too," Mrs. Lewis reminded from the back seat. "And you need someone to be a mother to you."

Mr. Lewis urged the horses to step along. The foolishness of our adventure had caused much trouble and worry. He looked out across the fields and there, not far away, sat a haystack. He pointed to it. "See that haystack over there?" He was talking to Dubby and me. We all looked. "Well, finding your father would be like finding a needle in that stack."

He turned to look at me as I stared at the pile. I had heard Aunt Carrie talk about "looking for a needle in a haystack" when she couldn't find something. He said, "It would be pretty hard to find a lost needle in there, wouldn't it?"

I nodded yes, but was wondering, as I studied it, if a

needle wouldn't fall through to the ground. I asked him
about that. He said, "It would be apt to get stuck in stems
and stay in one place." He looked amused and smiled
pleasantly. I didn't want to believe that anything was impossible, but the superintendent did make it seem that way.
Hopelessly that way.

He was still pondering his first question: Why had we run
away? "If your only thought was to find your father, why
didn't you wait until you heard from him and had some idea
of where to find him? If you were happy at the school,
except for missing him, I don't think you would have run
away. Tell me now — just what was the matter?" he asked.

We couldn't tell him we hated everything.

"Of course, we know you were lonesome. All children are
until they get acquainted." He tried to help. "What don't you
like about the school? Tell me at least one thing."

That sounded a bit easier. There were many things we
didn't like. "There isn't anything to do," Dubby said.

He had to think about that a moment. It was vacation, but
play and exercises were planned to fill the days.

"Don't you like to play?" he asked.

"Yes — but I like to do other things, too. And I don't like
to have to march everywhere we go." Though, she said, she
knew it kept order.

Then I bravely decided to tell what I hated most. "We
have to polish floors when they don't need it."

The surprised superintendent turned to me. "Do you think
you rub those floors only to keep them polished?" he asked.
I knew of no other reason to work so hard every day. My
questioning look made him hasten to explain. "Didn't
anyone tell you that is done only for exercising?"

I shook my head no.

"That's done for your own benefit. I thought the children had fun doing that floor work together. That is very good exercise." He was quiet for a moment, then continued, "And you thought we were making you polish floors just to be mean to you?"

Timidly, I admitted, "Yes."

Speaking directly to Dubby and me he asked, "What were you girls accustomed to doing every day before you came here?" No doubt he was beginning to wonder if we should be placed differently. He knew we had lived with our father and ran free all day, every day. We had been put in a cage that couldn't hold us. We had heard the farm lady say to him, "The girls appear to be refined, with good manners and good grammar." He looked puzzled.

Dubby answered his question, "We used to keep house."

"And I baked bread," I added.

"Yes," Dubby remembered with eagerness. "She made such good bread that a neighbor bought a loaf every week."

"And I like to sew," I told him. (Hadn't I made a waist for Dubby from a pink flour sack? And hadn't I worked on keystone cushions?)

Mr. Lewis could see where some of the trouble lay. We hadn't been kept busy enough, and we hadn't been doing what, to us, seemed worthwhile. He became thoughtfully quiet as we rode along. All the while Ellen sat silent. I knew she was not at all sorry to go back to her bed at the school. She had been unhappy mostly because she didn't get along well with other children, ever. Mrs. Lewis talked quietly with the two girls beside her.

Later on, as we came nearer the school, the certainty of punishment worried Dubby even more, and she asked, "Aren't you going to punish us at all?"

Mr. Lewis said, "I think maybe you will have to stay inside for the rest of the day. I mean, not be outside for the play period."

Dubby didn't care about that. She said she didn't want to see all the other children anyhow. But I was very disappointed, I wanted to sing after supper, and felt punished right then. Dubby could see the hurt look in my eyes, so she said to Mr. Lewis, "My sister shouldn't have to take any blame for running away. She didn't want to come and we coaxed her."

Mr. Lewis gazed kindly at me, sitting humbly beside him. I said, "I was going to run and tell the matron, and then I got scared when they left me."

He liked the way Dubby showed consideration, for he said to her, "Do you think then, that it would be all right to allow your sister to go outside and play, and you two stay inside?"

"Yes," Dubby said.

And that is the way things turned out. I answered curious questions from children on the playground, but the excitement lessened when they learned I had gone only because my sister did. They all wondered what was happening to Dubby and Ellen.

But Dubby was no longer in cottage 5. It was afternoon of the next day when she came to talk with me. She was smiling, anxious to tell about her new work.

"I'm taking care of babies," she beamed. "I'm over in the baby ward. And there are the sweetest babies there." She seemed the happiest girl at the school and never mentioned the midnight walk. Best of all, she wasn't facing her former companions.

Although she was younger than others working with babies, I knew she could do it, and the change did help. No longer would there be "nothing to do."

A different day was planned for me. I couldn't bake bread in the kitchen. The boys did that. But there was a wide screened balcony along the back of cottage 5 where older girls mended stockings. They took me there and found I could use a needle as well as anyone.

The others smiled doubtfully at my small size. I felt important holding the long black stocking over an egg-shaped piece of wood and carefully weaving across the hole in the heel, the way I had learned to weave in school. This was a thing worth the doing, not at all like polishing floors that didn't need polishing.

* * *

Although I had not wanted to run away, and hadn't planned it, I was the one that suffered all shame afterward. When our long line marched to the dining-hall, the older boys, watching from the kitchen door, singled me out. For all knew about the runaway, and my shoes were my undoing — marking me as one of the new girls from the north woods.

All marchers looked alike, in checked dresses and black stockings, and all wore black shoes except me. I could be spotted far up the line, coming in the hated orangey ones. Because the doorway was up several feet, they could see me even though I changed each time to walk on the far side.

At breakfast, dinner, and suppertime, I could see the aproned tormentors waiting for me and laughing. How I longed to jump out of line and dash ahead, even if I squeaked faster. I dreaded their loud announcement, "Here come the runaway 'jacks' (lumberjacks)." And as I cringed closer they shouted, "Hey — how'd you like the cornfields?" and sometimes, "Where'd you get the shoes?" laughing all the while. Other girls in line grinned back, while I burned with shame. Then, for another time, it was almost over, "There go the runaway jacks." On the return march the taunters were busy washing dishes, sparing me.

29

The Important Letter

It was now near the end of our second week. No letter had come from Papa Frank, nor from anyone who might ever come and rescue us. We began to think we might grow up at the school. Some children did, and some would "get adopted."

One day a carriage, drawn by a fine team, rolled through the grounds where beautiful flower beds bordered the drives. All the girls at cottage 5, playing outside, began to talk about the lady in the carriage. They were sure she was coming for one of them. Well, just maybe she was, and they were not at all sure they would want to go if she should ask for them.

I became as excited as the others. What if the lady should choose me? Would I want to go? What would it be like to have a new mother? I didn't know.

A small group of girls, now clustering close to the drive, were trying to decide if they liked the lady. Most of us said we hoped she wouldn't ask for us. The change to a strange home was a frightening thought to many. But to some, the hope of being adopted was what they liked most to talk about. It was fun to talk about it.

I didn't want to grow up at the school, but I didn't want to leave Dubby, either. And I didn't think I wanted to go to any more strangers. So I was glad when the lady left after talking to several little girls. Much excitement lasted the rest of the day. The lady would come back, she had said.

* * *

Then it happened!

It was Saturday night — just at bedtime — when wonderful news came. The children in cottage5, moving in long white nightgowns, were climbing the wide stairway from the lower hall. I was walking importantly at the end of the line for I had been chosen to be rear monitor that night.

After climbing but a few steps, the outside door, down behind me, opened suddenly, and Dubby rushed in, followed by one of the matrons. She saw me and ran forward to tell the joyous news. "Beeny Coony — they've come for us!"

My matron said I could leave the line. "Who? Where are they?" I asked eagerly and hurried back down the few steps.

"I don't know who's here. They're at the superintendent's office," Dubby rattled on so fast I had to listen closely, "but they said it's our uncle from the farm. So, I think it must be Uncle Albert. Hurry — they want us to come." Dubby grasped my arm, pulling me toward the now-darkened dressing room. Dubby's matron, too, was happily urging, "Hurry - hurry."

My clothes on the little chair, left folded only moments before, were grabbed and pulled on with shaking fingers. Four hands helped me get buttoned into dress and shoes, and we left within minutes.

Outside, it was dark, and the various yards were completely deserted, but not with the desperate desertion they had held two weeks before, when we arrived. Now, welcoming lights beamed from many, many windows. And it was fun to hurry along the empty curving walks to the big center building — even in squeaking shoes.

We entered the superintendent's living quarters. Mrs. Lewis led us to the office off the parlor, and there was Uncle Albert, standing in the center of the room with Mr. Lewis! Just the person Dubby said she thought it would be. And he was not alone! He had brought his own little girl to accompany her cousins back to Iowa. Dubby rushed to hug Valeria, and I waited behind. Then Uncle Albert squeezed us. How happy and grateful we were.

Oh - the joy of it! Someone did come after all! Someone had come to get us out of there!

Uncle Albert was impatient to start back on the 2:00 a.m. train. "We came to get them," he repeated, "and we're ready to go. We don't want to stay around here." He stepped back and forth nervously.

Mr. Lewis finally persuaded him it would be necessary to wait until the next day. There were papers to be signed before we could go. Mrs. Lewis insisted they remain right there with them over night, and so he sat down and visited.

"What's this I hear about you?" he turned an amused smile at us. Mr. Lewis had told about the runaway attempt. "Guess I didn't get here soon enough, did I? But we found out only yesterday, or we'd have come sooner. We got a letter from some woman, telling us you had been brought here. I got ready and took the first train to come and get you."

He paused a moment and chuckled, "Hardly knew where I was going."

"It's a good thing he had me along," Valeria explained. "Every time they asked him 'where to,' he'd turn to me, and I'd have to say 'Owatonna.' He just couldn't remember that name."

It was the kind farm lady who had written. She had remembered the name and the town that Dubby had talked about while they made cookies that day in her kitchen. What a kind lady!

"Now, aren't you glad we brought you back?" the super-intendent asked. "Just think, you might not have been here when they came for you. Wouldn't that have been too bad?"

A smile of compassionate humor played around his eyes.

It was a horrible thought just then. We were ashamed to talk about it, and wished we had never run away. Then Mr. Lewis reminded that it was past bedtime. For this one night, we returned to our separate cottages and dreamed of the wonderful tomorrow.

It was an exciting forenoon. Mr. Lewis showed his guests around. They visited Dubby at the baby ward, and then came to cottage 5 where I was allowed to walk along from room to room: to where I dressed, and where I slept — in the sea of beds.

On entering the gymnasium, with the glassy polished floor, I pointed down, and said, "Uncle Albert, do you know why that shines that way? Because we polish it on our hands and knees."

He roared. Mr. Lewis had told him my feelings and how I had misunderstood.

After they left, I was sent to change clothes and get ready to join them at the superintendent's office. Dubby came to cottage 5 to wait for me. She visited in the matron's office, like an out sider now, after being promoted to the baby ward. One of the matrons walked outside with her, while they waited, and Dubby said she was surprised to see all the beautiful flower beds that she hadn't noticed before, though they had been there all the time.

All her world had now turned golden. When I came she said, "You know — this is really a beautiful place. I never knew there were so many lovely flowerbeds. I've been talking to the matrons, and you know, they are just as nice as they can be." It was easy now to love everything.

The children of cottage 5, outside for the play period, clustered around to say good-by. I'm sure they envied us, for

Walking To A Waiting World

two reasons: We were going to our uncle's farm and could run and play every day freely, and we had received the new dresses and hats and shoes given to every girl when leaving the school.

And we were wearing every bit of it, and all was ours to keep! The dresses were the Sunday kind — white seersucker with gray stripes. And the hats, of thick shiny straw, were creamy white with stiff sailor brims, so they needed to be anchored with a rubber under the chin. I walked as if balancing a board on my head, but was very proud to wear it. A black ribbon, tied around the crown, hung over the brim at the back.

And I had a special reason to be proud! As I walked away with the matron, my head was high, the way Papa Frank would want it to be, and my heart was bursting with pride, for no longer was each step a squeaking torture. On my feet were shiny black shoes that matched my stockings, like Dubby's did. I tripped along smoothly, glad the boys would never again see the yellow runaway shoes, for the matron was carrying the blue canvas telescope that held them safely out of sight. Dubby, too, walked with head high, for I guess we were just naturally proud, as Papa wanted us to be.

I was walking toward an open world, where everyone was waiting. And I would some day see Aunt Nellie, and Donald, in Minneapolis. And Aunt Carrie in Emily. And most wonderful of all, I would somehow, somewhere, see Papa Frank. For I was sure he loved me.

Epilogue

Dubby and Beeny Coony didn't remain at the farm with cousin Valeria. Beeny Coony was adopted by her grandparents in Iowa where the sad funeral had been held three years before. Dubby was adopted by her mother's brother and his wife who lived in a town not far from there.

After Papa Frank learned where each girl lived he wrote letters but didn't go to see them feeling he wouldn't be welcomed. The letters told of his love and his continuing plans for a home. The girls answered. Dubby even wrote she would like a log house with a fireplace that would be in northern Minnesota where he was planning to live.

But time took care of everything. The girls were in school doing well and making friends. Letters came less often as the years passed. The girls did have homes but Papa Frank would never again be with them, or see them. He remained away from his elderly parents, and his entire family, nursing his regrets.

Years later, through outside information, it was learned that he had lived alone and had reached a satisfying old age.